JEWISH
SPIRITUAL GUIDANCE

Finding Our Way to God

Carol Ochs and Kerry M. Olitzky

Jossey-Bass Publishers
San Francisco

Substantial discounts on bulk quantities of Jossey-Bass
books are available to corporations, professional
associations, and other organizations. For details and
discount information, contact the special sales depart-
ment at Jossey-Bass Inc., Publishers (415) 433–1740;
Fax (800) 605–2665.

For sales outside the United States, please contact your local
Simon & Schuster International Office.

Jossey-Bass Web address: http://www.josseybass.com

 Manufactured in the United States of America on Lyons
Falls Turin Book. This paper is acid-free and 100 percent
totally chlorine-free.

Acknowledgments

Page 97: Eleanor Wilner, for permission to quote from the poem
"It's Not Cold Here."

Page 159: Sylvia Winner, for permission to quote from the poem
"Phenomenal Men and Women" by Robert Winner.

Library of Congress Cataloging-in-Publication Data

Ochs, Carol.
  Jewish spiritual guidance : finding our way to God /
  Carol Ochs, Kerry M. Olitzky. — 1st ed.
    p. cm. — (The Jossey-Bass religion-in-practice series)
  Includes bibliographical references and index.
  ISBN 0–7879–1059–7 (cloth : acid-free paper)
    1. Spiritual life—Judaism. 2. Jewish way of life. I. Olitzky,
Kerry M. II. Title. III. Series.
  BM723.O35   1997
  296.7—dc21   97–4877

FIRST EDITION

HB Printing 10 9 8 7 6 5 4 3 2 1

CONTENTS

PREFACE

EVERYTHING WE NEED for growing into a full, rich relationship with God is already available in our lives. We just need to pray, stay open, and not become discouraged. We don't have to study for years and get our theology right before we can begin our spiritual journey. Our experiences will correct us, and our theology will evolve through the life we live. Perhaps the greatest temptation is to feel that we can't do it, that other people are more worthy, but a spiritual journey is not a competitive event; we can *all* be on a spiritual quest. God comes to each of us in the native language of our soul. Gradually the language grows and expands, but no one grows in just the same way as someone else. God creates new individuals, not clones. We need to accept ourselves as we are and keep ourselves open to being changed and shaped by a life lived in growing intimacy with God.

The major function of the spiritual guide is to help the seeker remain on the way. Real changes come about not through some clever insight of the spiritual guide but because both guide and seeker are open to God's presence in their lives. The guide helps seekers overcome fear and resistance, encourages them to take their commitment seriously, and tries to keep them from despair by pointing out the many subtle changes that are taking place along the way. The guide helps seekers recognize that they are not alone, that all across our tradition, Jews have responded to God's call and grown in their relationship with God.

The purposes of this book are to explain what spiritual guidance is, to encourage people to seek it out, to aid them in supporting one another, and to help prepare them to serve as spiritual guides if that is their calling. Spiritual guidance can be given by lay people just as appropriately and effectively as by rabbis, social workers, and other professionals. Rabbis generally have a greater familiarity with Jewish religious literature than most lay people, enabling them to recognize and recall texts to fit particular situations that arise in spiritual guidance. Intensive study of texts—whether of biblical, rabbinic, or lay origin—and experience in drawing meaning from them helps the guide employ texts metaphorically and suggestively to help seekers recognize things about themselves that they cannot easily see.

A familiarity with psychology is useful, not because the spiritual guide will treat psychological problems but because the need may arise to assess whether psychotherapeutic counseling is warranted. Such counseling, which is usually short-term and problem-oriented, is entirely compatible with spiritual guidance, as long as the chosen therapist respects the subject's religious commitments. The therapist may well help someone explore the dark, but the spiritual guide is concerned with leading the seeker to the light. Wholeness is the goal of both, but the spiritual guide aims for the wholeness that depends on the seeker's relationship with God. To differentiate between the two approaches using the imagery of Exodus, the psychotherapist may help someone get free from the bondage of internalized pharaohs, whereas the spiritual guide wants the person to recognize that freedom is more than freedom from old habits, fears, and unresolved conflicts—that freedom is the rest of the journey to the Promised Land.

In the course of this book, we discuss various cases and incidents we have encountered in our work. In writing them up, we faced the dilemma of how to refer to ourselves in our roles as spiritual guides. We agreed that identifying which of us was involved in each of the stories and conversations related in the book would distract significantly from the ideas we are trying to convey and violate our own belief that authors of books on spiritual guidance, like spiritual guides themselves, should interpose themselves as little as possible between the subject matter and the seeker. We tried using *we,* but that made it sound as though we had somehow teamed up to guide the individuals we were seeing. We settled on maintaining the first person singular as it appeared in the notes we prepared for writing the book. This procedure has the advantage of allowing the reader to imagine either one of us in any—or all—of the situations we describe. If it seems jarring at first to have two coauthors refer to themselves as *I* and *me,* we hope and believe that readers will quickly become accustomed to this unusual solution to an unusual problem.

We have also drawn on a variety of traditional sources, particularly the Bible (from the authors' own adaptations of numerous translations, always using the verse numbering of the Hebrew Bible); rabbinic texts such as the Mishnah, Talmud, midrash, and codes; medieval ethical, mystical, and legal works; Hasidic tales and teachings; and contemporary wisdom by great thinkers such as Martin Buber and Mordecai Kaplan. Because this book is a reflective text for the seeker and the guide, we have chosen not to break up its rhythm by intruding with technical explanatory notes and references. Many citations have been included in the back-matter of the book. By omitting others, we mean no disrespect to the authors of these books or to the reader; instead, we aim to be reader-friendly and seek to honor the ancient oral tradition of citing teachings simply in the name of the teacher. This is particularly true with classic sources of Jewish literature.

Spiritual guides always see people individually. It is therefore of the utmost importance that all communication between the guide and the seeker remain strictly confidential; any violation of privacy by either one destroys the mutual trust both must have. For this reason, all the cases and incidents have been thoroughly disguised.

Although the facts of our education, careers, and publications are summarized at the end of this book, we thought readers might want to know something of our individual backgrounds, especially as it relates to spiritual direction.

———————— o ————————

CAROL OCHS: The daughter of two New York City Public School teachers, I spent my first twenty-six years growing up and being educated in what was then regarded as an outstanding municipal school system and benefiting from the city's rich cultural offerings. Philosophical and religious questions felt like a call that seemed to arise from within. So in the summer before attending college, I took my first course in philosophy and thus began my formal exploration of religion and religious thinking.

When I was graduated from college, rabbinic seminaries had no place for women, so I studied to enter the profession that seemed closest to the rabbinate—teaching philosophy at the college level. In this role I was able to do some of what had attracted me to the rabbinate: I could teach people who were eager to learn, even preach a bit now and then, and counsel those who were struggling with spiritual issues. In time, students approached me with questions they felt they couldn't ask the staff at the college counseling center. In order to better serve them and to help myself as well, I sought out a spiritual guide whom I saw for several years. Changing to another guide and, eventually, to a third and a fourth has exposed me to various approaches to spiritual guidance and enabled me to focus on different aspects of spiritual growth.

After I taught my first seminary course, a rabbinic student asked if I would see her for spiritual guidance. Within a short time I was seeing eight students in all. Although the majority of the seekers I now see are Jewish, over the years I have worked comfortably—as guide, seeker, and colleague—with people from a variety of faiths, and their background in spiritual guidance has been a most valued resource. Over the years, I have shared concerns with others who practice spiritual guidance, and while this sharing has not been formalized, it has been a great source of joy. I have learned both from my teachers and from those who have come to me as students and seekers. There can be no community more genuine than one that grows up around a shared love of God.

KERRY M. OLITZKY: My spiritual journey began in childhood, but—like many childhood encounters—I only realized it many years later. I grew up in a small Southern town, having relocated there from a large Northern city that boasted of a large Jewish population. So there I was in a foreign culture searching for a community that reflected a value system I was only yet beginning to form. The pivotal point in my search came during my first trip to Israel at age sixteen. Along with a group, I climbed Mount Sinai. While others rushed ahead to the top, I slowly and methodically climbed with my mentor, my own *moreh derekh*. It was a long climb, and the desert sun grew progressively more fierce as the morning wore on. After many hours of climbing, we could see the glistening peak of Sinai. Suddenly, my walking buddy—my teacher of the way—stopped abruptly. I too stopped out of deference, mistakenly thinking that his age prevented him from rushing ahead. He gently said to me, "You're not ready to finish the climb," and we descended the mountain in silence. I needed to go down the mountain before I could indeed finish the climb, ridding myself of youthful arrogance and precocious assumptions. It was five years before I even deigned to approach the mountain again—and finish my climb. Through the years, I have learned that I can never really reach the top. So I continue to climb to this day.

But I never climb alone. First, it was with fellow seekers: students with whom I studied as we prepared for the rabbinate. Then it was with colleagues. And now it is with my own students—for they have taught me the classic teaching over and over again: "From my teachers I have learned a great deal; but from my students I have learned most of all."

○

Our book is written for anyone who takes the spiritual life seriously and wonders how to approach it, how to tell whether they are on the right course, even how to talk about it and with whom. It is meant to sensitize readers, so that these urgent concerns can be discussed in our communities—adult education classes, *minyanim,* or prayer groups, with study partners, with close friends. Although we describe our work in terms of broad principles, it might better be thought of as two people, seeker and guide, journeying in the wilderness toward God and together encountering God's presence. Our program in spiritual guidance and the individual work that we do is thus not about vocational training. It is about helping individuals to journey on the path toward God and in doing so, to discover the various dimensions of their religious selves.

In the Bible, the Israelites were charged to be a kingdom of priests and a holy people (Exod. 19:6). Our mission thus has an ancient, biblical warrant, and we fulfill it by helping one another in the most important area of our lives. Spiritual guidance is not analogous to a profession like surgery. Surgeons must train on cadavers for many years before they get to work on living people. But the major operator in spiritual guidance is not the guide but God. The spiritual guide does need to learn certain skills, but the primary lesson is how to get out of the way so that God can be present during the time guide and seeker are together. This means that the guide does not initiate spiritual guidance; the seeker does. If no one comes, the guide is not called on to guide. Spiritual guides do not put up shingles, they simply make themselves available. Praying for all of those they work with helps guides focus on the reality that guidance is all about God's—and not their own—relationship to the seeker. All the lessons that the guide teaches the seeker—about prayer, listening, discerning, study, and so on—are lessons that the guide is also learning, again and again.

Why practice spiritual guidance? For three simple reasons: love, gratitude, and joy. Our love is inclusive and does not seek to be "alone with the All One" but to include all of Israel and every human being who sincerely seeks relationship with the divine. We are grateful to those who have supported and encouraged us on our way and have thereby helped pass on this gift. And our deepest gratitude goes to those who have shared their journeys with us. It is to them that this book is dedicated.

New York City   CAROL OCHS
Lag B'omer 5757 (1997)   KERRY M. OLITZKY

PRONUNCIATION GUIDE

Pronouncing Transliterated Hebrew

○ Pronounce vowels as in the following English words: f*a*ther, l*e*t, w*eigh*, mach*i*ne, br*oa*d, r*u*le.

○ Pronounce apostrophes (') like the *a* in *alone;* the apostrophe is also used to separate vowel sounds.

○ Pronounce *ch* or *kh* like the *ch* in *loch* (Scottish) or *ach* (German).

○ Pronounce *ch* or *ḥ* like *kh* or *h* (the actual sound does not occur in European languages).

○ Pronounce *r* as in French or as in Italian (both are used).

○ Accent the final syllable, and you will rarely be wrong.

INTRODUCTION

SEEKING AND GUIDING ON THE SPIRITUAL WAY

WE HAVE NO CONCERN more central than to live our lives in a deepening relationship with God. But this concern, at the heart of many people's lives, is often disguised as a vague disquiet, or is misnamed restlessness. Frequently we need the help of someone other than ourselves to understand our own heart's desire. Finding a spiritual guide can be the prelude to a transformative experience. Unfortunately, there is a dearth of spiritual guides in Jewish religious life, and even some of them are unrecognizable as such. They do their work quietly and with no fanfare. We have written *Jewish Spiritual Guidance* with the intention of detailing this neglected aspect of Jewish tradition, hoping that people will both recognize their need for spiritual guidance and reflect on their capacity to guide others.

Spiritual guides do not help by virtue of their expertise. Rather, they help through their capacity to get out of the way and enable seekers to deepen their relationship with God. Guide and seeker embark on a journey together. The greatest strength of spiritual guides is their own evolving personal relationship with God, not some psychological acumen. And it is not the ability to articulate that relationship intellectually that matters most but the genuineness of the relationship and the fact of having entered into a covenant with God that forms the focus of their lives.

It is also crucial that anyone giving spiritual guidance be spiritually guided. We may be tempted to think it is *we* who have made the difference in another's life or to ignore essential boundaries between ourselves and the person we are helping. A humble posture will remind us that we are always at risk of letting the seekers' gratitude go to our heads, thinking the directing comes from us rather than from God, and trying to dispel ambiguity by hastening the process. We need our own strict, regular, consistent spiritual practice: prayer, meditation, study. Like the person we are guiding, we have to give someone else permission to correct us, even offer us what the rabbis through the ages have called *tokheḥah*, rebuke. And we need regular stretches of silence and solitude to clear out periodically all the noise that keeps us from hearing God's word in the world.

So often—far too often to be accidental—those who come to us raise issues that we have recently been struggling with or that we are still confronting on our own journey. On the one hand, that is what allows us to hear their story and understand it. On the other, we may project our own unresolved issues onto the seekers. In order to avoid doing this kind of harm, we must deal with the challenges of our own spiritual lives. Giving the best spiritual guidance we can allows us to heal ourselves while we are helping others.

The hard work of spiritual guidance may feel effortless while we are doing it, lifting us up at the same time as it lifts the other. But toward the end of the day, we find ourselves exhausted from having focused so fully on helping the seeker discern God's voice. Later, when we pause to take stock of our own selves with a spiritual accounting (in Hebrew, *ḥeshbon hanefesh*), we sometimes realize that in the course of providing guidance to another with a specific problem, a similar problem in our own life has reached resolution.

Those who come for spiritual guidance frequently thank their guides, who in turn often feel gratitude for the shared journey. This sense of mutual benefit illustrates the workings of a "spiritual economy." In the material economy, the larger your piece of the pie, the less there is for me, but in the spiritual economy, your gain is also my gain. The more joy you achieve and the greater love you feel, the more there is to reverberate among everyone else.

Because the ability to provide spiritual guidance is a gift whose actual practice benefits both the guide and the guided, it seems inappropriate to charge a professional fee for such guidance. Although some spiritual guides have no other way of earning a living, most—including all of those who have helped us personally—have given their guidance without charge.

We have already noted that Jewish spiritual guides are few in number and generally inconspicuous. The best way to locate a qualified guide is to tell people you know and respect that you are looking, and then wait patiently. In time the right person will come into your life. Be wary of anyone who hangs out a shingle or actively goes looking for people to guide. Once you have made contact with a potential guide, use these four points to determine whether you and the person are compatible:

1. You must always feel safe and comfortable in your guide's presence.
2 The only agenda for discussion should be your relationship with God.
3. You should be discovering your own spiritual strength.
4. Your relationship with the guide must be one of equals.

If you feel unsafe or uneasy; if the discussion wanders into areas outside your agenda or you sense that the guide is leading you; if the guide or the process makes you feel bad, guilty, or inadequate; and, most important, if you ever even *begin* viewing the guide as master, expert, or guru, you are far better off with no spiritual guide but your own instincts.

———— o ————

The story of one particular seeker and her spiritual guide will help to illustrate what may happen when an individual becomes aware of an inner spiritual prompting and seeks help in responding to it.

Rebecca's Call

When Rebecca was in her mid-forties, she went to see Sarah, a hospital chaplain who also counseled people privately, for spiritual guidance. Rebecca was married, comfortably settled in the suburbs, established as a teacher of art history. Her sons were recently graduated from college. She came to Sarah because, as she tried to explain, she felt a vague unease. It was all so amorphous and intangible that she was almost embarrassed to seek guidance, but Sarah was neither surprised nor disconcerted by Rebecca's inability to explain what she wanted. Sarah asked her for a brief autobiography and then suggested that she take a few days to think about committing to a schedule of sessions. If she felt comfortable with the idea, they would see each other monthly as long as Rebecca found it useful.

In the ensuing months, Rebecca came to name her restless feeling "the call." It took time for her to apply that name to her own experience because *call* implies a voice, and listening. When we speak of a voice, we are implicitly speaking of word. But word is definite, and the call as Rebecca experienced it was vague—it gave direction but not a goal. Rebecca's call was so formless that she found it hard to relate to the concept *call*, which she associated with Abraham's departure from his father's house and the country of his kindred to the land that God promised to show him. But Rebecca learned that the call need not literally be a voice calling you. It can be a subtle urging requiring attentiveness and openness—and frequently restlessness as well. Perhaps we sense a call when we turn around and affirm that we have been going in the wrong direction. Perhaps it is the time when we shake our heads, open our eyes, and say, "Now I'm really awake." Perhaps it is the moment when our shuffling feet are poised to leap toward some great aspiration.

These are all reflections after the fact. Rebecca experienced her call long before she began to think about the many ways in which we are called, the many forms the call takes: we are called from outdated responses, for example, and called to fullness of life. Her initial call took her into spiritual guidance. We are called into ever deeper relationship with God, and so there are calls all along the way.

After Rebecca had been working with Sarah for a year and a half, her call took a more dramatic form. It was the last week of December. She had finished commenting on her students' final papers and at last had arrived at that cherished time between semesters when she was free to read, write, and pursue her thoughts. At Sarah's suggestion, she chose to stay alone in her house in the Berkshire Hills of western Massachusetts with her previous year's journal, a blank notebook, and three books to read. She would use this time as a concentrated retreat, though she wasn't sure what that meant or what sort of agenda she should have.

She foreswore vacationing and began by working on her spring semester courses. But the next day was bright and cold—in the twenties—with the sun glistening off the snow. After a walk up the block, she built a cozy fire in the fireplace. At first, as she later reported to Sarah, she just sat there drinking in the silence. Her house was the last on the road, so no cars passed by. The snow muffled any sounds. The phone did not ring. But with quiet filling the house and the brilliant sunlight reflecting off the snow onto the white walls, Rebecca, rather than slipping into a state of hibernation and sleepiness, felt an awakening sense of urgency and yearning.

She began reading in the books she had brought, and every line seemed personally addressed to her. She alternated between reading van Gogh's letters and looking over her previous year's journal. She found herself underlining such passages in her journal as "My major vice is impatience," "All is gift, I need only be open and aware," "Real change comes less from will than from trust and abandon." She also found herself envying van Gogh's dedication to his work and decided then and there that she would not be satisfied until she had become just as dedicated.

She had always cared about the spiritual life. Was she now ready to stop "playing" at it and make it her central focus? In the quiet of that sunlit room, she prayed to be as dedicated in her religious life as van

Gogh and Cézanne were in their artistic endeavors. Later she would report to Sarah that she had no idea what she was actually praying for and couldn't imagine what would follow as a result. Only in retrospect could she describe what happened on that quiet morning as a call. At the time, she thought that she had initiated the call; she later came to believe that she was responding to something.

Rebecca returned to the college the day before classes began and learned that a severance package was being offered to any faculty members whose age and years of teaching together added up to sixty-five. The offer was unexpected. She was shocked. Was someone trying to tell her something? Was it possible that these events were connected in some way with that prayer she had uttered in the solitude of her retreat? How could she know? Her first response was to see Sarah. Together they recalled the story of the Israelites wandering in the desert. Rebecca identified with these people who had allowed themselves to be guided by a pillar of cloud. Their way, too, was unclear.

She was given only six weeks to accept or reject the severance package. Her decision, it quickly became clear, would not be based on logic. She wasn't sure how to think about what was happening and found herself returning to the Bible. The Hebrew Scriptures provide examples of the many ways we can become enslaved and supply models of people who found liberation.

Were Rebecca to leave her tenured teaching position, she would be entering the desert. She had no illusions about finding another position easily. After a lifetime of working, she would suddenly be unemployed. She would move from a settled, comfortable—if somewhat predictable— state to one of great uncertainty. Yet she sensed on some level that her unease, feared and even hated though it might be, was still a gift. She wrote in her journal in capital letters (because she wasn't quite sure she believed what she wrote), "GOD WANTS ME TO BE HAPPIER THAN I WANT MYSELF TO BE!" Rebecca had no idea how her dislocation would, or even could, bring about a new-found wholeness and happiness. She just decided to trust.

Given Rebecca's reasoning about the call, it should have been the easiest thing in the world for her to accept the severance package. But to paraphrase some lines from T. S. Eliot's poem "The Hollow Men," between the essence and the existence falls the shadow. One part of her knew she was responding to something much larger than her institution's plans to restructure itself. But another part heard her colleagues' questions and her family's concern: What will you do when you're no longer working? She was no longer certain. Sarah's quiet confidence was a precious gift during this time. She helped Rebecca recognize her own aliveness and sense of adventure.

On the last day of March, three months after her retreat in the Berkshires, two months after the severance package was announced, Rebecca resigned her teaching position. She was willing to answer the call, willing to go into the desert. But she hadn't admitted to herself that her response came with conditions. She thought it was perfectly reasonable to believe that she would suffer dislocation for the sake of some greater comfort to come, that the end of her journeying would be something she would recognize as home. She was willing to suspend anticipations about what shape this home might take, but she neither expected nor accepted that home might be the desert itself.

The semester drew to a close. Rebecca gave her last lecture, said goodbye to her students and colleagues, and headed off to the Berkshires again for a long retreat.

Many things happened to Rebecca in the five years after she responded to the call to focus more seriously on her spiritual commitment. For example, she was present when a member of her family died, and noticed in that situation that her fear was lessening and her sense of trust growing. She found herself able to help her dying relative say the ancient deathbed confession of faith in God. She also moved from a house in the suburbs to a much smaller city apartment. As a result of that move, she lost friends, gave up possessions, and noticed a waning sense of competence and familiarity with her environment. But these losses themselves led her to recognize the distinction between appearance and reality (apparent versus real friends), the transience of physical objects, and the contingency that underlies our sense of mastery over situations.

When Rebecca left her job, she temporarily lost focus; she thought that the point of the change was to find another job. But subsequently, with Sarah's guidance, she came to see that all the calls she had responded to were invitations to deeper intimacy with God. She rediscovered her love of painting; she turned her study into a studio and gave private art lessons. The long hours alone in the new studio became for her a time of worship.

What exactly did Sarah do during this process? Sarah helped Rebecca turn a vague restlessness and dissatisfaction into a conscious love that gave energy and direction to Rebecca's life. She accomplished this over time. In all our years of giving spiritual direction, we have never had a person come to us with the explicit desire to grow in intimacy with God. They may, and frequently do, reach a point when that desire can be articulated, but initially they find it hard to say why they have come. It may seem obvious to an outsider that they have chosen to consult with a spiritual guide rather than a psychologist, a marriage counselor, or a career planner, and that this makes plain what they are seeking, but rarely can those choosing guidance identify the precise nature of their quest.

Before beginning our detailed exploration of the spiritual way and the role of guidance within it, we offer the following outline of the topics we will be addressing in the rest of the book.

A Preview of the Chapters Ahead

In Chapter One, we will discuss maps for the spiritual way. These maps are linguistic rather than visual. They might be compared with a book on how to drive a car. Such a book can be very helpful and, in fact, its value increases once you start to drive and realize what the author meant. But you cannot learn to drive by reading a book, no matter how fine the book is, and the same is true of learning how to follow a spiritual way or to give spiritual guidance. In the work done by Sarah and Rebecca, the major function of the biblical texts they studied was to give them a shared language with which to express what Rebecca was experiencing.

Sarah and Rebecca had dissimilar backgrounds. Sarah had been born abroad and came to the United States as a young woman to complete her education; Rebecca had not left America's shores when she married at age twenty. Sarah had grown up in a rural setting; Rebecca was a city girl through and through. They shared a concern for the spiritual life and the text of the Bible. A different spiritual guide may well have chosen other maps to help the seeker name her experiences. In our own guiding, where we have worked with people of different faiths, we have recommended a variety of books, each carefully chosen to fit a specific person in a particular situation. Among these titles are Etty Hillesum's *An Interrupted Life,* Rainer Maria Rilke's *Letters to a Young Poet,* Aryeh Kaplan's *Jewish Meditation,* Doris Schwerin's *Diary of a Pigeon Watcher,* Oliver Sacks's *The Man Who Mistook His Wife for a Hat,* Dag Hammarskjöld's *Markings,* Herbert Mason's *The Death of Al-Hallaj,* and the book of Psalms. In this book, we give particular prominence to Exodus and the Song of Songs because they have repeatedly served as powerful tools for the Jews we have worked with.

Sarah helped Rebecca grow in her prayer life, which became the major support in Rebecca's journey. Rebecca already had a developed prayer life when she began working with Sarah: she had been saying the morning service, reading psalms, praying before going to bed. But it was Sarah who helped Rebecca go beyond the formal text of prayer and bring the questions that were troubling her directly to God. In Chapter Two, we discuss prayer and its centrality to the spiritual way. We have observed that people find it very difficult to talk about their prayer life. It is an extraordinarily intimate subject and usually arises more easily after trust has grown.

Sarah taught Rebecca to really listen and hear, a subject we discuss in Chapter Three. She communicated what she heard when Rebecca spoke, and also how Rebecca could learn to hear God in and through other people's words and in her own deepest desires. Spiritual guides try to make themselves obsolete. Sarah shared with Rebecca whatever she was doing and learning so that Rebecca could acquire those skills herself.

Rebecca was very hard on herself. When she had a positive mammogram, her first reaction was to consider herself a failure. Sarah explained that a mammogram was a test that you could not study for and could not "fail." When she asked Rebecca what advice she herself would give to a hypothetical friend who had a positive mammogram, Rebecca's response was wise and compassionate. Sarah simply repeated Rebecca's words back to her, and at last Rebecca could hear both her own wisdom and the strange dual standard she had for herself and others. Rebecca was not yet ready to be her own spiritual guide, but she was growing to be a strong support to many other people.

Beyond learning how to hear, Rebecca was helped by Sarah to learn other signs that indicated when she was on or off her path. She had to learn the difference between the agitation that was a necessary accompaniment of rapid change and the agitation that was a sign of a breakdown in trust. In Chapter Four, we discuss this and other aspects of discernment.

Much of what Sarah was giving to Rebecca was encouragement in the face of her hesitancy and fear. There are many fears along the spiritual way, and a major role of the spiritual guide is to serve as the angel crying "Fear not!" In Chapter Five, you will read about some of the fears that seekers have brought to us over the years. Not all of them experience all these fears, but they have all experienced some fear, and it is essential that this be discussed with the guide.

Sarah helped Rebecca grow in the ways she imaged God. They never formally addressed questions such as, How do you imagine God? What is God like for you? Rather, Rebecca's fears made it evident that she had unexamined assumptions about God. Later, during a time of real closeness with God, she found, through Sarah's gentle prodding, that she had a new sense of divinity. In our own work, we have had a number of explicit discussions about images of God, especially with women studying for the rabbinate who are disquieted by their experience of a God whose image is not found within traditional rabbinic writings. They wonder if their God image disqualifies them for the rabbinate, or whether they can expand the literature on how God may be imagined. In Chapter Six we explore images of God.

Since the destruction of the second Temple in 70 C.E., study has been central to Jewish spirituality. It played a very minor role in Sarah and Rebecca's relationship, in part because Rebecca was so academic in approach and so cognitive that Sarah tended to downplay study. In their eight years together, Sarah recommended only one book and photocopied only one article for Rebecca to read.

In my own practice,* I have not only recommended books, I have even read books that my students have recommended to me so that we could discuss them together. In one case, a woman lent me a book about goddesses in an attempt to reconcile her Jewish commitment with her attraction to Greek deities. I read the book not to agree with or disapprove of her interest but to have a shared language with which to discuss what was going on in her spiritual life. The text served its purpose, and I was able to communicate feelings that previously she and I had no common language to express.

It is our hope that *Jewish Spiritual Guidance* can serve as a shared text so that guides and the people they are assisting can talk about issues of mutual concern. In Chapter Seven we will present some more traditional approaches to study, all of them serving the objective of encountering God.

Over the years that they worked together, Rebecca turned to Sarah to discuss experiences of temptation and failure. Sarah took these concerns seriously but never let Rebecca forget that the central issue was her relationship with God and that no temptation or even sin should cut her off from that relationship. In Chapter Eight, we discuss various forms of temptation and definitions of sin, but our fundamental concern remains a growing intimacy with God.

Sarah helped Rebecca understand that the spiritual quest was a lifelong adventure. It was not a matter of screwing up one's courage for a single monumental feat: Rebecca's entire life had to be shaped by her growing relationship with God. In Chapter Nine, we discuss the role of practical advice during the inevitable times of trial. For example, Sarah suggested that Rebecca keep a journal and that she return in such times to entries she had made when she was experiencing peace and joy. The purpose was not to indulge in nostalgia but to reawaken the sense of God's presence. Sarah also encouraged structure in Rebecca's prayer life. Rebecca put a lot of energy into both formal and informal prayer, and this energy returned to support her self and her values when the way became rough.

---

* The authors' use of first-person pronouns is explained in the Preface.

Sarah helped Rebecca see how her separate quest was really part of a relationship with a series of communities in which she participated: the community of seeker and guide that she shared with Sarah, the community with which she worshiped, and the larger historical community of her faith tradition. Gently, Sarah helped her see that each community entailed an obligation. Rebecca's spiritual growth was not only for her sake but, as we discuss in Chapter Ten, for the sake of family, community, and the Jewish people.

Our final chapter reviews all the principles discussed in the previous ten, first in terms of one seeker's experience in spiritual guidance and then in terms of the feelings, attitudes, and supplications expressed in Psalm 119. We examine each of the twenty-two stanzas of this psalm, showing how they reflect essential aspects of the ongoing relationship between the seeker and God.

———————— o ————————

The process of writing this book has been an opportunity to reflect on the many years of experience we have had working with others and to try to systematize some of what we have learned. *Systematize* may be the wrong word. Spiritual guidance is less a science or a craft that can be mastered with the help of a "how to" book than it is an art or a gift. Throughout this book we speak as both guides and seekers because we are, in fact, both. The text is not addressed first to one and then to the other. At every moment, we are all learning both to guide and to be guided.

FINDING OUR SPIRITUAL MAPS

Adonai will guide you always.

—Isaiah 58:11

SPIRITUAL GUIDANCE is the process that helps us recognize God's direction, which is there for us if only we can be open to it. In this book we attempt to share what we have learned in the process of both receiving and giving spiritual guidance over the course of more than a decade.

What Spiritual Guidance Is

Spiritual guidance is a relationship between a spiritual guide and a seeker that is focused on the growth of the seeker. The relationship is maintained between two mature people differing in competence but not authority. Guides place their knowledge and experience of the spiritual life at the service of seekers who wish to grow in the life of faith. The seekers, in turn, are open and responsive, but must never abandon their critical judgment and their own sense of personal responsibility. In spiritual guidance, the central relationship is *not* between the seeker and the guide but between the seeker and God. The guide assists the seeker, helps the seeker discover patterns, articulate insights, remain faithful. The guide is a companion who accompanies but does not direct the seeker.

Although we can find examples of spiritual guidance throughout the Hebrew and Greek Scriptures, the first formal discussion of the practice occurs in the writings of the Christian Desert Fathers, who lived in Egypt, Palestine, Arabia, and Persia in the fourth century of the Common Era.

The Desert Fathers left the temptations of the pagan world in search of salvation, which they thought to gain through the discipline and trials of solitude. But they soon recognized that solitude presents its own dangers, so they advised newcomers to the desert to put themselves under the direction of a spiritual parent. These individuals were the earliest spiritual guides we know of in the Western world.

Spiritual guidance remained largely a Catholic practice (both Roman and Eastern Orthodox) until Protestants began to recognize its value in the eighteenth and nineteenth centuries, with the increased emphasis on personal religious experience. Now, at the dawn of the twenty-first century, Jews and people of many other faith traditions are embracing the principles of spiritual direction as they seek to deepen their relationship with God.

Psychotherapy, Pastoral Counseling, and Spiritual Guidance

At a time when many different forms of counseling and guidance are available, it is important to distinguish spiritual guidance from its two most closely related practices, psychotherapy and pastoral counseling. We can draw this distinction in terms of four essential factors: the qualifications of the person practicing, the types of problems addressed, the role of God language, and the objectives of the encounter.

Qualifications

The psychotherapist is a specialist among other specialists, possessing academic credentials and, usually, certification by some professional organization or governing body. In the United States this certification varies from state to state but almost always includes academic training at the master's level and, frequently, at the doctoral level. Within the fields of Freudian psychoanalysis and Jungian analytical psychology, therapists must also have undergone a training analysis.

The pastoral counselor is usually ordained. (The main exceptions to this pattern are women whose denominations allow ordination only to men. Such women nevertheless have a thorough grounding in their own faiths and may have taken holy orders.) In addition to completing the course of study for ordination, the counselor is expected to have studied psychology and frequently meets the requirements for qualification as a psychotherapist.

Spiritual guides have no specific academic training, and although they may be ordained, they frequently are not. Many have studied psychology, but not necessarily in any formal way. The two essential qualifications for spiritual guides are that they themselves have been and continue to be in guidance and that they have a deepening relationship with God. While this latter attribute cannot, of course, be certified, it is the single most important qualification for the spiritual guide.

Types of Problems Addressed

Psychotherapy addresses problems in living: the therapist helps the patient explore fears, obsessions, compulsions, and unresolved issues from childhood. Pastoral counseling addresses the same problems but does so within the context of faith. Whereas in psychotherapy religious issues might be interpreted in nonreligious terms, in the context of pastoral counseling they form part of a shared conceptual framework.

Spiritual guidance has only one focus: the relationship of the seeker to God. In the course of exploring issues such as fear or resistance, the spiritual guide may also look at the seeker's interpersonal relationships, but the purpose of doing so is only to further the seeker's primary relationship with God. Janice (we'll call her) approached spiritual guidance with a very specific question in mind: she was trying to decide whether or not to stay with her husband. When Deborah, her prospective spiritual guide, asked why she didn't consult a marriage counselor, it became clear that Janice saw her marriage in a larger spiritual context. Whatever reservations Deborah may have had about Janice's view of spiritual guidance as an alternative to marriage counseling, she did not voice them. She explained her basic rules: that they should meet once to determine whether there was a fundamental compatibility and whether Janice truly wanted spiritual guidance in which she would focus on her relationship with God. Because Janice was entering into spiritual guidance during a life crisis, they began by meeting once a week rather than the more usual once a month. Within two weeks it became apparent that Janice had very deliberately chosen to approach her marital problems through spiritual guidance. As a result of Deborah's careful questioning, Janice revealed that she had experienced infidelity by her husband as an indication of her own unworthiness and—she found this very hard to voice—as a sign of God's abandonment of her.

Spiritual guidance is not structured for short-range problem solving, but in this case there really was a moment that transformed the entire nature of the discourse. As Janice detailed yet again the ways in which her husband had betrayed her, Deborah asked why she stayed with him. Janice responded, "Because I take covenant seriously." Very softly, Deborah said, "And you don't think God does?" Janice was silent for what seemed a long time as she took in Deborah's question. Deborah was comfortable with the silence and let Janice absorb what the question had brought out: if covenant is serious, then God could not have abandoned her. If God hadn't abandoned her, then she could look again at the incidents she had been relating and see them in a new way. Janice continued to see Deborah over the course of the next two years, but the focus of the discussions never again returned to the problems in her marriage.

While carefully maintaining Janice's privacy, Deborah brought up the issues raised in this case at a peer meeting with other spiritual guides, an informal group that met in her area. One of the other guides said that the seeker's decision to work with Deborah even after she had suggested marriage counseling must have been what tipped Deborah off to the real nature of the seeker's problem. Deborah shook her head in contradiction. "What you say makes sense, but I agreed to work with the seeker because it felt right. I did not consciously analyze why it was appropriate for us to meet. As for what I said, I hadn't planned it, I just suddenly heard myself saying those words." Jack, who earned his living as a high school teacher but functioned as a spiritual guide, added his agreement. "I know what you mean, because that happens to me all the time. I don't plan what I'm going to say, but somehow the appropriate questions just pop out."

The Role of God Language

Ever since Freud published *The Future of an Illusion,* psychotherapists have been suspicious of religion and God language. The patient's spiritual yearnings are often viewed as symptomatic of unresolved issues. In short, God language is viewed not as referring to God but as expressing the patient's problems. The pastoral counselor, by contrast, takes religion seriously and accepts God language as natural rather than problematic. The spiritual guide not only appreciates that God language refers to the seeker's relationship with God but helps expand the language, teaching the seeker to have more flexible images of God, to understand different experiences as indicative of the deepening relationship, and to make subtle distinctions that will facilitate the spiritual life.

Objective of the Encounter

For the psychotherapist, the purpose of therapy is to help the patient adjust to life in this world. A major tool in the process is transference, which leads the patient to project onto the therapist feelings that first arose in earlier relationships. The therapist lets the feelings arise in the new safe environment where pain and anger can be healed.

The pastoral counselor also helps the client adjust to difficult life situations—in marriage, in parenting, at work. There are issues of transference in this situation as well, and when properly handled, they can have curative functions. Pastoral counseling is problem-oriented and can therefore frequently be productive in the short term.

For the spiritual guide, the objective of the encounter is to foster the seeker's relationship with God. Both guide and seeker should guard against transference and countertransference (the projection of personal feelings by the guide onto the seeker) because the real guide is God, not the person who is simply facilitating the developing intimacy. (Avoiding the transference makes it doubly important for the guide to continue in spiritual guidance.) Spiritual guidance is growth-oriented and may continue throughout a person's life. The spiritual guide helps seekers learn to recognize and pay attention to God's personal communication and to respond to this direction throughout their lives.

The Goals of Jewish Spiritual Guidance

A prayer recited in the Jewish morning worship service clearly and concisely outlines the goals of spiritual guidance:

> Inspire us to understand and discern, to perceive, learn, and teach, to observe, do, and fulfill gladly all the teachings of your Torah [revealed law, specifically the Five Books of Moses].

To Understand and Discern

God speaks to the individuals in the Bible directly. God calls out to Adam in the Garden, "Where are you?" (Gen. 3:9). Of Cain, God inquires, "Where is your brother Abel?" (Gen. 4:9). God commands Noah, "Make yourself an ark of gopher wood" (Gen. 6:14), and tells Abraham, "I now establish My covenant with you and your offspring to come" (Gen. 9:9) and "Go forth from your native land" (Gen. 12:1). God addresses Hagar, "Go back to your mistress, and submit to her harsh treatment" (Gen. 16:9), and informs Rebecca, "Two nations are in your womb, two separate peoples shall issue from your belly" (Gen. 25:23).

Although written with carefully crafted words, these biblical utterances are similar to many directives we seem to encounter throughout our own lives. We are tempted to ask when God stopped speaking to people. The answer, as spiritual guides affirm, is never—we just have to find the means within ourselves to listen for God's voice. So a major goal of spiritual guidance is to help seekers recognize that God still speaks to us, unceasingly. In Hebrew, a spiritual guide is called *moreh* (for a male) or *morah* (for a female) *derekh*—literally, teacher of the way. The way is clear if we follow God's guidance, and the teacher of the way—the spiritual guide—helps us listen, discern, and remain open to the many ways in which God speaks to us. As we go about our daily routines, doing the chores that occupy our ordinary lives, the voice of God is always present. We learn how to listen to that voice and to discern the directions in which it is leading us.

Discernment will be discussed more fully in Chapter Four. For now, let it suffice to say that the guide must discern when the guidance offered really illuminates God's way. A spiritual guide does not use "techniques," nor does the guide succeed because of books read or analytic skills sharply honed. The effective guide simply gets out of the way and allows for the expression of God's will. What that feels like is effortless assurance. When spiritual guidance is done properly, there is no strain or second guessing, just clarity, calmness, and confidence. After the seeker leaves, the guide may wonder how just the right questions arose that took the seeker on the right path. A good session proceeds easily, like a well-practiced musical recital. Effort precedes the performance, analysis follows it, but during the recital there is only music. And when the guide, after personal practice of prayer and attentiveness, can be open to God's guidance during the session, we can say that there really is "music."

Learning to distinguish God's speech from other messages we perceive and from noise means recognizing God's caring concern, not only in the obvious statements articulated in the biblical text, but also in the revelation at Mount Sinai and in the providential care of the daily manna, the mysterious food that provided sustenance for the Israelites in the wilderness of Sinai. The spiritual guide points out to the seeker that even in the Bible, God's speech is not restricted to the direct declarative statements made to the patriarchs, matriarchs, and prophets. The example of the manna allows us to notice the variety of forms God's speech can take in our lives. To perceive these forms, it is not necessary to look to the supernatural or beyond the ordinary at all. We receive them in the miraculous reality that surrounds us—as we put food in our bodies, as we go about the daily routines of living, as we lay our weary bodies to sleep at night and wake up renewed, as we bring children into the world and nurture them while they evolve into independent selves, and as we let them go.

Learning how to understand the meaning of God's words also means learning to recognize the signs that lead us on our way. In the desert, God led the Israelites, who were fleeing slavery in Egypt, with a pillar of cloud by day and a pillar of fire by night. According to the biblical text, the cloud was also positioned temporarily between the Israelites and the pursuing Egyptians (Exod. 14:19). Once the Egyptians no longer posed a threat, the pillar of cloud embodied a different message. It was then used to tell the Israelites when to set out on their various forays and when to remain in camp.

We have to look for similar signs. How do we know when to stop our journey and when to continue? The spiritual guide helps us see that the pillar, in its many guises, continues to lead us if we can only discern it. Sometimes it takes the form of a still, small voice that emanates from our soul, and sometimes we find God leading us through the voices of others. In rare moments, the voice of God—heard through discernment—overwhelms us when we least expect it, revealing the right decision we have been desperately struggling to find. Many of us have heard it on the Sabbath in particular. We have been lifted heavenward by music, by the lilting chant of the liturgy. And we carry those moments with us, praying that they might illumine our path.

Someone recently told me, following a worship service, "I was finally able to hear God's voice in the silence of prayer." Jewish prayer addresses the many things that concern us. If we look at the subject matter of the psalms, we find that they are filled with the concerns of ethics, war, enemies, relationship with God, fear, protection, wonder. The psalms actually provide us with the opportunity—and the permission—to say things we would otherwise feel uncomfortable saying. The psalmists were individuals like us, who saw every aspect of their lives in the context of their relationship with God. At some point along the path of life, we may cease to nourish that relationship through prayer, but when we are ready, spiritual guidance offers one means of reviving it.

In the Bible, God speaks in a variety of ways: directly, in dreams, through the inner self, and through the voices of others. Nature speaks to us of God. As the psalmist writes, "The heavens declare the glory of God." The heavens have always been there, but not everyone sees them as the work of God. Similarly, texts, even sacred ones, require interpretation—and so does personal experience. One friend told me, "I pray for the guidance to come to know the self that I want to return to." The spiritual guide must help seekers interpret the events of their lives. But the guide must be careful: when the interpretation is hasty or superficial, the seeker may be worse off, understanding, say, some loss, pain, or suffering as a punishment or a withdrawal of love. The guide's task is to push the question, Where is God in this experience?

Here the story of Joseph offers us a potent image. After the death of Jacob, Joseph's brothers feared that, without their father to protect them, Joseph would now exact retribution from them for selling him into slavery. Joseph reassures them: "Although you intended me harm, God intended it for good, so as to bring about the present result—the survival of many people" (Gen. 50:20). Joseph's statement comes from his understanding that God was playing a significant role in his life.

As difficult as it may be to accept rationally, a series of painful circumstances can bring us to a profound discernment of the role that God plays in our lives. The Baal Shem Tov (1700–1760), the founder of Hasidism, which takes a mystical approach to Judaism, taught that only suffering makes for proper insight and compassion. Like Joseph, we too can come to understand the meaning of suffering.

Later in the Bible, when Moses asked to behold God's presence, God answered, "You cannot see My face . . . I will put you in a cleft of the rock and shield you with My hand until I have passed by. Then I will take My hand away and you will see My back" (Exod. 33:18, 20, 22–23). Some commentators have taken this passage to mean that we cannot see God's actions in the present, that it is only when we look back over our lives that we can recognize God's presence and caring concern in the events of our days. Often we get a glimpse of God in our lives, the feeling of God's presence, only after it has gone. Like Jacob, we may be moved to respond, "God was in this place and I did not even realize it" (Gen. 28:16). We need a method of interpretation so that we may indeed experience God's presence in the moment.

There are other models of interpretation that also influence spiritual guidance. Sigmund Freud's psychoanalytic work was profoundly informed by his Jewish background. Like Judaism, psychoanalysis has freedom as its goal. And the psychoanalytic task is to discern the meaning behind "texts." Freud found these texts in dreams, slips of the tongue, patterns of relationship. In his later writings, Freud even echoes the injunction found in Deuteronomy, "I have put before you life and death, blessing and curse. Choose life" (Deut. 30:19). Freud posited both a life force and a death instinct but neglected the primary relationship that underlies the entire text: our relationship with God. The spiritual guide must never forget that there is meaning in life and in the activities of life because there is God. The *moreh/morah derekh* is not the healer but simply the one who helps seekers discover—discover, not create—the patterns in their lives.

Although spiritual guidance resembles Freudian analysis, the differences remain crucial. Like Freudian analysis, spiritual guidance weighs in on the side of life and freedom, but it recognizes that true healing and liberation come from our deepening relationship with God. Thus the spiritual guide is simply the one who fosters that relationship.

To Learn and to Teach

Learning and teaching inevitably flow into one another. Responsible spiritual guides are themselves in spiritual guidance. They know that their relationship with God never ceases to grow and change, and that they can best help others when they are actively exploring that relationship with the help of their own guide. In informal contexts we find that we give advice to one person and seek advice from another. In our many roles, we are both guide and guided.

The guide turns to others to be guided, and the seeker is frequently able to help others. It seems that we always teach what we most need to learn, almost as if a part of us knows what we need to know, and the process of telling others helps us meet our own need. We can also help others because our own struggle has taught us how to help discern the way for someone else. The spiritual guide and the spiritual seeker share the same world, face the same challenges, experience the same pain, yearn for the same pleasure, and establish a covenant with the same God. They are both people who take their spiritual lives seriously and feel that they have been called. But guides can rarely guide themselves.

A story in the Jewish folk literature illustrates three aspects of spiritual guidance. The story is told of a man who came to an elderly rabbi and said, "I have heard that you Jews employ a special form of reasoning, called Talmudic, which explains your cleverness. I want you to teach it to me." The old rabbi sighed and offered him this problem to solve. Two men fell down a chimney. One emerged filthy, covered with soot; the other emerged clean. Which one washes his face? The obvious answer, the one with the dirty face, is wrong, because how would he know his face was dirty? The man with the clean face, on the other hand, seeing his fellow with the dirty face, assumes his own face is dirty and so goes to wash. The rabbi then repeats the question and supplies a new answer: once the man with the dirty face sees the other one washing, he figures out that his own face must be dirty, and so he washes too. But then the rabbi shows that even this third answer is no better than the first. Why? Because no one can fall down a chimney and emerge with a clean face.

How does this story relate to spiritual guidance? First, it shows us that we need another to see ourselves; second, that other person also needs to be helped by another to achieve self-knowledge; and third, we are all coming out of the same chimney, that is, we all share the human condition and therefore need one another to become whole. The Baal Shem Tov put it this way:

> No truly righteous person would be able to see the wickedness in others. The real *tzaddik* [righteous person] would not know if men and women are guilty of offenses. The *tzaddik* could not, therefore, under these circumstances serve as an example to others, and could not teach people. It is for this reason that there is no one on earth who does not sin. The sin makes the righteous human and enables them to guide others [Midrash *Ribesh Tov*].

Samuel, the Kaminker Rebbe, wrote,

> The leader complains that multitudes come to him for guidance though he still needs guidance for his own conduct of life. He then muses, "Because I have not yet perfected my own ways, I must suffer the punishment of guiding others. It is painful, also, that I must lead others to perfection while I must constantly endeavor to perfect myself. Every day, therefore, I must set aside many hours for self-improvement" [quoted in Rabbi Pinchas Shapiro of Koretz, *Beth Pinchas*].

It is embarrassing to recognize the many ways we hide from God and resist a more intimate relationship. But this awareness does not merely serve the purposes of remorse; it can also become a tool we bring to the task of really hearing the doubts of others as they come for spiritual guidance. Mark, a systems analyst, spoke to me about a moment of profound closeness with God's presence and then immediately switched to discussing a text. How well I recognized, from personal experience, that move from heart to head. As deeply committed as I am to the spiritual life, I am almost too skilled in the cognitive domain, where I wield my mastery and control. Mark had the "disadvantage" of being very articulate, an accomplished academic thinker, but I had to remind him that he was affected by his emotions. In my role as spiritual guide, I encouraged him to go back to the actual experience of God's presence and not think about it but feel it. The experience of feeling his own emotions and attending to them was all the education he needed. And it was my own awareness of the ways I express resistance that helped me recognize the same thing in my seeker.

To Observe and to Do

The effort to discern God's will is not like learning any other skill. Unlike learning how to play chess, whose application is only to the game itself (although avid chess players will no doubt argue this point), learning spiritual discernment bears on all the relationships in our lives regardless of the context. Our relationship to God expresses itself in and through our commitment to our partner, our child, our parents, our community. God is the ordering principle that sets all the other loves in our lives within their right framework. (A fuller discussion of this idea appears in Chapter Ten.)

When spiritual guidance is successful, it motivates us to action. Sometimes it involves changing the course of our lives: a new career, a new job, going back to school. Often it includes examining our relationships with others and repairing them—particularly those with our parents and our children. Spiritual guidance begins with the inner life of the soul, but it must include the outer life as well.

To Fulfill Gladly the Teachings of Your Torah

We follow the teachings of the Torah so that we can learn, as Noah did, to "walk with God." The Hasidim (followers of Hasidism) take this one step further. They not only want to walk with God, they want to cling to God. This clinging is called *devekut*. For most of us the full meaning of living in unity with God will only gradually become clearer after years of personal growth and often as a result of being guided. It very rarely happens overnight. Spiritual guidance is not a quick fix for whatever ails us. It fosters the growth of a relationship with God over the course of a lifetime. It has been said that a true friend is one with whom you have eaten a lot of salt. Obviously that requires a long period of time. Spiritual guidance has as its aim to help us become true friends of God.

The Focus of Guidance: Our Relationship with God

This, then, is the subject matter of spiritual guidance: our *relationship with God*. If we examine these three key words, we discover that their simplicity is deceptive. Our focus is single-pointed but not narrow, because our relationship with God includes and transforms all of our other relationships across time: in the past (for example, with our parents and our tradition), in the present (with our partner and our contemporaries), in the future (with our children and the next generation), and, outside of time, in eternity, which imbues all other times with meaning.

Our *Relationship with God*

Ours. Not the Israelites' relationship with God. Not all of humanity's relationship with God. Ours. Ours alone—and yet we learn through this relationship that we are never alone. We all left Egypt. All Jews participate in the Jewish people's history, all beings pass through experiences in this life that embody the same forces as are represented in the exodus story. We all left Egypt collectively with our people and also individually, personally—in relationship with God.

Our Relationship *with God*

We know about relationships. As teachers and learners, we must now apply that knowledge to God. We know that relationships require constant contact. In order for us to have a relationship with someone, we need to meet them, see them, speak to them, communicate with them on a regular basis. If our relationship with God is to work, then we must not consider God an explanatory principle, a historical idea, a cognitive construct. God has to be the God we have met in our personal journey through life.

Is it really possible for an ordinary person to have a personal experience of God? Yes. It is not only possible, but the life of the ordinary provides the foundation for genuine religious experience. This notion is somewhat baffling, and we will circle back to it shortly. If we return, for the moment, to our human relationships (which can also be frightening to contemplate), we may ask, "What, in addition to contact, is required for a relationship?" The philosopher Martin Buber (1878–1965) taught that our human relationships should reflect the divine relationship we are trying to maintain. The minimum requirement for this relationship is that it be an intrinsic, not an instrumental, good, that is, we like people for who they are, not for what they can do for us. Buber described this relationship as "I-Thou" and distinguished it from superficial relationships, which he named "I-It."

In Judaism our relationship with God is described as a covenant, one that was initially established on Mount Sinai. A covenant is like a contract, only you can't hire lawyers to find loopholes to get out of it! A covenant is also like a promise, but unlike most promises we make, we rarely know what we are promising at the time we enter into a covenant.

According to one midrash (a rabbinic legend woven around a Bible story), when our ancestors were invited to enter into the covenant at Sinai, God asked them whom they would name as guarantors. They replied, "Our children will serve as guarantors." That includes us and our own off-spring. The covenant was a promise whose full implications could not be understood at the time it was made. It also transforms the original covenanters' descendants as they try to live up to it.

But just as the Israelites' marriage to God was not an arranged marriage (it grew out of a prior experience of God and a growing love and trust), our own entry into the same covenant is not—as our spiritual guide helps us see—merely the inheritance of our ancestral traditions but the result of our personal experience of God. There is a difference between a relationship that holds simply because of the status of our parents and one that we con-sciously and conscientiously develop. Most of us have cousins with whom we are related in name only. We rarely visit with them, don't remember their children's birthdays, are not really part of their lives, but the status of cousin applies nevertheless. We may have other cousins with whom we have found genuine companionship: we strive to keep in touch, share experiences, and be involved in each other's lives. Here the automatic relationship has become a deliberate and carefully nurtured one. Something analogous hap-pens in terms of our covenant with God. We inherit the covenant from our ancestors, but it becomes central to our lives, nurturing and shaping us, only when the "given" relationship becomes a self-consciously "chosen" rela-tionship. The Gerer Rebbe (1845–1905) stressed the importance of estab-lishing one's own relationship with God in an exhortation to his followers:

> Let me be candid with you. You cannot depend on me to be an inter-mediary between God and you. I can merely attempt to point out to you the right paths in good conduct, leading to Godliness. But you must walk thereon without my aid. Learn to stand on your own feet, and even if your rebbe is not a great person, you will not fail [quoted in Abraham Alter, *Meir Einei ha-Golah*].

Our Relationship with God

Clearly, we can never fully understand or characterize God. We can get only glimpses, brief insights. But we must confront all the God images we have formed throughout our life. A *God image* is one of the many ways we have come to understand God, and its nature is usually affected by the age at which we form it.

For example, when we were six or seven years old, our teachers may have wanted us to learn us that Abraham was the great founder of the

Jewish faith. They may have told a story from the midrash about how the young Abram (as he was called before God declared the covenant with him) destroyed nearly all the idols in his father's store and then placed a stick in the hand of the largest remaining idol. When Terah, Abram's father, asked who had done this, Abram replied that the large idol had. Terah replied the idol could not have done such a thing. Retorted Abram, "Then why do you worship it?" To a seven-year-old, this is a very satisfying story. It possesses a clarity any child can grasp.

The story of Abram and the idols, however, is not recorded in the Bible, which understands that idolatry is not conquered by destroying statues. Idolatry involves far more than bowing before images of clay, stone, or metal. Long after Abraham had recognized the true God, the Ten Commandments still had to explicitly forbid idolatry, because the Israelites at Sinai, as well as many who came after them, were slow to recognize that idolatry is one of the most difficult heresies to uproot. We think we are relying on God but discover that we are really relying on idols of wealth, status, luck, or even technology. Abraham's profound recognition of God is not something a seven-year-old can understand. But no harm is done by the earlier image of Abram destroying idols, as long as the question of what constitutes idolatry remains open.

We formed our images of God at around the same age that we formed images of Abraham's greatness. The images are similarly incomplete and structured for a child's consciousness, but though we reexamine the story of Abraham through each yearly cycle of Torah reading, we tend not to reexamine our image of God. We may become adults and hold on to an image constructed out of aspects of our parents, grandparents, first-grade teacher, or even a police officer or other authority figure. Then suddenly, many years later, we might face a major life crisis. We reach for our God image, the one we left hidden in the recesses of our memory. Now our idea of God might seem embarrassing—as irrelevant to our present situation as the teddy bear that we clung to at the time our early image of God was formed. Recollecting this inappropriate and inadequate image, people will sometimes reject God entirely instead of ponder how God might look through the eyes of a mature adult.

In Chapter Six, we will discuss God images further, but an example will show how one actually functioned in the life of an individual woman.

Janna had been raised in a traditional religious home where God was a surrogate for all the parents' values. When her parents could not watch their very active daughter, they invoked God's all-seeing eyes and wrath to control the girl. Before Janna's twelfth birthday, both parents died, and she went on to reach adulthood under very trying circumstances. In her forties, having managed to survive her childhood losses and having built a life for herself and raised children of her own, she found comfort in the sense of a loving presence. It never occurred to her that the presence was God, because her God image was judgmental and wrathful. This presence was loving, assuring, and appreciative of her courage in fully living her life. It was only after several sessions of spiritual guidance that Janna even mentioned this sense of loving presence, because she really did not recognize it as being religiously relevant. Gradually she was led to see that what obstructed her relationship with God was not God but the way God had been portrayed to her childhood self. The day finally came when she could trust her own present experiences and name them as being experiences of God.

One of the first things, then, that a spiritual guide has to do is help those seeking guidance to ascertain how they relate to God and where they find God in their adult lives. Spiritual guides help seekers expand their God images, making sure to include the insights that have come over years of growth and maturing. Along with the change in our image of God comes a change in our understanding of who we are in relationship with God.

In relationships we have to try to see others as they are and not just as they function for us as *my* friend, *my* parent, *my* child. Seeing the other through an independent prism, not one we have crafted out of the experience of our own life, is never easy. Nowhere is it more difficult than when the other is God. It is hard to contemplate God and not think about our own needs and fears. How can we ponder God and not reflect on our finitude and vulnerability? We may try to find comfort in thinking of nature—the whole of which we are a part. Nature does turn out to be one context where we can just delight in God's Creation. We become centered watching the waves crash against the rocks, we marvel at the infinite expanse of the starlit sky, we feel tenderness in the presence of the delicate buds of spring. There is divine majesty expressed even in a paralyzing snowstorm. But sometimes our experiences of nature bring us back to the theophany in the book of Job. Job, the just man who suffers the loss of all that mattered to him, demands that God explain why the just suffer (Job 31:35). God does answer Job, but commentators have not found it easy to connect this speech and Job's demand. In fact, God never offers an explanation for his pain and suffering.

Just what was God showing Job in that speech? How is it related to Job's question about suffering? God's soliloquy focuses on different aspects of nature, as if Job, in coming to understand Creation, might also come to understand the mind of the Creator. God describes the lion, the hind, the wild ass, the ox, the ostrich, the horse (Job 39:19). If we rationally explore this speech, trying to understand how it relates to the problem of evil, we're stumped, just as we are when we try to apply the orderliness we have discovered in nature to the evils of the world. *Olam k'negdo:* the world follows its own order. We might study the many interpretations that have been put forward of the theophany in the book of Job. But we were reminded of the speech because we took the time to really enter nature. Our question about the reason for suffering arises—as does Job's—in the context of the experience of living. So the answer will be revealed in the form of an experience in life. All we have to do is to stay open, responsive, and honest. And through the experience, we may gain insight into meaning.

How do we feel in nature? Not one way, but many ways. We feel awed, delighted, moved, overwhelmed. We want to love and accept; we want to change and control. We think of all the many forms of water we have experienced—oceans, rivers, clouds, snow, dew, ice, frost, hail, even tears and life-giving rain. The psalmist talks about the waters knowing their boundaries, but we've seen floods and the destruction caused by waters overrunning their boundaries. We have recognized, with the psalmist, that we are "awesomely, wondrously made" (Ps. 139:14), but we've also seen one instance after another of human cells overrunning their boundaries in rampant malignancy. We stand in awe, we stand in anger and fury. We respect, we despise. Such is our relationship with nature. It is not simple. Our relationship—and our struggle—is neither easy nor superficial. Nor do we have a simple relationship with God. This we come to understand through spiritual guidance.

Sacred Texts as Maps for the Spiritual Way

Our spiritual texts contain many models for spiritual direction. The book of Exodus and the Song of Songs offer us two models, or maps, that we can employ to help us along the spiritual way. But this use of texts is not about scholarly exegesis. The spiritual guide does not give a reasoned interpretation of what is happening in the text. Instead, the guide helps the seeker (1) attend to the seeker's own experience of God, (2) begin to recognize the seriousness of the seeker's own life, and (3) start to shape that life around this ongoing relationship. Exodus and the Song of Songs have a way of balancing one another: one deals with a call to depart from a place of oppression, the other with a call to enter into the arms of love.

Exodus

Journeys exhibit some common features: they require preparation; there are various stages or landmarks along the way; and always, there is a clearly defined destination—a journey has to take us somewhere. The encounters along the way enrich the journey because they help us reach and better understand the goal that lies at the journey's end.

The standard journey model for Jews has always been the exodus from Egypt and the trek across the wilderness to the Promised Land. That journey is instructive for the spiritual life because we, like the Israelites, have been enslaved, even if we are not immediately aware of it. When we can affirm that we are enslaved, we can begin our exodus from slavery. Some say we cannot even taste our freedom until we have experienced what it is to be enslaved. We come to recognize patterns of bad choices and thereby learn that we may *not* be free. We seek to understand the purpose and meaning of these repeated actions. We have to identify our chains of slavery. Our careers, for example, may drive us and simultaneously chain us. We can be enslaved to resentment, jealousy, insecurity, ambition, competitiveness, anger. But "nearness to God is my good" (Ps. 73:28) and also my freedom.

The old patterns of behavior don't have to continue. We can change— let go of old angers and outmoded viewpoints. The Israelites suffered their earliest enslavement not at the hands of the Egyptians but in the surroundings of their own family. The biblical record of enslavement begins with the conflicts of Eden, long before the Israelites set foot in Egypt. Did the mutual blaming of Adam and Eve eventually find expression in the deadly rivalry of Cain and Abel? Again, we raise this question not for the sake of biblical exegesis but to search our own lives for the contagion of jealousy, competitiveness, differentiated familial love. We read the Bible, and suddenly there is a shock of recognition: "This message is addressed to me" or "This story is about me." We'd love to identify only with positive figures, but everyone portrayed in the Bible is flawed, and the text pulls us in at disconcerting moments. However, there is no point in mincing words, no reason to try to turn the Torah into a gentler document that radiates only divine light and sheds no darkness, a sacred text that elevates the spirit while avoiding the existential realities of human life.

According to our understanding of the biblical text, the Israelites finally recognized that they were slaves when Pharaoh's dictates became harsher and he told them to make bricks without straw. It was at this point that their future appeared hopeless. They had grown used to their lives as slaves and did not want to leave the familiar routine—however miserable— behind them. Moses saw the Israelites' enslavement more clearly because he had been raised outside the slave environment. He could recognize the injustice. It seems that we cannot fully appreciate our own condition of servitude until we have some experience that allows us, even for just a moment, to transcend our chains. We must then identify our enslavers: egotism, narcissism, subservience to external standards, grandiose goals.

The exodus is instructive in another sense. The Israelites traveled a circuitous route that frequently took them back to places they had already passed through, so they could not define their progress. They traveled many more miles than necessary to cross the desert. The journey took forty years, enough time to transform an entire generation. In fact, we learn that the journey to the Promised Land is measured in character transformed rather than in distance traveled. If we can follow our own spiritual way without trying to measure our progress by some yardstick or by comparing it with someone else's spiritual life, then the journey model can be useful. The exodus story helps us understand our own enslavement, deliverance, revelation, and redemptive freedom.

Freedom. We know about freedom from bondage, and we know we are invited to something more than that, for otherwise simply getting out of Egypt would have been the end of the story. We are invited to freedom from meaninglessness, to the inclusion of our stories in the larger story of creation and redemption.

So much of our journey requires following a cloud. What does it mean to be led by a pillar of cloud? It means that the way is mystery and that mystery is a gift. If we really want all things to be new (Lam 5:21), we must accept mystery, filled as it is with surprises, bewilderment, and a level of fear. The fear does not have to paralyze us: it can be a frisson of excitement rooted in deep trust. We may remember when our grandparents tossed us in their laps; we were afraid but excited—fully trusting.

We know now that we must circle back on routes already traveled and not lose heart or faith. We cling to the memory of God's miracles and the sense of God's presence. But to pass back over familiar ground, see the remains of our abandoned encampments, and recall what we knew and believed in those earlier times is to feel doubt, anguish, and despair, because everything has changed in the course of our wanderings. What enables us to go on? "It is Adonai who goes before you . . . do not fear or be dismayed" (Deut. 31:8). That belief alone is what allows us to journey. We are being led, and the guide is true and trustworthy.

Song of Songs

The journey to freedom, as portrayed in the book of Exodus, is one model that can be used in spiritual guidance. A second model is a relationship of deepening intimacy, the kind potentially developed between the individual and God, as described in the Song of Songs. The text, a collection of passionate love poetry that commentators have understood to refer to the love between God and the people of Israel, reminds us that covenant is central to our lives. At first it seems that the map of the Song of Songs will be a much easier map to follow than that of Exodus. Love has always drawn us. But love is not only nourishing, it is also painful—it can, indeed, be its own kind of desert.

The more deeply we allow love to transform us and our world, the more we find ourselves beyond known lands, in the uncharted *midbar,* or wilderness, of our lives. Love takes us out into the far reaches of vulnerability. When we love someone, our own sense of well-being becomes contingent on our beloved's being and well-being. What allows us to love that which death will take away is the sense that all our memories and loves are held by God. "For love is stronger than death"(Song of Songs 8:6). Each human love potentially opens us to the love of God, which is always offered to us.

The Song of Songs is a textual tool that allows us to explore how love changes us—not merely our feeling love but our loving another and mutually interacting with that person. As we have all learned, love grows, matures, and changes over time. But what other changes result from being in relationship over a long period of time? The spiritual guide can help the seeker explore this question within the context of human relationships and then raise the question, What if the other is not a person but God? We bring the insight of the Song of Songs to bear in our understanding of the forty-year relationship with God described in Exodus in terms of the daily presence of the pillars of cloud and fire.

Using the Maps

Why consider the Exodus story and the Song of Songs together in one context? Because their spiritual models complement each other, together giving a fuller picture of the goals of the spiritual life. Neither the map of the journey in Exodus nor the map of a relationship in the Song of Songs expresses our experience adequately.

Language confers the power to create and destroy worlds. We read in Genesis that God called the world into being by word alone. Adam, the first human, was given the task of naming all the creatures. And we his descendants, created in God's image, do the same thing in our world. When, for example, we call something a "weed," we are not giving a botanical description, we are simply saying that the plant in its present context is noxious and should be pulled out. Similarly, when we call something a "dream" or an "illusion," we disarm it and diminish its importance.

Spiritual guides help seekers notice how they have been naming their experiences and teach them how not to "undername" their lives. To be free is to let no one else name us. We are selves that can be fully understood only in terms of our relationship with God, which allows us to name ourselves and our lives. Anything that offers less undernames us and thereby trivializes our lives.

Developing a map is a painfully slow process, and we could die of spiritual starvation before we learned how to express our needs, let alone fulfill them. That's why we start with the maps we already have—Exodus and the Song of Songs—and use the time we save to modify them. We can then figuratively move out of Egypt and cross the Red Sea, but we are stopped short at Sinai. We realize that before we can continue on to the Promised Land, we must first return to our personal Egypt and recover valuable memories from an earlier time in our lives. So our journey is not quite the same as the journey of the Israelites. We discover that we each must journey in our own way, but the shared language of collective memory allows the biblical journey to contribute to our understanding of that way.

We have seen that spiritual guidance is a process concerned with the seeker's relationship with God. The spiritual guide fosters this relationship by helping seekers recognize the ways in which God still communicates with us. In the next chapter, prayer—the seeker's part in this communication—will be discussed. The spiritual guide wants to think about and articulate the subtle motion entailed in the seeker's growing intimacy with the holy. To this end, the guide makes use of the language and road markers located in our shared texts, the story of Exodus and the Song of Songs.

2

MEETING GOD
THROUGH PRAYER

Hear my cry, O God,
heed my prayer.

—Psalms 61:1

THE CENTRAL EVENT in the spiritual life is prayer. Prayer, as far too many people understand it, is usually limited to "saying prayers," repeating a liturgical text from a standard prayer book, or reciting a personal wish list of some sort. Spiritual guides try to expand people's concept of prayer so that it opens up to a relationship with God.

What happens when a person prays? It seems like a simple question. Yet we realize that before we can answer any question about prayer in general, we need to ask ourselves about our own prayer life. Why do we pray? How do we pray? When do we pray? What is prayer for us? There could be an anthology of answers, but our emphasis will be on remembering that spiritual guidance begins with our own experience.

Why Do We Pray?

Before we can examine our experiences in prayer, we must answer the question, What motivates us to pray in the first place? According to Jewish tradition, there are set times for prayer and specific rules for saying spontaneous blessing. But what about prayer itself? What is it that sweeps us heavenward, that causes the words to erupt from our souls, the music to escape from our hearts? We all have occasions in which we might have prayed—we attended services, read the prescribed texts—but nothing genuine seemed to have occurred. We discover to our disappointment that having set hours guarantees nothing. For even when we go through the motion of routine prescribed prayer, it does not mean that we are necessarily praying. Instead of focusing on fixed hours of prayer, we turn our memory toward moments, outside of more formal prayer situations, where there were intense feelings that left us speechless or where our despair suddenly lifted. Those who are led to reflect on their prayer experience try to recapture those moments, create them, call them on demand. We all recognize that this one nagging question about why we pray has generated a quest, a search in time and memory, for experiences of authentic prayer. Once we identify them, we might be able to begin to answer the question, What happens when we pray?

Levi Yitzchak of Berditchev (1740–1809) was concerned that his congregants tended to come to the synagogue only on Rosh Hashanah (New Year), ignoring all the other times of prayer throughout the year. One Rosh Hashanah evening, with the synagogue full, he told the story of a shopkeeper who lost his business in a fire. The man was distraught and shared his tale of woe with his friends at the local inn. What really concerned him was that he was indebted to a provider of raw materials—someone with whom he had done business for many years. The merchandise whose sale would have enabled him to pay the supplier had gone up in flames.

The shopkeeper's spouse advised him to tell his creditor exactly what had happened. Mustering up a great deal of courage, he made his way to the supplier's home, an exquisite villa on the edge of town. As he approached the front door, he broke into tears. He was unable to go further and sat down on the steps. Hearing the sound of sobs, the homeowner opened the door to see who was there—only to find his old friend and longtime customer hunched over in front of his house. He asked the shopkeeper why he was so upset and was told about the fire. He responded, "Don't you worry about what you owe me. I will forgive you the debt and even loan you some money in order to rebuild your business." Delighted, the shopkeeper returned to the inn to tell his friends of his good fortune.

A neighbor, not well-acquainted with the shopkeeper, overheard the story and reported it to his own wife. In turn, his spouse coaxed him to approach the same individual, tell a similar story, and receive some funds. And that's exactly what he did. When the homeowner heard the noise on his steps and opened the door, he was surprised to find a stranger there. After hearing this stranger's fabricated story, he replied, "I do not know you. I do not have a relationship with you. The shopkeeper and I have done business for many years. We have been friends for a long time." And with those words, he threw the man off his property.

After telling this story, Levi Yitzchak said: "It's the same thing with God. We can't approach as strangers and expect God to do whatever we ask. Just as it takes time to develop a relationship with other humans, it takes time to develop one with God."

It is a *mitzvah,* a divine commandment (the word also means "righteous act"), to pray every day—one among many that inform our lives. Like the ancient Temple sacrifices called "service of the heart," prayer is considered the service of the heart. But the word we translate as "worship" is *avodah,* which actually means "work"—a duty. Unfortunately, many find prayer—like work itself—to be a burden. It is a regimented discipline that is undertaken to sharpen the spirit, as daily exercise is pursued to tone the body. But if we look more carefully at work, we may come to understand something more about prayer. Work opens up a world of spiritual potential for us. We tend to associate work with expulsion from Eden, but that is not what the biblical text actually says:

> Adonai, God, took Adam and put Adam in the Garden of Eden to till it and keep it [Gen. 2:15].

Human life in the Garden included work, duties to be performed.

We must recognize, then, that work is an aspect of Paradise. We may think of some of our own experiences in which we so loved our work that it felt as if we weren't working at all. Work, rather than being onerous, adds meaning to our life. Freud taught that love and work were among our primary needs. One characteristic of work, and singularly important in our connection of work to prayer, is that work can be devoted, directed to greater meaning than that of the particular task at hand. Work can be spiritual, elevating, God-like—when we want it to be. Just as God can promise, "I will be with you" (Exod. 3:12), we can promise, "I will come to you," both through the dedication of the actions I perform and the devotion of the "work" of prayer. Morning, afternoon, evening, whether we feel like it or not, we will come, study, read texts, be reminded of our relationship—as we work our way through a life of prayer.

Why did we work in Paradise? Work can be an expression of our identity. It can offer fulfillment, absorbedness, self-forgetfulness, transcendence. It can connect us to the earth and its permanence. Work is one of the activities we share with God. According to a midrash, God intentionally left the world incomplete, inviting humans to become co-creators and finish the work of creation. This work is part of our obligation, which grows out of our relationship with God. And we perform the work of prayer because we are responsible for that relationship—it does not just come to us.

One great sage taught that in developing a spiritual life for ourselves, we have to become like the desert, free of encumbrance. Perhaps the only things that "belong" to us are the things we have shaped through the amount of time in our lives that we have poured into them. The Hebrew language says it best. It does not allow for the construction of a phrase that implies ownership. We can never actually own things. We are merely in relationship to them for a limited period of time. Yet what we love is not merely the object we created but the process of creating. The process is a form of prayer that takes the raw materials God created and the skills that God implanted in us in order to reshape the world and add beauty to it, to recreate paradise—*Gan Eden*—in our midst.

Henry Moore, the sculptor (1898–1986), commenting on work, might just as well have been commenting on prayer:

> The secret of life is to have a task, something you devote your entire life to, something you bring everything to, every minute of the day for your whole life. And the most important thing is—it must be something you cannot possibly do!

Prayer is an intrinsic good, something we devote our entire lives to, and something we cannot possibly do.

At the start of our coming to prayer, we may think of it more in terms of magic than prayer: we seek to effect a certain outcome. We equate prayer with petition. But the "inutility" of prayer is very important. If one has a goal, it is the wrong goal. Prayer is opening oneself to relationship, an approach to life lived in companionship with God.

We originally answered the question "Why do we pray?" in terms of work, an obligation, and this work opened up to reveal its positive aspects. But we haven't really explored to whom we are obliged to pray. There is a wonderful story told of a Hasidic master who traveled to a new town. On entering the town, he noticed a man cleaning the streets and inquired, "For whom do you work?" Instead of directly answering the rabbi's inquiry, the street cleaner responded, "And for whom do you work?" Hearing this question, the rabbi decided on the spot to offer the worker a job. The new employee would have only one duty: each day he must ask the rabbi, "For whom do you work?" With this query, the rabbi would be reminded of the awesome responsibility he had to God.

Prayer is about relationship. It is a form of focusing, of paying attention, of intentionality (the literal meaning of the Hebrew word *kavanah*, attentiveness in prayer). It is also a way of changing perspectives. We begin with our narrow, self-centered perspective, but once we pray we are forced to see things or situations in the context of God. To pray is to bring a concern to God, and that can transform our perspective. To illustrate by example, Luissa had a recurring blood disease and asked me to pray for her. I initially began to pray with my concern being only that she become well. But lifting Luissa in my prayer to God allowed me to see her in a different light. She was so much more than a person with an illness, she was part of a whole community related through our shared love of God. Praying for Luissa was no longer just adding a name to a list of those about whom I was concerned, it became a way to celebrate the interconnection of all of our lives.

If we start out with the understanding that prayer is an occasion for an encounter with God, we can never confuse praying with saying prayers. It would be like confusing a genuine conversation with repeating a set piece. There are texts in the prayer service, but it is not on the literal level that they function for the person praying. Some parts of the institutionalized service, repeated once or several times a day, keep the conscious mind occupied while some more hidden aspect of ourselves opens up to an encounter. The words drop away and a deeper engagement occurs.

During the time of the Bible, our people had no prayer books, no collected body of texts that a person referred to when it was time to pray. Even the psalms, the earliest known prayers of our people, whose texts can be found scattered throughout our prayer books, were generally used only in public assembly at the Temple in Jerusalem. As a result, no one could confuse the simple rote recitation of words in the prayer book with the act of praying (a distinction that is often lost today). Real prayer involves opening our self to the reality of God's presence. In the midst of prayer, we can learn to talk to God about everything—our needs, our fears, our sense of shame and guilt, our gratitude and wonder. We are able to transcend the words of the prayer text. Our capacity to do so—to "fly"—is based in part on our deep rootedness in the tradition. We are familiar with this language, these images, the world view presupposed by the tradition. That comfort is precisely what allows our thoughts the freedom to use the given text as a springboard for a wordless relationship.

The prayer book, which is built around fixed prayers (*keva*), recalls our shared yet personal history:

> My shape was not concealed from you
> when I was shaped in a hidden place,
> knit together in the recesses of the earth.
> Your eyes saw my unformed limbs;
> they were all recorded in your book.
> —Ps. 139:15–16

—and a history that belongs to the whole people:

> Give ear, my people, to my teaching,
> turn your ear to what I say.
> I will expound a theme,
> hold forth on the lessons of the past,
> things we have heard and known,
> that our ancestors have told us.
> We will not withhold them from their children,
> telling the coming generation the praises of Adonai
> and Your might,
> the wonders You performed.
>
> —Ps. 78:1–4

—or even to all of Creation:

> Adonai, You have been our refuge in every generation.
> Before the mountains came into being,
> before You brought forth the earth and the world,
> from eternity to eternity you are God.
>
> —Ps. 90:2

The different answers we can offer as to why we pray can be explored in terms of one seeker's experience. Fred had written an article on computer applications. He was very excited about the article and sent it off to a prestigious journal. Although he was somewhat embarrassed about it, he began praying that the journal would accept his article. After a few months, the article was rejected and returned. A colleague of Fred's suggested that the material in the article was too rich for a single article and that he ought to turn it into a book. Fred remained excited about the material, although dubious about his chances of publishing a book given that he couldn't even get an article published. Nonetheless, he did write the book and in time it was accepted and published.

Subsequently, with the help of his spiritual guide, he began to reflect on his earlier prayer that his initial article be accepted, something he had deeply wanted. He had thought that would be his greatest good. He realized now that he hadn't known his own greatest good and that having the article rejected and then having to rework and expand the material had been a greater good. Still, the difference between having an article accepted and having a book accepted is not that great. He might simply have learned postponed gratification. He might not, from this experience alone, have learned the more significant lesson. We do not know our own greatest good. Our good is to live a surrendered life, a life steered by God.

How we can come to recognize and cooperate with that steering will be taken up in Chapter Four.

With the help of spiritual guidance, Fred learned two things: by *not* getting what he initially desired, he discovered that that failure was good; and by getting what he later desired (the publication of his book) he discovered that that did not appreciably change his life. Then he learned that the real joy lay in the process of thinking the thoughts that formed the article and the book—that this process was a gift. He began to look for other areas in his life where he experienced this sense of joy. When he let go of goals and focused on process, when he used himself instead of focusing on himself, he found this joy. His discomfort with his original prayer was a good indication. He had sensitive "antennae" and began to affirm his own inner sense of rightness.

But regardless of Fred's experience, for most of us the first form of prayer is petition. We learn it early in life from the popular culture. We ask for what we want and believe we need. And when our prayers are not answered, we frequently begin to doubt the efficacy of prayer and our relationship with God. Even when we have learned that prayer is not the same as magic—it is about a relationship in which we try to be open and to bring all of our concerns to God—still we cannot help praying for a positive outcome when someone we love is in trouble, perhaps ill or undergoing surgery. We think that because we make a request, God has the responsibility, the obligation, to act on it. But it doesn't always happen that way.

Prayer is about relationship. This may appear to be a dogmatic statement, but it is not. Rather, it is a discovery along the path of prayer. We were created to live in relationship with God, and prayer is an intrinsic part of that relationship. Thus we never really live alone, never need to feel isolated or estranged. Life is a journey with God. God accompanies every action of our lives. We therefore pray to be mindful of God's presence. It is this presence that is both gift and promise: "I will be with you." God's felt presence in our midst is called *Shekhinah*. We invite God to be with us. We struggle to stay awake and mindful of God. We want to be heard, we want to be seen, we want to be *known*. And because of God's knowing, loving acceptance, we begin to know, integrate, and love ourselves. Only after we learn to love ourselves is the love of others possible. According to Rabbi Akiva (40–135 C.E.), the primary principle in the entire Torah is "Love your neighbor as yourself" (Lev. 19:18).

The first negative statement in the Torah is God's observation about Adam, "It is not good for Adam to be alone" (Gen. 2:18), which precedes the creation of Eve. But God's statement reminds us that we are not alone, that we are with God. We need to learn how to be with God, and one way is by entering into covenant with a human partner. Our loved one can teach us how to be with another. Sometimes we forget that God is always with us, ever present. We walk blindly among God's miracles.

All the various forms of prayer—and there are many forms—are part of our human relationships, extended to help us learn how to be with God. The different kinds of human interactions we have become models for our interaction with God. We begin as child to parent (God, then, is our mother or father), and we move on to friend or companion, perhaps even continuing (as in the Song of Songs) to God as lover. In each of these contexts our form of communication finds its parallel in one or another form of prayer. We can be the young child asking for what is desired; we can be with our friend trying to amend a breach in our relationship; we can be with our beloved praising and celebrating the wonder of our closeness. We pray to become conscious of being with God.

What Happens When We Pray?

We may pray at fixed times and seasons, but there is nothing automatic about what happens when we pray. Sometimes prayer quiets us, centers us. Sometimes it leaves us with a sense of the holy. Sometimes prayer is merely mechanical, and at other times it is urgent and desperate. Sometimes prayer is just a friendly checking-in—looking up from work to rejoice in the presence of our beloved. The answer to the question, What happens when we pray? turns out to be as complex as the answer to the question, What happens when we talk to our beloved? It must take into account why we are talking, what we intend to have happen, the ways in which we are surprised by the response. And all of this takes place within the context of our relationship. We've learned about that in our own lives, in our interactions with others. And we have come to learn that about our relationship with God as well.

One of the most difficult tasks in spiritual guidance is to get the seeker to focus on what happens during prayer. It is far easier to focus on theories of rite and ritual than on prayer itself. When pushed, a person might answer, "Nothing that I know of happens when I pray." Such a response may come from someone who has never been encouraged to focus systematically on what actually transpires during prayer. Although this discipline might be taxing, it is potentially transforming. Often, it is because we lack a vocabulary for thinking about these experiences that we do not focus on them. Sometimes reading accounts of other people's experiences allows us to recognize ways in which they resemble our own, as well as ways in which they differ. All of this is part of a process of claiming more of our own relationship with God.

The quiet in the room deepened as Joel, a teacher, took in the question, "What happens when you pray?" His eyes darted around—under the chair, at the ceiling. Finally he grew still and began to reflect on the question. He first said he wasn't sure he ever really prayed at all. Yes, he recited the morning service, but did that count? As he reflected on prayer, he listed five practices he thought might be prayer. He prayed the morning service daily. It centered him. Occasionally (and he emphasized the occasional aspect of it) a line jumped out of the text and addressed him. He specifically mentioned the *amidah* (the standing prayer, consisting of eighteen blessings) as a point in the service where he could lift all his concerns to God.

His second practice was reciting psalms. Here the phenomenon of a line jumping out of the text happened more frequently. Joel also meditated regularly. He wasn't certain whether or not to consider that prayer. As he reflected on that experience, he saw that it opened him to trust. He couldn't rush the meditation; it took as long as it took. Meditation led into darkness, but he was more and more comfortable with that darkness. Something was going on in and through meditation, but he could not say more than that. He also thought his work as a teacher was, perhaps, a form of prayer. He would find himself saying what he himself needed to hear. Finally, he considered his painting a form of worship.

His embarrassment and discomfort gone, he was able to recognize that he had a rich prayer life, one he wanted to think about and reflect on. Encouragement to focus on our prayer life and broaden our understanding of what prayer is helps us to take our relationship with God seriously and to discover that we are already deeply engaged in it.

Forms of Prayer

If we explore our relationships with our friends, we will notice topics of conversation analogous to the different forms of prayer. This should not be too surprising, because one of the principal ways in which we learn to relate to God is in and through the people given to us in this world. Ultimately, as audacious as it may sound, we are to move in the direction of becoming a friend of God. It is a role we are to grow into. We begin as the child who obeys because the way is laid down by our Creator/parent figure. But if we are to become co-creators and take responsibility for *tikun olam* (repair of the world), then even if it seems rationally unthinkable, we must move beyond the role of child to the role of friend.

Rabbi Akiba even suggests we can go beyond that role, to become the lover of God. The motion of our progress in prayer can be charted in terms of the motion of change in relationship found in the Song of Songs. The different forms of prayer exhibit the following stages: (1) recognition of the call of the beloved; (2) the growing sense of discipline and faithfulness in persevering in response; (3) the joy of connection in the relationship and the dark night of abandonment (the moment when the beloved does not respond to the lover at the door); and finally (4) complete reconciliation and union. Throughout this process, the spiritual guide supports the person in continuing the prayer life and in recognizing when forms of prayer have become mechanical and something else is being asked for.

Petition

Bakashah, petition, which is so central in the prayer of childhood, would ideally be rare in our adult human communications. We shouldn't associate with people just because of what they could do for us; we should associate with them only for their own worthiness. (We can recognize the persistence of self-interest in human relationships as being symptomatic of those who have not grown beyond childish relationships.) And maybe that will become increasingly true as we pray more and get to know God better. In one section of the Talmud, *Berakhot,* the rabbis dedicate several pages to some of their own prayers—personal prayers that they regularly added to the prescribed core of liturgy. Many of them are particularly apt for the spiritual seeker. A favorite one is attributed to Rabbi Alexandri:

> May it be Your will, Adonai our God, to place us in an illumined corner and not to place us in a darkened corner. Let not our heart be sick nor our eyes darkened [Babylonian Talmud, *Berakhot,* 17a].

Although petition is so common in early life, adults in spiritual guidance frequently have to be encouraged to ask for what they need. They feel that such asking is akin to magic and has no place in a mature spiritual relationship. The spiritual guide aims throughout to encourage authenticity in the relationship between the seeker and God. If there is something on a person's mind, the guide suggests praying about it. It may seem like petitioning, but the deeper reality is that it is a sharing of what is most on the seeker's heart and mind. Expressing one's needs makes it easier to enter into other forms of prayer.

Intercession

Intercession is a special form of petition. We take our concern for someone else into the context of our relationship with God. The *mi sheberakh* prayer for healing is an example of this form of intercessory prayer, one that is increasing in popularity among Jews today. It is generally said during the course of the Sabbath or festival Torah reading, in the assembly of the entire congregation, in the context of community—one of the most powerful settings for healing. But individuals frequently pray for those they love outside of congregational services.

A schoolteacher underwent a grave illness that required major surgery. As she was recovering in the hospital, someone told her how many people had been praying for her. "I know," she replied. "As I recovered, I could feel their prayers helping me along the way."

We pray for those who come to us for guidance—and as we lift each person in thought, individually, to God's concern and care, we find it is impossible to pray for them and not grow fonder of them. Of course, that presupposes the distinction between saying words and praying. Going through a list of names is not the same as taking each person into our consciousness and lifting our concerns for them into this larger perspective.

Thanksgiving

We do notice and appreciate what our friends do, and say so. The moment we recognize some of the gifts around us—holding, nurturing, supporting, and sustaining—we begin to notice still more. As we first open our eyes each morning we give thanks for the restoration of consciousness. Each of the prayers in the early-morning blessings reminds us of all that makes it possible for us to function: all the ducts and tubes in our body working properly, the strength we gain, the sleep being removed from our eyes. We go on to recognize that it is not only we who are restored, and so we bless God's daily renewal of the work of Creation.

Confession

And then come our moments of confession, *vidui,* when we admit our shortcomings and failures. We make mistakes. We all do. We are careless, thoughtless, and we are sorry. Confession is not about warding off punishment. Rather, it is about healing and the maintenance of love and friendship. Moses Maimonides, the renowned medieval philosopher

(1135–1204), wrote an entire treatise on the rules and regulations for making *teshuvah,* the act of contrition and renewal. In the process of preparing to admit our sins before God, we learn how to "beg *meḥilah*" (as our folk tradition calls it), or ask forgiveness from others. According to Maimonides, if we commit a sin, we must confess the sin by saying the following:

> I implore You, God. I sinned. I transgressed. I committed an iniquity before You by doing _____. I have been chastened and shamed by what I have done. And for as long as I live, I shall not return to this act.

Confession is an act of cleansing, of purging ourselves of the stuff that poisons the soul and obscures our vision of God.

Silent Prayer

A genuine friendship is more than just a series of monologues. Real friendship demands an ongoing, honest dialogue—the kind we may find with spouses and lovers or intimate friends. Sometimes we just need to be together in *silence.* It is astounding how long we can go before recognizing that we need to listen for God's word as well as pouring out our words to God.

Prayer usually begins with an emptying out of all the busyness of our days. We have to rid ourselves of the preoccupations that bog us down. One colleague invites people, as they come into the synagogue to pray, to leave all of their mundane concerns outside so that they might truly be able to pray. Sometimes we have to struggle just to reach the point of stillness where we can open ourselves up to true prayer and an encounter with the divine. True prayer moves toward silence because its ultimate aim is the indwelling presence of God, *Shekhinah:* "To You silence is praise" (Ps. 65:2).

Some will argue that prayer can be replaced, in principle, by silence. Silence is really part of prayer. It is the spaces between the words. It is the intention, the *kavanah,* behind each of the words. Some Ḥasidim build entire relationships in silence, as the novelist Chaim Potok describes in his novel *The Chosen.* A therapist has related that she sits for long periods of silence with her patients, just waiting for them to speak. Sometimes they do. And when they don't, she sits and waits longer. Even writers of prayer, whose tools are words, finally understand that all the words of prayer are really inadequate. At best, words can only approximate what we feel, what we want to say. So we may be moved to dance, whether in spontaneous forms or in the swaying motion of the traditional Jew at prayer. It is a different way of maintaining a beat to a different kind of music. One of the central images we have of early Judaism is the empty shrine at the heart of the Temple: the Holy of Holies. This is the place where the High Priest entered only once a year—on Yom Kippur. That empty shrine points toward the silence to which prayer leads. A hospital chaplain sat in silence as he waited out the time of his young patient's surgery, wanting to pray but not even knowing what to pray for. He learned to just be still and enter into God's presence.

We know what that silent presence can mean in our human relationships. Sometimes it is just holding hands with someone in pain. A simple hug. A caring touch. Our tradition teaches that we have no right to judge another's pain. The only thing we can do is reach out and share it. The comfort comes, the burden is lessened when it is shared with others. We know all too well people who turn away when real trouble hits; and we know those few special friends who are there. They cannot change the circumstances, but they choose to be with us, and their presence is a very special gift. That's one of the ways God sends healing presence into the world: through the sacred acts of others. They help us bear our pain.

Something analogous to the presence of friends is found in the silence of prayer. This does not rule out the possibility of prayers of petition and intercession for healing and for cure. We believe in the healing response of God. But prayers of silent presence are at the heart of our growing relationship with God.

When people try to explain and justify silence, entering into quiet, they frequently offer rationales that appear to trivialize the experience: silence relieves stress, lowers blood pressure, is restful and centering. The physician Herbert Benson calls it the "relaxation response" (Benson and Klipper, *The Relaxation Response*). But the health benefits of silence point to a larger reality. Silence is the place where our restless, uneasy, discomforted, and confused minds can yield up to God and find rest. Afterwards, we are thrust back into life with renewed psychic energy, seeing the world from God's perspective.

O Adonai, you have been our refuge in every generation [Ps. 90:1].

The ratio of rest to activity changes throughout our lives. Sometimes—particularly in our youth—we are so busily engaged in activity that rest and centering occur only in momentary flashes of connection. We like to call these "Sabbath moments."

A friend with four children under the age of five says she has no time for formal, fixed prayers. Any formal prayers she attempts are interrupted by a cry, a need for help, another demand. So for now her prayer takes the form of silent blessing, an intense focus during the busy activities of the day—on her children, her home, her spouse. She finds a way to just let the gratitude "sink in," as she likes to say. She knows God is with her, beside her, in her love for her family. For a while this has to be implicit. Later, when the two older children are in nursery school and kindergarten, and she can put the younger ones down for naps, she will attempt a more explicit approach to a prayer life. But her prayers are no less authentic.

Communal Prayer

It is an awesome thing to encounter God. But as we repeat the prayers said by generations and generations of Jews, the words remind us that we do not stand alone. Never. Others have said these words, and all around us others are saying them now. Their faith upholds our own. At points of deepest engagement and maximum fear in our spiritual life—at entry into covenant, at moments of transition, at the joining of marriage, and at death—we are encouraged and comforted by the words that have been used by our ancestors. Words sometimes convey new meanings, and sometimes merely say what has been said before, reminding us, "I will be with you."

The daily worship has aspects that are communal and moments that are intensely private. It's just like singing in a chorus. We must learn our part and integrate it with the whole. But sometimes we lose our place in the music, have to take a breath, or just can't sing what we are supposed to sing. So we look to someone else who may have the place when we've lost ours. We are liable to lose our place not because we cannot follow the text rapidly enough, but because we cannot own all the words of the prayers. Some may have expressed what we felt in the past—before we suffered a profound loss, for example—but now we say the words with great difficulty; some we hope to grow into, but at present represent beliefs that we have yet to make our own; and others we're not sure we'll ever be able to agree with. We don't want to restrict ourselves to saying only those words that we currently believe, because we want to be stretched by our prayer. When praying feels the most difficult, the genuine belief and fervor of some in our congregation can carry us. Likewise, when we are carrying either the melody line or the harmony, our voice needs to blend and be in balance with the other parts so that the whole harmonious sound can emerge. We can, in our faith, help carry our fellow congregants. Music and prayer involve much more than our individual voices or even our individual line. When communal worship works, we do experience transcendence. Referring to music, T. S. Eliot wrote, "You are the music while the music lasts." The same applies to prayer.

Prayer adds sacred rhythm to our daily routine. Regular prayer helps to steady us in the turbulent seas of time. To the uninitiated, communal worship may sound like a cacophony of sound, but to one with spiritual insight, it is a melody that binds the generations.

> You shall be praised forever, our Rock, our Redeemer, our Sovereign. You fashion angelic spirits to serve You; beyond the heavens, they all await your instruction. In a chorus, they proclaim with reverence words of the living God, eternal Sovereign. They are all adoring, beloved, and choice—in awe they fulfill their Creator's will. In pure sanctity, they raise their voices in song and psalm, extolling and exalting, declaring the power, praise, holiness, and majesty of God, the great, mighty, and awesome Sovereign, the Holy One. Vowing to one another, they swear loyalty to God's rule and hallow their Creator with serenity, pure speech, and sacred song, in one voice singing with reverence: "Holy, holy, holy is *Adonai Tzeva'ot*; the whole earth is full of God's glory." Then the celestial *ofanim* and the holy beings, rising with a loud sound toward the *seraphim*, respond with praise and say, "Praised be the glory of Adonai throughout the universe." To the God of blessing, they sweetly sing; to the Sovereign, the living God, they offer hymns and praises [Adapted from blessings following the morning call to worship].

This prayer offers images of singing in unison, in antiphon (response), and in perfect harmony. It offers us an image of *kedushah* (holiness), of the heavenly angels that must have inspired the Levitical choir of the ancient Temple.

Using the words of the prayer book allows us to stand in community across countless generations. Our people have said the *Shema* prayer ("Hear! O Israel, *Adonai* is our God, *Adonai* is One") almost as far back as we can trace our ancestors. As we say these words, we close our eyes and gather in all our senses to focus on the meaning of this short phrase. But we are not alone in doing so. The Levites join us, as do the throngs in ancient Jerusalem. As we say these words, we are joined through time and space with the generations of Jews who share our unity of faith—and who cry out alone in the night, as we do, reaching out to God.

Resistance

Communal prayer is one support for our prayer life. But even in communal prayer, or even after the intimacy of silent prayer, it may seem surprising that we suddenly seem resistant to entering into prayer. Spiritual guides recognize the many different forms that resistance takes. We may pray when we're afraid, but sometimes prayer itself can cause fear. The spiritual guide encourages the seeker to persist, and the regular structure of prayer helps maintain the relationship with God. Prayer is transformative. Sometimes we hesitate, afraid that we'll be asked to change too much or to change into someone we don't recognize; or we may be asked to change too rapidly or urged to do something beyond our present courage and strength. Sometimes the joy itself, inherent in the sense of intimacy with God, frightens us. And ecstasy (*hitlahavut* in Hebrew), which we may experience on occasion, can be very scary. We may also feel unworthy, or we may become uncertain who we are as we find ourselves doing things without the accustomed strain. We don't think we like strain, but it is our usual mode of operation and is one of our assurances that the effort we are making is really our own. When things happen without stress, we wonder whether we made those things happen or whether they just happened "through" us. We have no sense of control. We must learn to give up control and let God back into our lives. We cling to the old principle we learned in physical education class or in the local health club: "No pain, no gain," yet it is contradicted in this situation. Our usual view of causality has become jeopardized.

Is this ease worth it? Sometimes we simply withdraw from this time of intimacy because it leaves us exposed, our selves naked. At other times it seems simply to end by itself. The experience suggests a different way of understanding ourselves and our way of being in this world—and we're not sure we're ready for it. So busyness is not all that stands in the way of explicit communication; some other obstacles are shyness, a sense of unworthiness, and a feeling that our words are no longer appropriate to the person we have become. For so many reasons, the conversation breaks down.

The spiritual guide can remind the seeker of some ways to begin again. Once again, human relationships serve as a model: sometimes sincere appreciation can restart a long-broken conversation. We may be far from ready to share with God our fears or even the events of our days, but we do notice the wonder of a tree or a gathering storm, and we simply voice that wonder. A small beginning, and yet prayers have a strange tendency to gather other prayers around them. We start with an initial awareness, and this awareness expands. The tree, the storm, everything we sense in the world that surrounds us is connected to other things we admire and appreciate. Still, there is usually something left unsaid—and until those unarticulated thoughts are expressed, the communication is incomplete and the relationship unhealed. But when we finally release what we've been holding back, then words emerge from our hearts and enter our souls.

Rather than honestly confessing all that obstructs our communication, we might resort to other strategies. Prayer is not the only route to God, we tell ourselves, so we get busy performing various *mitzvot,* or we become immersed in study, plunging deeply into texts so that we don't have to face others or ourselves. Both are indeed paths to God; they are forms of prayer because they acknowledge God's presence and our relationship to God. But when there is no communication in that relationship, these other paths of prayer may become blocked. They may look promising, but when we get to the point of approaching God's presence, we draw ourselves back, just as we did when we were praying in the synagogue or communing with God at home. Study becomes abstract—removed from the events of our lives. This is one reason why we study with a *hevruta,* or partner.

Complaint and Outrage

A major cause of resistance is angry feelings that we are ashamed to artic-ulate. In our human relationships, we have to really trust someone before we will have a real fight. Lovers do fight, spouses do argue—it helps love to grow, not falter. The alternative is simply to avoid spending time together or making that time safe and sterile through formality and polite-ness. But a genuine fight can really be a profound communication and, although very difficult and frequently painful, can deepen the relationship. Do we care enough to avoid falling into formal, correct behavior and really struggling for a genuine relationship with all its ups and downs and the possibility of total honesty?

Honesty is not only about what we think but about what we feel. We may "know" that what has happened is for the best, but we feel bereft. Both of these experiences, knowing and feeling, need to be brought to our relationship with God. Many of the attributes of God (which are described in religious texts in a variety of ways) reflect God's empathy for our human feelings. We may therefore say, "God doesn't need to be told what I'm thinking or feeling because God already knows everything." But the spiritual guide must explain to the seeker that it is not a question of knowledge, it is a question of relationship. Though prayers of complaint and outrage are an ancient Jewish tradition, it is always scary to tell God just how hurt and angry we are. Consider the thirteenth psalm, where the writer expresses explicit outrage:

How long, Adonai; will you ignore me forever?
How long will you hide your face from me?
How long will I have cares on my mind,
grief in my heart all day?
How long will my enemy have the upper hand?
Look at me, answer me, Adonai, my God!

—Ps. 13:2–4

"Look at me, answer me!" Can we really say that to God? We might think about writing our own psalms or imitate one that exists in the biblical canon. All of our feelings are part of the relationship, and we need to communicate them, even though it may be frightening to share them. We may have survived a major trauma. We've survived, but the world will never look the same to us. We can't even look at our pain. True, God may say there is a limit to the flood waters, and that they will not overflow their boundaries:

Who closed the sea behind doors . . .
When I made breakers my limit for it,
And set up bars and doors,
And said "You may come so far and no farther,
Here your surging waves will stop"?

—Job 38:8–11

But we believe that if we ever let our grief out, we would drown in it. It takes a lot to get "well-brought-up" people to finally express their anger. It just doesn't seem like the right thing to do. We have been taught to suppress our emotions, particularly if we are men. We may have to learn the expression of such emotion anew. Even dancing on Simḥat Torah (at the completion of the annual Torah-reading cycle) or donning masks on Purim (which celebrates the victory of the Jews over their Persian enemies, as described in the book of Esther) is an extraordinary challenge for many.

Joan had lost her job and had gone out to the country for some time to reflect and reevaluate. During the first three weeks of her country retreat, she received no mail, and no one called her. Had she really disappeared from everyone's consciousness so quickly? Finally, a letter came; it was a rejection of a manuscript she had submitted for publication. Then the phone rang. The caller announced the death of a friend. Whatever renewed sense of meaning, transformed vision, and hope she had acquired on her retreat were knocked out of her. So, mindful of what her spiritual guide had told her about authenticity in her relationship with God, she took her outrage to the Creator. It had been growing for some time.

God I am angry! So much has been taken from me and I just wanted a
little support. I am ungrateful—probably. But what can I enjoy? What
can I celebrate? What can I hope for? I get "wooed into the wilderness"
only to have everything taken from me. I'm furious. I don't want to write,
I don't want to work again, I don't want *anything*. I'm just furious and
sad and bitter and resentful, and there is a limit to my resilience.

Joan received no immediate answer to her outburst, but also no withdrawal of a sense of presence. She could say what she was feeling and still
be faithful. Something lived deeper than her feelings, and this something
was a relationship that was becoming increasingly clear to her.

Dan goes to the synagogue and sits there silently, in protest. He
believes—and challenges God within the context of that belief.

Simple but honest words are part of the poetry of prayer, even when
there are no carefully constructed passages of verse. We don't always
know what to say or how to say it. We know only that we want to say
something. Relationships cannot live without honesty. All falseness—any
measure of it—destroys. All politeness, diplomacy, formality—all ways of
not saying what we most deeply feel—are forms of denial. The psalms
remind us of the degree of honesty in the psalmist's relationship with God.
We can begin by entering into a psalm and making those words our own;
then we can modify the psalm so that the deep hurt we are experiencing
can find expression.

The psalms model the penetrating honesty we need in our own lives. They
help us give voice to what has succeeded in choking off prayer for so long—
and the "answer" we receive is usually not an explanation. It is the ever-reas-
suring statement of God in Exodus: "I will be with you." That's all we need
to know, even though we have to repeat it to ourselves often so that at
last our heart may feel what our head has begun to know. (One of the reasons the *amidah* prayer is said in a hushed undertone is to create a quietness in which our hearts may hear the deeper communications of God.)

We may need to express our anger, hurt, and outrage more than once.
They have been bottled up for years. But now letting them out is easier, and
after a while, we come to recognize that the relationship has survived our
outbursts and that, in fact, it was ongoing even when we were unable to pray
at all. God's faithfulness in the face of our coldness awes and humbles us.

Spiritual Guidance and Prayer

In spiritual guidance, the fundamental questions that seekers need help in
facing are about changes in their prayer life. Among these changes are a
shift in the relative emphases of petition, thanksgiving, and confession;

fluctuations in the experience of peace or ease; the ebb and flow of felt presence; the development of dryness or boredom; and breakthroughs into a sense of timelessness. Also needing examination are changes outside of prayer, such as the healing of intractable anger or hatred.

We know that hatred distorts and deforms us, but we can't seem to get beyond it. We may try a psychological approach: who does Tom (or Linda or Elaine or Jim) remind us of? We try to get ourselves to think of how distressing and deprived Tom's childhood must have been to have made him so difficult. It does no good. There is Tom, and once again our stomach knots. The hatred is as virulent as ever. Finally—and it is often a very long time in coming—we may pray about it. It's the same thing that Beruria taught her spouse Rabbi Meir (according to the Talmud) when he was concerned about the evildoers who lived in their neighborhood. "Do not pray for their end. Rather, pray for the end of their actions." Once we pray to be healed of our hatred, shifting our focus from changing Tom to changing our relationship with Tom and taking responsibility for our own feelings, a wonderful softening takes place. What could not be accomplished by will, gritted teeth, or psychology has been accomplished by prayer. It truly is a miracle, a liberation from our personal Egypt, where we were enslaved, bound by shackles.

However, when Linda shows up, evoking all the same old responses that Tom had triggered, it may again be a long time before we return to prayer for our own healing from anger and hatred. These emotions are too intimate to us, too closely connected to what we understand to be our identity. The spiritual guide usually does not respond to such a transformation as our healing of hatred for Tom by offering some theory of, say, how an appeal to a higher reality can transform our emotions and still leave us as a free self. Rather, the concern is to make us aware of our deepening life with God. The guide will help us recognize that we can pray to go beyond hatred and irritation so that we can become capable of loving.

Changes in our prayer life are fundamental, because it is in prayer (using the term to include religious study and righteous acts) that we meet God. Prayer is not a mechanical exercise, and it can make the most significant demands on us. We approach God with our petition only to discover that God is asking us to change our lives in certain ways. The spiritual guide encourages the seeker to keep the relationship going, even when feelings of resistance to praying arise. The guide also affirms that prayer should take the form that is most natural and authentic to the seeker. The guide can move easily between the two maps of the Song of Songs and Exodus, helping the seeker recognize the move from a kind of enslavement to a sense of deeper connectedness with God. The seeker may learn the surprising truth that ecstatic prayer experiences are more common for beginners than for those further along the spiritual way, just as miraculous events occur more often in the early chapters of Exodus than in the last third of the book. In the beginning we need more encouragement and more wonders. Later our focus shifts, from God's gifts to God. Just as we recognize our prayer experience as one mapped in Exodus, we come to realize that we are indeed part of the Torah, that we participate in the ongoing relationship between our people and God. Then we begin to see that it is not enough to talk. We have to listen—we have to give some space for God to speak with us.

The Kotzker Rebbe (1787–1859) was asked by his students, "Tell us, rebbe, where is God?" Came the rebbe's response, "Wherever you let God in."

3

LISTENING WITH SPIRITUAL ATTENTIVENESS

Hear, O Israel!
Adonai is our God,
Adonai is One.

—Deuteronomy 6:4

THE CENTRAL CREEDAL STATEMENT of prayer in Judaism is based on hearing. The familiar *Shema* begins, "*Hear,* O Israel!" It does not say, "*See,* O Israel!" Like other religions and cultures, Judaism is distinguished by one particular sense that is emphasized in much of its liturgy. For the Greek world, the dominant sense was sight: the philosopher saw and enjoyed. The touchstone for reality was seeing (compare the English adage, "seeing is believing"), and to understand something was to see it (as we say, "I see what you mean"). For the Jewish world, the central sense is hearing. *Na'aseh venishmah,* "We shall do and we shall hear" (Deut. 5:24), said the ancient Israelites as they were presented with the Torah. The Jew hears and responds. The distinctions between sight and sound may seem somewhat abstract until we consider the challenges presented by the task of spiritual guidance. If the primary sense in Judaism is hearing, we must learn to grow quiet, to shut out noise and busyness, in order to truly hear. In the resulting calm we may discover that God is still speaking in the world—and to us.

Judaism: A Religion of Sound, not Sight

In order to understand what is at the core of the difference between sight and sound, we should ask what appears to be a rather simple question: Why don't we confuse sight with sound? Even three-year-old children are not mistaken in making this distinction. At first, we might respond that sight comes through our eyes, and sound only through our ears, but that is not what allows us to be so clear about the difference. In fact, when neither eyes nor ears are operating, when scientists simply stimulate the corresponding areas of the brain, we can still distinguish a sight from a sound. The distinction is based on the different fields the two senses deliver. Sight gives us the fields of shape, color, and texture, while sound gives volume, pitch, harmony, and rhythm. The significance of each of these characteristics of sound finds its analog in the religion that is centered on hearing: harmony becomes not only the relationship between sound frequencies but the blending and consonance of viewpoints; rhythm becomes not only the temporal component of the music but the structuring of time by the worshiper (into sacred and ordinary time); both pitch and volume lead to questions of discernment and discrimination. How can we distinguish all the sounds around us so that we can recognize the voice that has a sacred imperative?

We take our senses for granted until they are at risk—ask anyone who has been challenged by a limitation or loss of any of them. Even the transition to bifocal lenses as we enter middle age helps us understand what is at stake. But as we try to explore the deceptively familiar senses in an attempt to understand them anew, we become aware of two important characteristics: sight is instantaneous; sound unfolds over time. Judaism and other religions that give priority to sound also give priority to sacred time. On the other hand, religions that emphasize sight tend to emphasize sacred place. With this distinction in mind, we consider it natural that Judaism, a religion in which historical events play such a basic role, should also be centered on hearing.

The relationship of the self to what it sees differs from the relationship of the self to what it hears. When we view something, what we see becomes an object to our subjectivity. But when we listen to something, what we hear displaces our own consciousness: This distinction between sight and sound in terms of the relative distance to our own subjectivity has been acutely drawn by the philosopher Hans Jonas, who points out that sight is the ideal distance-sense, the only sense in which the advantage lies not in proximity but distance. "The best view is by no means the closest view . . . we consciously stand back and create distance in order to look at the world, i.e., at objects as parts of the world" (*The Phenomenon of Life,* pp.149–152). What we achieve is not *objectivity* but *objectivism*— the mistaken belief that we are not involved and not invested in our perception of the world. Sound, on the contrary, usually requires closeness to even be heard. "You are the music while the music lasts" (Eliot, *Four Quartets*). Anything we see is outside ourselves, but we also have the ability to hear from within. We can hear our own heart beat and, in the vast silence of the desert, we can even hear the blood coursing through our veins. This subtle distinction may explain how and why our religion of hearing recognizes both transcendent and immanent aspects of God.

Our breathing, both within and without, becomes something to focus on as we prepare to pray. We hear it. We feel it. Breathing represents the force of life itself. It is the first thing we do upon entering the world; and when we stop, our life is at an end. Listening to our breathing also helps us connect with what was taught on Mount Sinai in the form of Torah. Some biblical commentators say that all 613 commandments were given at Sinai; others claim it was only *aseret hadibrot* (literally, the ten words or utterances), commonly referred to as the Ten Commandments. According to Maimonides, the Israelites heard only the inarticulate sound of God's voice; only Moses heard the words in their meaningful articulation and communicated them to the people (*Guide to the Perplexed, ii,* p. 33). Rabbi Mendel of Ryamanov carried these ideas further, saying that the Israelites heard only the letter *aleph,* with which the first word (*Anokhi*) of the Hebrew text begins. But, as Gershom Scholem points out, "In Hebrew the consonant *aleph* represents nothing more than the position taken by the larynx when a word begins with a vowel. . . . To hear the *aleph* is to hear next to nothing; it is the preparation for all audible language" (*On the Kabbalah and Its Symbolism,* p. 30). In other words, what the people heard was the billowing of their lungs. So when we take cognizance of our breathing and listen only to it, we are listening for the voice of Sinai once again. The psalmist said it best: *Kol haneshamah tehallel Yah,* "May every living thing [everything that takes breath] praise God" (Ps. 150:6).

Both sight and sound can be used to convey meaning. A printed book can convey time duration by spacing, but how does it convey vocal inflection and tone of voice? That takes a masterful construction of language. In the earliest extant scrolls that contain the Torah text, the scribes used a variety of methods to approximate sound, including spacing. The Song of the Sea (Exod. 15:1–18) is a wonderful example: the layout of the passage in the Torah itself clearly conveys that it was a song. In rabbinic times, the Masoretes supplied the biblical text with a rudimentary system of music notation that served to phrase and punctuate the sentences and to provide a hierarchy of emphasis for the words and syllables. The notation also codified how the text was sung in public readings. And in rare moments, as the Torah is chanted in the synagogue—a re-enactment of revelation itself—we can feel swept back to the moment of first utterance, hearing the echoes of the original revelation across the desert sand.

A central image in the biblical story is the revelation at the burning bush. Moses, while shepherding the flock of his father-in-law Jethro, comes upon a bush that is aflame but is not consumed in the fire. As he watches the unusual conflagration, he hears God's voice, which tells him that he is standing on holy ground (Exod. 3:1–5). The burning bush episode appears to favor the sense of sight. However, if we examine the characteristics of the burning bush episode, we soon discover that its salient feature—which it shares with other spiritual experiences—is that it unfolds over time. Moses saw a bush that burned but was not consumed—an event that could only take place over time. Visually, it is possible to rush ahead and see the end point; aurally, that can't be done. A musical phrase, for example, unfolds over time, one note after another. We cannot hear the last note before we've heard the next to last. Dancing is the same. We have to be on this beat, at this step, at a particular time. If we rush ahead, we will be "out of step" with the music. What is central to this distinction between instantaneous sight and the unfolding of sound over time is that sight is about the whole and some end; that you finally see or "get," but sound is about presence, this moment. At its very core, sound is about a developing relationship.

In Exodus 33, Moses asks to see God's presence:

> "Oh let me behold your Presence." And God answered, "I will make all My goodness pass before you, and I will proclaim before you the name Adonai, and the grace that I grant and the compassion I show. But," God said, "you cannot see My face, for no one may see Me and live." And Adonai said, "See, there is a place near Me. Station yourself on the rock and, as My Presence passes by, I will put you in a cleft of the rock and shield you with My hand until I have passed by. Then I will take My hand away and you will see My back; but My face must not be seen [Exod. 33:18–23].

Moses is informed that he cannot see God and live. The author of the text implies that seeing is immediate and instantaneous. Instead, Moses is told that he may hear God's name. In addition, the expression "see My back" implies that he—and we—may recognize God's presence in retrospect. With the help of others, we can be taught to recognize God in the events in our past. While there are interesting exceptions (notably Hagar and Jacob), the Torah teaches that we cannot see God and live. Something analogous to that belief is suggested by Ernest Becker: "The great boon of repression is that it makes it possible to live decisively in an over-whelmingly miraculous and incomprehensible world, a world so full of beauty, majesty, and terror that if animals perceived it all they would be paralyzed to act" (*The Denial of Death,* p. 50). In the present, the beatific vision would be more than our fragile vessels could hold, and we would be destroyed. But, in retrospect, we can—like Jacob—recognize that "God was in this place, and I, I did not know" (Gen. 28:16). With this per-spective, we can be sensitized to God's nearness in the unfolding events of our lives. It should also prepare us for the encounters with God that lie ahead. Although we might expect our past to be sealed into history, this outlook on God's role in our lives allows the past to remain alive through our current attempts to grapple with it. In the process of this grappling, we can come close to God's presence. The rabbis put it this way: "The eye is shown only what it is capable of seeing and the ear is given to hear only what it is capable of hearing" (*Avot d'Rabbi Natan* a:2).

Marilyn had been married for fifteen years. She worked in a law office, but her real joy was her religious study. She had been seeing her spiritual guide, a fellow student in her Talmud class, for many months when she came in one day quite irritated. Her husband, not for the first time, had forgotten her birthday. Her guide listened to her complaint and then asked her to read Exodus 20:4, 20:19, 32:1–4, 33:18, and 34:33–35. Marilyn quickly jotted down the numbers and checked the Torah. The first quotation was the text of the second commandment, "You shall not make yourself a graven image or any likeness of what is in the heavens above or on the earth below or in the waters under the earth." The sec-ond was the puzzling text "Thus shall you say to the Israelites: You your-selves saw that I spoke to you from the very heavens." The third was the story of the building of the golden calf. Then came Moses' request "Oh let me behold your Presence!" And the last quotation was the account of Moses' face so radiant from nearness to God that he had to wear a veil when he was with the Israelites.

Marilyn looked up at her guide when she had finished reading the texts and asked what their meaning was. He explained that here the Torah was recounting the move of a people focused on sight to one that could hear the word and be transformed. Marilyn was intrigued. She could certainly see that in the second commandment. The second quotation was a con-flation of sight and sound—seeing that God spoke. Even Moses, in the fourth quotation, was not exempt from wanting a visual indication of

God's presence, but what he got was the view of God after God has passed—in other words, not the instantaneous satisfaction of sight but the unfolding over time of sound. The building of the golden calf resulted from the Israelites' inability to make the move from sight to sound. And the immediate consequence was that Moses, who could draw close to God, had to present his own understanding in a veiled, mediated way.

Marilyn was pleased with this explication but became puzzled when her spiritual guide added, "And how does this apply to you?" Suddenly she laughed. "Sight is immediate and tangible, but reality for us Jews is tested not by appearance but by constancy over time. So I shouldn't be so annoyed because my husband doesn't remember my birthday but should ask myself about his faithfulness over time."

Hearing God's Call

God's call to us unfolds, as it did with our biblical ancestors, progressively through the events of our lives, in much the same way that, according to Reform Judaism, God's revelation evolves over time. In the Bible, we see this in the progressive stages of the call to the patriarch Jacob: crisis (Esau's rage), discipline (twenty years in the house of Laban), admission of his own powerlessness (at the banks of Jabbok), and living his transformed life (signaled by his change of name from Jacob to Israel, a life of faithfulness).

Crisis

The first call to Jacob drew him away from the existence he knew, the comfort and settled aspect of life in the tents of his parents. God called Jacob to set out on a new adventure, although Jacob focused only on fleeing Esau's fury (Gen. 27:43). We find ourselves faced with a similar challenge in our own lives when all that made us settled and complacent is suddenly called into question. Sometimes the challenge is forced on us when we pass a milestone in our lives or suffer a life-threatening illness. Our perspective changes dramatically, and we are often able to hear God's call to us more clearly. So we seek to change the direction of our lives. We are called *away* from something much before we can consider what we are being called *toward*. It's frustrating, unsettling, and sometimes painful. We may not yet know to what we are being drawn, what we are being called to do; we know only that we cannot stay where we are.

Some crises involve thwarted hopes and dreams: losing a job, ending a relationship, having to leave home. But some involve things we have wanted and dreamed about. Beth and her husband knew they wanted a child. Her pregnancy was normal; the delivery was normal; the baby was normal. But Beth now felt anything *but* normal—at least, what she had previously thought of as normal. She gained a great sense of the miraculous, and she also became aware that never again could she sleep peacefully unless she knew that her daughter was well. Her entire center of gravity had shifted. She was suddenly free from the bonds of narcissism, but she had no idea how this new identity as mother would be integrated with other senses of herself. This "crisis" evolved in Beth into the discipline of parenthood.

Discipline

The next twenty years in Jacob's life saw his transformation from powerless alien in the home of his uncle Laban to husband of four wives, father of twelve sons and a daughter, and owner of myriad flocks. Sometimes the journey of our lives takes us somewhere unplanned and unanticipated. But it is a sense of personal discipline that keeps us in that place and prepares us for the next phase. However we define and understand it, Judaism demands of us a life of discipline.

God's call does not precipitate the immediate change we might expect. Instead, over time, we are drawn to develop a lifestyle compatible with our commitment. This is the aspect of discipline. Most of us can muster our courage for a single heroic feat requiring a burst of inner energy, but God's call is about the shaping of our lives. Spiritual heroism is based in the reality and routine of everyday living. This kind of dedication is not easy. It does not contain a quick fix that offers an immediate high—even a spiritual one. The spiritual life is a centered life, balanced between the extremes, with an occasional glimpse of the holy. It offers neither constant peaks nor constant valleys; most of the time, one is living on the plains. Jacob's life was shaped by the twenty years he spent working in his uncle's house. This is daily living, the kind of life we all lead.

One of the roles of the spiritual guide is to help seekers name their experience with proper dignity. Many of us have been led to take other people's lives more seriously than our own, but our own life's experiences are as significant as any life that has ever been lived on this planet. Beth, the woman who recognized how markedly her life had changed when she became a mother, also had to recognize that faithfulness to the routines of caring for her daughter was a way of shaping herself for her relationship with God. Her covenant with God was, in part, embedded in her covenant with her infant daughter.

Admission of Powerlessness

Despite material prosperity, Jacob came to an awareness that he lacked control of his life. Nothing he had acquired in the twenty years he had spent in the house of Laban stood with him as he wrestled with an unknown force at the river Jabbok. He stood alone, as we all do, in the nakedness of self. Yet Jacob came away from that confrontation blessed and wounded, or perhaps blessed by his having been wounded (Gen. 32:24–29). Survivors of life-threatening illnesses often tell us that their being so sick taught them something important about their lives. Nakedness of self, extreme vulnerability, can bring families together and to God in profound ways.

Many things happen to us in the course of our lives, but somewhere along the way we begin to notice the difference between the plans we make for ourselves and the larger pattern in which we play a role. The Talmud discusses fatalism and free will. In the end, the rabbis decide that God knows all that will happen even as we exercise our free will.

Beth, our wonderful, conscientious mother, came very close to burnout in the first nine months of parenting. Certainly she needed to be careful, to childproof the house, to recognize any sign that suggested she should consult a doctor. But she also had to learn that she could not control the child's inhaling of breath. She could do what she could do, but ultimately the child's life or death was controlled by God. Recognizing the limits of what she could control was surprisingly liberating. Her daughter would need her help long after she was walking by herself, feeding herself, and going off to school. But even now, her daughter's needs were not solely Beth's responsibility.

Living a Transformed Life

In the Bible, Jacob is no longer a dominant force during the years of his life. Instead, he is acted on by his sons and by other forces. Relinquishing leadership while continuing to live a full life is an important aspect of the third stage of life. Nevertheless, throughout his declining years, Jacob retains a sense of meaning and covenant. We can never know the larger trajectory of our own lives, but as we look at the biography of this spiritual person whose character looms large in the Bible, we resonate with him. It might even be said that the three biblical patriarchs represent the spiritual life of one individual, beginning with Abraham and attaining fruition in the character of Jacob. We, like Jacob and the other patriarchs and matriarchs, recognize that the call takes different forms at different stages in our lives, but that it is always an invitation to deepen our relationship with God.

However we describe this call—even if we are uncomfortable with the whole concept of a "call"—we understand that God's purpose will be revealed to us gradually as our life unfolds. Purpose does not take the form of one particular action isolated in time. Rather, it is a shape for the entirety of our lives—a life of relationship and passionate commitment.

Obstacles to Hearing the Call

The call to set out on the spiritual way is not a one-time event; it comes throughout our lives. It is reassuring to discover that we don't get only one chance to respond. And even when we respond to the call, we continue to be called to deeper and deeper levels of commitment. Because the call is an ongoing process, we sometimes turn a deaf ear to its charge. Our refusal to hear the call arises from a variety of factors.

Noise and Busyness

The immediate practical obstacle to listening and hearing is our refusal to grow quiet. Silence is not a central fact of Jewish worship. Synagogues themselves are rather noisy. People come there for community, to be with other Jews. Even the "silent" *amidah,* the prayer at the heart of the worship service, is not really silent; it is simply not said very loudly. The distinction is an important one. When we pray the *amidah,* we are not listening, we are saying words in our mind and in our heart. Listening requires that we have no thoughts in our mind and that we be open and receptive to what may emerge. Now, it is impossible to will our minds to be empty—as impossible as to obey the command, "Don't think of a white elephant." But there are methods by which we can free the mind. One is to repeat something so frequently that we can say it on "automatic pilot," thus freeing the mind to be empty and receptive without having to obey the paradoxical command not to think about anything. We can stand truly silent during the *amidah,* listening for the words of others to form our prayers. Another method for promoting the experience of true silence is simply to wait for all the noise to exhaust itself.

This was the path I attempted with Jackie. Jackie was very busy. In addition to the actual busyness of her work and studies, she created an interior busyness by maintaining as much background noise as possible. As soon as she came home, she turned on the TV to keep her company. When she was not actually asleep, she was either engaged in conversation with people who were present, talking on the phone, or surfing the Internet. Even when she was alone, walking from one place to another, she worked on lists in her mind.

I suggested a weekend away from her phone, her computer, her books, other people. The idea terrified her. She came up with all sorts of objections. Her first objection was that it was very un-Jewish. Judaism is a communal religion—why practice silence and solitude? I reminded her of the psalmist's statement, "Be still and know that I am God" (Ps. 46:11). She thought she would be bored. I assured her that the person she would meet in solitude would be sufficiently engaging to make boredom impossible. She still came up with one excuse after another. I kept returning to the same suggestion. I told her there were stages of solitude, that it would be mapping an unknown territory, and although I would have preferred no words at all, I agreed that she could take a blank journal with her. Jackie would spend a weekend at a friend's empty house. She was as anxious as if she were going on a safari in uncharted territory. And like the safari traveler, she prepared for her two days of silence with great care.

Although each person's journey is different, I did give Jackie a few suggestions to help her along the way. She should be firm in her practice, with set hours for prayer and for reading the texts I recommended, and she was to eat three meals a day. I also warned her about the difficulties of the late afternoon. Around four o'clock, many people are at their lowest psychological and physiological ebb. This is the hour when fevers tend to spike in hospitals. Spiritual guides also know it's the time when doubts attack us. The energy of the early morning hours is gone, and it is not yet time to prepare the evening meal and see the day come to an end. She was to plan activities for that time of the afternoon.

Jackie returned animated. She had thought her greatest accomplishment would be to have survived the two days. She viewed the retreat as analogous to her annual fast on Yom Kippur (the Day of Atonement) and the major challenge to be simply getting through it. In fact, she discovered that the two days of silence and solitude were a gift. Although there had been a few frightening moments, she had now met herself and would not be reluctant to enter into silence again. She was just beginning to realize the wealth of inner resources she had.

Impatience

Sound, as noted previously, unfolds over time. This temporal aspect applies directly to our discernment of God's role in our lives. Such discernment requires regular communication and trust, both of which deepen over time. As we grow in our relationship with God, we begin to understand how the revelation of God's word is gradual. However, when we first start out on the spiritual way, we often suffer from impatience. We want things quickly, immediately. This is particularly true in the computer age, as ever faster and more efficient computer systems condition us to instant responses. Electronic communications—beepers, cellular phones, E-mail, voice mail, faxes—provide worldwide access at the touch of a keypad. It's not surprising, therefore, that we experience waiting, which is a requirement of spiritual growth, as a form of testing and trial. We want to actively storm the heavens rather than grow slowly in our openness toward, and trust in, God.

Patience, the capacity to wait, is a quality too little valued in our society. The rabbis expressed the importance of waiting in *Pirkei Avot* where they wrote that we had to wait until we were forty years old before studying the *Zohar,* the central Jewish mystical text. Before that age, they argued, the guidance offered in the text would have no meaning for us. In fact, it could lead us astray and sever us from our spiritual moorings.

Illness is one context in which we begin to understand waiting. In hospitals and medical centers, we get treated, we get "done to," we become objects of decision making by others. Exercising patience means depending on factors not controlled by our own efforts and initiative. Loving also teaches us patience. When we are in love, we place our greatest interests into the hands of another. We wait for the phone call, the letter, or just the smile that affirms love. Waiting is directly connected to caring, to finding that things matter. When we care about something that is important to us, we are willing to wait—and we do so with a calming anticipation.

When we love God, we are presented with many occasions to wait. The seeker can expect from the spiritual guide support through periods of uncertainty, encouragement to endure them, and help learning how to wait. Sometimes seekers feel as if they are being pushed in one direction and pulled in the other. The Hebrew folk expression *yihyeh tov* (literally, it will be for good) is a salutary reminder that the story is not yet complete.

What is at stake in the spiritual life is an intimate relationship with God. But our most significant relationships are not characterized by instant intimacy. Rather, they grow over time as shared history, memories, and trust accumulate, as misunderstandings are corrected, and as we effect some genuine change in ourselves. What is true in our human relationships is also true in our relationship with God. Long after we can name the desire to grow closer to God, we still have to discover what that may mean, what it may require, how we will have to be changed. So we feel pulled toward God even as we learn, with the spiritual guide's assistance, "Do not wake or rouse Love until it please!" (Song of Songs 2:7).

Feelings of Unworthiness

The spiritual guide must recognize the major obstacles that prevent the seeker from responding to the call. The first is simple disbelief: "I'm not being called—I'm too unworthy." We have all had these thoughts. Even Moses felt this way: "I am not a man of words, neither heretofore, nor since Thou hast spoken unto Thy servant; for I am slow of speech, and of a slow tongue" (Exod. 4:10). The Baal Shem Tov recalled a person who once complained to him, "I have labored hard and long in the service of God and yet I have not improved. I am still an ordinary and ignorant person." The Besht (as the Baal Shem Tov is often referred to) responded, "You have gained the realization that you are ordinary and ignorant, and this in itself is a worthy accomplishment" (Midrash *Ribesh Tov*). When we consider the great prophets in the history of religion, the thought that we too might be called seems presumptuous. We were never meant to live our lives in such a large panorama. And indeed we aren't worthy, but saying yes to the call is opening ourselves to the potential of becoming worthy to enter into relationship with God. Responding to the call forces us to face many truths about ourselves, not for the sake of remorse or penitence, but to help us see ourselves in wholeness and love. Once we accept that we are loved, we gain a capacity to love ourselves, as beings in relationship with God.

Laura, who was very serious about the spiritual way, was surprised to discover herself suddenly taking an interest in clothes, even in jewelry. She was ashamed of this new interest, as she had always associated spirituality with asceticism. Working with her spiritual guide, a math professor at a neighboring college, she was able to discover that God delighted in her eye for color and in her joyousness and sensuality, and that she was as responsible for celebrating the goodness of Creation as she was for avoiding its temptations. She was encouraged to read some of the exquisite descriptive poetry in the Song of Songs, and as a result she came to accept her love of beauty as another way of relating to God.

Fear of Change

How do the self we would become and the life we would be living differ from our present self and life? We know we have flaws and limitations, but even our imperfections form part of our identity. Will this identity be lost if we respond to the call? How can we know that our real self will be found and released as a result of our entering the desert? As seekers we count on the spiritual guide to help us understand that what we now claim as our self is a mixture of a genuine self, cultural accretions, and historical accidents. One aim of spiritual guidance is to scour away the accretions so that at last our genuine self can be expressed in all its fullness. It is in this context that the spiritual guide exercises the most important mission, calling out "Fear not!"

With many of the people I have worked with, the answer "Fear not!" and my own patient presence are all I can offer. Over time, these seekers come to recognize that they feel more comfortable, less strained. Only when they have found this new ease within themselves can I help them realize that the relief they feel comes from no longer playing a role but from finally being more and more their authentic selves.

The Language of the Seeker

> Let us, then, go down and confound their speech there, so that they
> shall not understand one another's speech [Gen. 11:7].

Confronted with a multiplicity of viewpoints and philosophies, we find ourselves unable to understand one another. Instead of living in harmony we live in disharmony. If we are to serve as spiritual guides for one another, we must be prepared to move easily from one "language" to another—from an intellectual language, say, to a spiritual one—in our efforts to really hear what the other person is trying to say. Some people feel comfortable with religious language. Other people need the language of creativity, psychology, or science. It doesn't matter which language we choose for expressing ourselves in. Our objective is to make the way accessible, so we do not elevate one language over another but try to talk in the native language of the seeker's soul.

Jeannine was trying to distinguish between healing and cure. She was concerned for her mother, who had recently been diagnosed with breast cancer. I recommended Doris Schwerin's *Diary of a Pigeon Watcher,* an autobiographical account of her own bout with the same disease. After Jeannine had read the book, we explored Schwerin's statement, "I'm standing here, different, not the child, not the growing girl, not even the woman Papa knew in his old age. I'm standing here with one breast. I'm different, and yet strangely, whole, more whole than I've ever been" (p. 236).

Language is what we speak to one another, but it is also how reality "speaks" to us. Any aspect of reality that we attend to deeply enough can lead to God. All phenomena that we carefully observe and enter into with openness can lead to an awareness of God. This is the premise on which a famous "proof" for God's existence is based. The cosmological argument for the existence of God starts from some fact in the tangible world—such as motion, causality, contingency, or order—and argues back to a first cause of that fact. Proofs for the existence of God have fallen out of fashion; yet whether or not the cosmological argument makes belief in God more acceptable, it serves the experiential purpose of getting us to pay attention. We tend to take the world and all its processes for granted. But paying attention can be a profound form of prayer, the acknowledgment of God's presence in our lives. When we finally do pay attention to the world around us, we recognize many different ways of coming to God. We find that God speaks to us through the intricacies of the structure of DNA, the magnificence of a mountain in a storm, the tenderness of an unfolding leaf, even the pain of an individual in the throes of death. We need to look at the many different languages of living that confront us. Then we can hear the underlying harmony.

Our capacity to hear God is directly related to our capacity to be open to the world and to perceive its subtleties, because God speaks to us through the world. That's why we are taught to bless God for the good and the bad, or, as a favorite contemporary Hebrew song has it, "for all these things, for the bitter and for the sweet."

Our task as guides is to teach people on the spiritual way the importance of growing quiet, shutting out noise and busyness, and becoming open to the ways in which God and God's Creation speak to us. Hearing is one of the primary ways of making judgments about our way, but as we will see in Chapter Four, discernment goes beyond learning to hear.

4

RECOGNIZING
THE SPIRITUAL PATH

"Grant your servant an understanding mind to
judge your people, to distinguish between good and bad;
for who can judge this vast people of yours?" . . .

"I now do as you have spoken.
I grant you a wise and discerning mind."

—1 Kings 3:9, 11

DISCERNMENT IMPLIES a relationship and forms part of a relationship. Our capacity to understand what we hear is based on a prior relationship. Because we know someone, we understand what they are trying to say when their speech is impaired or their meaning exceptionally subtle. This is how love works. When Baby Deborah first learns to speak, someone unfamiliar with the child's attempt to form specific words or word groups may have no idea of what she is trying to say. Yet her parents readily understand her. They don't *hear* any better than other people; they understand Debbie's words because of the ongoing relationship they share with her. We learn to understand because we love. The same principle holds true for our relationship with God. Learning how to listen to God is learning about our relationship with God. We grow in our capacity to listen out of our love.

Discerning is also a form of acceptance, a willingness to let go, a conscious decision to try not to control another person. As we listen to Jessica in silence, we let her tell her story the way she wants to, however long it takes for it to unfold. While we are listening, we may get impatient with her pauses, but we must yield to them. We have to call on our inner strength and not rush to fill empty silence with empty noise. That silence is filled with potential, and we must listen for it. If we hurry her, interrupt her, finish her thoughts and sentences, or anticipate what she intends to say, we will not be able to hear what she is actually saying. When we are talking, we are unable to listen. That's why the Hebrew word *hakshavah* implies attentive listening.

One of the things the guide tries to convey to the seeker is the importance of being attentive to all the interior road signs: peace, a release of anxiety, a sense of fittingness. Such signs are present for all of us, but when intuition is not honored, our responsiveness to them seems to diminish. The more we attend to our own inner gyroscopes, the more adept we become at recognizing direction.

Discerning is a form of active waiting. And it's not easy. We are moved to take action. What makes discerning *active* waiting is that we have prepared for this encounter. We prepare by prayer, by study, by performing *mitzvot,* by cultivating an openness to God's word. Moses prepared himself to receive God's word on the mountaintop, and we too must prepare—in our own way, in our own time. Revelation comes to the prepared heart. The spiritual guide helps the seeker to prepare, to recognize that God's voice can be heard in our world—although it takes many forms. The greater our reverent attentiveness to the world, the greater our love for God. And so it follows: the greater our love for God, the more aspects of reality will speak to us of God. And they will convey God's instruction to us to direct our lives.

How God Speaks to Us

Sam had to make an important decision. He came to me in a quandary, but my job was not to give him my opinion; I was there only to suggest tools he might use to discern the best choice. I suggested a method he came to call "applied meditation." I advised him to do all the research he would normally do before making a decision—for example, discussing the issues with people whose judgment he respected, making lists of the pros and cons—then when all the preliminary work was done, he was to allow himself to become quiet. He could listen to the voices in his own head, but I hoped that the process would lead him to realize that *he* was not the source of the voices. There was an aspect of self that was independent of all the viewpoints he was weighing. Sam's task was to allow the still, small voice of his deeper consciousness to surface. I explained that this voice might bring a reframing of the question rather than a new answer.

Sam left excited about the prospect of trying this method. He was open to the suggestion that silence was not merely refreshing, but that it was opening him to contact with a self too often drowned out by the voices of those around him. As he gave himself to the silence, he learned that God speaks through things, events, words, and texts—and above all, through people we encounter. Sam also discovered that God speaks in our own voice, in the context of our deepest emotions.

Things

Many things may speak to us, communicate with us, have meaning for us. Things are not only silent; they may carry the voice of their Creator within them. It is not a question of looking for signs and omens but one of being open to entering into a relationship with the Creator through the created thing. In many ways we are oblivious to the gifts that surround us or can be found within ourselves. Often we are unaware of God's courting because we are focused on other things, and it can take someone else to point out the many cues that are being sent our way. Like people who for a long time remain unaware of the love felt for them by another, it takes us time to recognize who has been sending us all the flowers and gifts of the world.

Jake's friend Alice was visiting his home for the first time. The visit was a special treat for Jake because Alice's enthusiasm for all of his decoratings allowed him to see his apartment in a new light and once again take pleasure in his home. Alice paused before a portrait of Jake painted by his late father. Alice looked long and hard at the portrait, then at Jake, and after a while said, "I thought you said you weren't sure your father loved you. How could you doubt it with a portrait like that?" Jake looked at the portrait that had hung on his wall, almost unseen, for twenty years and suddenly saw what Alice was showing him. The words, "I love you," which his father had never been able to utter, were apparent in every aspect of the canvas. After a time Jake tried to thank Alice for the gift of what she had shown him, but Alice deflected the thanks to the true source of the healing between Jake and his father. "He shall reconcile fathers with sons and sons with their fathers" (Malachai 3:24).

Events

Events in the world around us also tell us about God and our relationship to God. History has a strong impact on the spiritual way, and in a historical religion, revelation is found through the unfolding of events in time. Learning to hear God's voice and recognize God's word in all these events requires us to be sensitive and perceptive. Merely observing the events that take place in our nation, our town, our family, and our personal life will not give us a sense of God's word. Spiritual interpretation depends on a subtle form of awareness, through which we learn to connect the events in the world to the role God plays in them. Our life in the world and our life with God are inextricably intertwined. Our challenge is to sew together this vibrant tapestry of life.

Esther had lived through a terrifying childhood. She had survived a Nazi concentration camp but had witnessed the deaths of her mother, sister, grandparents, and cousins. For forty years she had felt fury and outrage toward God, but increasingly she found good in this world as she married, had children, and even grandchildren. After working with me for many months, she began to talk about her experience in the camp and the tiny moments of respite she found amid the daily terror. I reminded her of her current practice of entering into the silent presence of goodness, and suddenly she began to cry in recognition. "God was present with me even then. God couldn't prevent what happened, but God was with me."

Words

What does it mean to say that God creates by speaking? We read about the force of such speech in the opening verses of the book of Genesis. Fashioned in God's image, we also create the world with words. But inherent in the power to create is also the power to destroy. For this reason, among many others, the litany of sins recited during the Yom Kippur confession is replete with sins of speech. And borrowing words from the rabbis, we conclude the daily *amidah* prayer with these pleas:

> Guard my tongue from evil and my lips from speaking guile. Let my soul be silent to all who would insult me.

We know the power of words to create and destroy worlds. The rabbis call it *lashon hara* (literally, the evil tongue). They even make a pun on the word for leprosy *(metzora)* by describing the disease as *motzi shem ra* (slander), what emanates from evil speech. The only thing that neutralizes the effect of *lashon hara* is *lashon hatov,* good speech (literally, the good tongue). "A wholesome tongue is a tree of life" (Prov. 15:4). One nineteenth-century Polish rabbi, Israel Mayer Kagan (also known as the Chofetz Chayim), wrote an ethical treatise on the dangers of gossip and evil speech. In the book *Shmirat Lashon* (literally, the guarding of the tongue), he contended that each of our words must be guarded, guided, and well-directed. Each holds the potential for good, but when wielded like a sword, also embodies the potential for evil. It is up to us to determine what effect our words will have.

We use words to make vows that shape our world. We enter into covenant, we name children, we bless, we confess, we say *kiddush* (the prayer of sanctification), thereby consecrating time, and we even declare that night has begun. We bring the Sabbath to an end by reciting the *havdalah* service. We pray, we speak, we listen—to other people, to the text, to what comes to us out of the silence. Words tell us that what we thought was unique has in fact been experienced by others; that's why there is already a word for it. Words, unlike perhaps any other force in the universe, can create community across time.

Words may be those carefully chosen by a friend or teacher, or those of our sacred texts. But sometimes they are chance words overheard in a conversation or read on a billboard. Susan related how she had left the hospital where her younger brother was a patient and, terribly shaken by seeing him attached to feeding and medication tubes, got on the subway in deep despair. But as she settled in her seat, she heard a mother comforting her sobbing child: "Don't cry. It will be all right. I'm right here." The words seemed to be addressed to her.

Texts

For Jews, the most important sacred text is the Torah. The Torah is God's love letter to us. That's why we treat it with such care. We caress it often, read it and reread it, consider every aspect of it looking for any hidden message that speaks of God's love for us. Texts, whether the Torah or a lesser writing, are alive—when we are prepared to enter them. How we can study in such a way that texts are likely to take on such immediacy will be discussed in Chapter Seven. This approach is at the heart of sacred study.

We all know how to read a text from a distance, keeping our own lives, thoughts, and emotions separate from our study. We were trained in school to keep our reading objective—to intellectualize, to get at the meaning supposedly intended by the author. But we know that words sometimes seem to jump off the page and personally address the sacred story of our own lives. That's when the text becomes sacred and invites us to engage with it. It not only illuminates the events of our lives; it seems to be actually *about* our lives. When we are thus joined with the text, it is no longer about someone else's revelation; it is our own, addressed to our very being. This is the experience that makes the Bible the Torah in the fullest sense of the word. The saying goes that when we pray, we talk to God, and when we study the Bible, God talks to us.

People

Toby was teaching an unusually difficult class of students and was feeling that his job was a distraction from his primary goal of growing spiritually. I asked him to focus on his last encounter with the class. As he talked, he recounted the remarks of one student he really liked. We continued to talk, and he quoted a very insightful response from another student. He then mentioned how some of the class had become involved with a news story he had brought up in class. Suddenly he stopped. "In the last ten minutes, I have told you three wonderful stories about this class. Is it possible I'm not seeing how great they really are?" The class was very challenging, but he came to see that the students were advancing him on his spiritual way rather than distracting him from it.

Although we know we have to listen to God, we sometimes forget that God speaks to us through the voices of other people, including our own children. They often remind us of our own words by reflecting them back to us. Jonathan, a very caring father, came to see me one day, delighted with a story about his fourteen-year-old daughter, with whom he had been experiencing the usual teenage rebellion. He had told his daughter repeatedly that if she ever phoned him asking for a ride home, regardless of the hour or place, he would come to pick her up, no questions asked. He was determined that she never ride with a driver who had been drinking. That past weekend, concerned about his family and undergoing stress at work, he had gone on a business trip. When he opened his suitcase he found a quarter taped to a card that read, "If you need a ride home, just call." In listening to one another, we may hear God's voice speak to us. But we have to be willing to listen, because we never know where the Messiah's voice may be concealed.

> As he was standing at the entrance to the cave of Rabbi Simon bar Yochai, Rabbi Joshua came upon the prophet Elijah. He asked Elijah, "When is the Messiah coming?"
>
> The other replied, "Go and ask him yourself."
>
> "Where shall I find him?" asked Rabbi Joshua.
>
> Came the reply, "Before the gates of Rome."
>
> "And how shall I recognize him?" asked Rabbi Joshua.
>
> Elijah responded, "He will be sitting among the poor people, covered with wounds. The others unbind their wounds all at once and then bind them up again. But he unbinds them one wound at a time

and then rebinds it immediately. He says to himself, 'If I am needed—I must be ready to go and not be late.'"

So Rabbi Joshua went to the gates of Rome and addressed the Messiah, "Peace be with you, my master and teacher."

The Messiah answered, "And peace be with you, son of Levi."

Rabbi Joshua continued, "When are you coming, master?"

Thereupon the Messiah answered, "Today."

So Rabbi Joshua returned to Elijah and said to him: "He has deceived me. He told me that he would come today, but he has not come."

But Elijah responded, "This is what he told you: 'Today—*if you would hearken to God's voice*'" [Babylonian Talmud, *Sanhedrin*, p. 98a].

Emotions

> I will put My teaching into their inmost being and inscribe it on their hearts [Jer. 31:33].

We have to learn to listen carefully to everything around us and in us because, as we have seen, God speaks to us in a variety of ways—through the voices of others, through events that occur along our journey. Now we learn that God speaks to us through our own thoughts and affections, so our emotional life has something important to tell us. Therefore, we need to attend to what goes on within us as well as around us.

The psalmist instructs us to attend to our own emotions as important indicators of the way.

> Commune with your own heart on your bed and be still [Ps. 4:5].

As the psalmist suggests, we must learn to trust a sense of naturalness, ease, and peace. When we recognize that we are doing God's will, one of the hallmarks of that experience is freedom from anxiety and tremendous joy. We may have thought that we were simply doing what was demanded of us; that alone would have given us a sense of profound satisfaction. We never imagined that it would unleash such deep feelings of love and joy. But, repeatedly, that is shown to be the case in the context of spiritual guidance.

Joy, naturalness, ease, and peace are genuine signposts that we are going in the right direction, but pain, discomfort, and agitation do not necessarily mean we are going in the wrong direction. There are discomforts along our journey toward God. Running into obstacles, uncertainties, is part of going in the right direction. From time to time we need to be shaken to the core. Our emotions, whether unpleasant or pleasant, inform us of change. The very word *emotion* derives from the Latin word meaning "move." Emotions come and go, and discerning motion becomes its own adventure.

In exploring our emotions, we need to learn the positive uses of negative states: just as pain is a messenger before it is anything else, so too are boredom, agitation, even depression. As if our unease were personified as an angelic messenger from the Almighty—the kind we might encounter in biblical narrative—we must ask ourselves what it portends. We need to explore the depths of our feelings, probing them for what they have to tell us.

Motion

After living through many significant changes in her life, Joan, whom we first met in Chapter Two, suddenly felt stuck, as if nothing new would ever happen again. She had to be shown how to perceive motion, how to recognize that she really was growing, even though it was not as apparent as it had been during a time of rapid external change. She was instructed to follow a few simple clues that would reveal movement and to try following the direction that the movement was taking. Up to this time, "motion" had not been something Joan had been taught to name and reflect on. Over the course of several meetings, she learned about different forms of motion. The particular schema she used was really based on the work of Aristotle, as understood by the Jewish philosophers of the twelfth century. It identified six distinct types of motion:

1. COMING TO BE. As we think about our spiritual growth, it makes sense to ask ourselves: What's new? What is true now that wasn't true before? In any loving relationship, we can expect to find some fruitfulness—new life. What has grown? We might expect to see growth in trust, in peacefulness, in a sense of tenderness for being.

2. PASSING AWAY. As a result of our growing intimacy, we realize that there are places that we will not revisit. Certain things must be left to the past. We are reminded of the warning given to the Israelites in the wilderness: "You must not go back that way again" (Deut. 17:16). So we stop pursuing some questions, because their answers provide us with no benefit. Some hatreds, those that burned a mark on our soul, will pass away from our midst. We will no longer have to contend with them. As these things withdraw themselves from our consciousness, we feel relieved, especially if they have troubled us for a long time. But we also feel a sense of loss; we had grown comfortable in our pain. As we continue on the spiritual way, we must turn our backs on other things, some that just yester-

day had given us pleasure (even if only from the familiarity of the routine). After a while, we discover that the things we gave up were neither as pleasurable nor as valuable as we once believed. Undoubtedly, we will re-encounter them later in our lives—surprisingly transformed as a result of our own spiritual development.

3. INCREASE. Because love is the impetus behind the motion on the spiritual way, there will be an increase in what we see and value as a result of this love. For many of us, it will take a long time to get used to this notion. We understand love between parent and child, spouse and partner, brother and sister, and friends, but to take the notion of love as a governing principle in our lives may still seem strange and somewhat awkward to us. This is one of the things to be learned on the spiritual way. In our human relationships, we strengthen those intrinsic characteristics that are admired by our beloved; the warmth of their approving gaze seems to foster the development and growth of some of these traits. Similarly, we grow into a person shaped by our loving relationship with God.

4. DECREASE. As a result of our spiritual journey, we will experience a decrease in what we had previously ignored and devalued. We don't have to grit our teeth and determine to overcome every bad habit, one by one. But living the spiritual life helps us to lessen many of the negative traits we have been trying to outgrow. They may not, or even by their nature cannot, pass away entirely, but we can learn that traits such as anger, jealousy, and hatred, though never dead, can be quiescent.

5. LOCOMOTION. This is the form of motion that Joan and most people tend to focus on because it is material and can be much better quantified than increase and decrease. It includes major points of transition: change of job, change in marital status, or change of residence. Locomotion also provides the foundation for the journey model of spirituality—the first major component of the Exodus story. We *moved* out of Egypt toward the Promised Land. The story of the physical crossing of the desert parallels the journey of the spirit. But the real motion is not the change from one location to another. It is the transformation of self.

6. BECOMING OTHER. The most significant motion on the spiritual way is that of transformation. It differs from other forms of motion in that it results from all the other changes. Transformation is a change in both quantity and quality. Something has become genuinely new. As we know from experience, nothing renews the world as thoroughly as love.

When we are in love, we see the entire world through the eyes of love. It centers the world. It provides us with perspective.

After learning about different kinds of motion, Joan stopped looking for motion outside herself and focused on the movement of her own thoughts and feelings.

In fact, we have all encountered the motion that Joan had to be taught to recognize. In childhood, it is the motion of increase. How many times did people say to us, "My, how you've grown!" when all they meant was that we had grown a bit taller. We didn't feel any different. Sometimes people would comment that we had become more adept at a particular skill. On occasion, people noticed other changes in us as well. But real change, the deeper forms of motion, are left for us to discern for ourselves. A spiritual guide can help us, but we are left on our own to discover real growth.

We don't have to go off in anxious search; we can wait and gradually see a pattern emerge. Rather than go looking for a pattern, our task is to sit, inviting motion to move toward us. We need help in learning the vocabulary of motion. We should be encouraged to talk and reflect on our lives, taking seriously all that has happened to us.

The Central Question: Where Is God in This?

Although discernment can be very subtle, in one respect it is much simpler than we imagine. Throughout spiritual guidance, there is really only one subject: the seeker's relationship with God. Where is God in what is happening at this very moment? For Fred, whom we met in Chapter Two, this commitment to the one subject changes his reaction to everything that is happening to him. Instead of the accusatory "Why me?" when he faces adversity, he asks, "Where is God in this experience?" Discernment is grounded in God's promise throughout the Torah: "I will be with you." That is the heart of all discernment. The more we look back with the help of a sensitive guide, the more we see God's presence and caring throughout our life.

In Genesis, Joseph twice suggests that the conscious, deliberate actions of his brothers were not the true cause of his sojourn in Egypt: "Now do not be distressed nor reproach yourselves because you sold me here; it was to save life that God sent me ahead of you" (Gen. 45:5) and "In any case—although you intended me harm, God intended it for good, so as to bring about the present result: the survival of many people" (Gen. 50:20). These two statements reveal a belief in God who infuses the world with design and meaning. Spiritual guidance presupposes this belief. Discovering God's presence in and through the events of our lives is indeed a warrant for hope and trust. It is this ongoing relationship that makes letting go possible.

Roadmarkers on the Path of Discernment

Whether we choose to focus on the Exodus story or the Song of Songs, we will find that there are certain experiences and qualities that serve as roadmarkers on the path of discernment: peace, clarity, empowerment, tenderness, the conquest of fear, and the release of joy.

Peace

Shalom—the opposite of agitation, division, anxiety. We tend to think of peace in terms of stillness—the still pool, the sleeping cat. But peace can be intensely active—the gracefulness of a deer running full force across a meadow. Here the emphasis is on *shalom* as wholeness. We find ourselves at peace not only when we are resting, but when we are absorbed in an activity that draws on all our abilities. A chaplain, after a long day's work, was asked to make rounds on one more floor before he went home. His exhaustion left him as he spoke to the patients. The effort energized him. Somehow he was doing the activity that best suited him, and he was at peace in the midst of his rounds.

Clarity

Clarity, purity, simplicity. Clarity is hearing the music without any background noise or static. Over the course of our lives, we have internalized many different voices. When we are faced with making a decision, we can hear the disapproving voice of a former teacher, the encouragement of a parent, the doubt of a former colleague. Which of those many voices is our own deepest nature that directs us to our own greatest good? We arrive at clarity not by silencing those inner voices but by letting them talk themselves out. If we can listen to them, we are not *identified* with any one of them. We are the observer watching them argue with one another. It's the same when we study a sacred text, giving ear to the teachers who have commented on the text in generations past until we are prepared to interpret it on our own. This practice gives us the perceptual distance to listen without conflict or agitation. With patience, silence emerges—and then we can begin to listen for our deepest good:

And lo, Adonai passed by. There was a great and mighty wind, splitting mountains and shattering rock by the power of God; but God was not in the wind. After the wind—an earthquake; but God was not in the earthquake. After the earthquake—fire; but God was not in the fire. And after the fire—a still small voice [1 Kings 19:11–12].

Conquest of Fear

An important signpost on the spiritual way is an increase in trust. We may spend many years with a cloud of fear hovering just behind our present pleasures. Underlying and compromising our sense of delight is the fear that pleasures cannot last. We grasp and clutch, thereby distorting what comes gently to us. We are creatures who live in time. How can we go beyond our discomfort with the transitory? The solution comes as a sense of fundamental trust rather than as a reasoned argument. We learn to love and release. And in the process, we experience a sense of love without shadow, a sense of freedom that comes from finally being beyond fear.

But there are other causes of fear (as we see further in Chapter Five). One cause is simply our lack of understanding. We do not know, cannot understand, predict, or control. Discernment involves the acceptance of this uncertainty, acceptance of a species of darkness, a letting go of purely rational assurance. This is hinted at in the representation of God in the dark cloud surrounding the peak of Mount Sinai (Exod. 19:9). But as lovers, we come to know that darkness need not be an occasion for fear; it can just as readily be an invitation to intimacy. Darkness, too, is a way of knowing God.

A rabbinic tale related by Martin Buber in *Tales of the Hasidim: The Later Masters* (p. 213) describes an encounter between two people lost in a forest. One asks the other the way out of the wood. "I don't know," the other replies. "But I can point out the ways that lead further into the thicket, and after that let us try to find the way together."

The spiritual guide, then, cannot remove the darkness or clear the way but can help the seeker avoid the thickets and can serve as a companion.

Empowerment

When we are whole, undivided, clear in our vision, and unafraid, we have both strength and joy. The absence of many little fears and doubts that previously impeded us make us now feel almost invincible or, at least, ready to undertake any task. This experience of empowerment is central to the story told in the book of Numbers about the so-called spies sent out to explore the Promised Land (13:1–14:10). Most of the spies, scouting out the land, could see its goodness but feared its inhabitants, who looked like giants to them. But two of the group, Caleb and Joshua, trusted that if the land had indeed been promised, there was no need to fear. Ultimately, these two were able to lead; the other spies were not. The Israelites did not enter the Promised Land for another thirty-eight years. They had much yet to learn along the way. But when they did enter Canaan, it was under the leadership of Caleb and Joshua.

Tenderness

Along with a sense of power, of freedom from fear, and of clarity, goes a sense of tenderness for all beings and a recognition of both our shared vulnerability and our common value. For men in particular, such tenderness might be difficult to acknowledge. We have lived too long in a world where it was considered a sign of weakness, a threat to the masculine self. And as women have ascended in what had been previously a man's world, some of them may have become hardened too, mistakenly believing that they had to mimic the "tough" male approach to life in order to succeed. Fear blocks our perception; noise obscures our capacity to appreciate. When we at last experience even some slight glimmer of inner peace, we begin to perceive the world as it is.

Shulamith, who was allergic to wasp stings, discovered wasps in her attic, so she decided to call an exterminator to destroy the nests. Her eight-year-old daughter, who still retained her tenderness toward all of God's creatures, made an eloquent plea for the wasps. "They also have a right to live," she protested, in a voice that has been given only to young children. Shulamith's fear was very real, but she couldn't easily dismiss her daughter's sensitivity. So she sat quietly in the attic watching the wasps fly in and out of the windows, trying not to disturb them, observing the rhythm of their routine. As her quietness deepened, she noticed a tiny sound they made both before entering the nest and when preparing to leave it. There was nothing random about their flight pattern. By the end of the afternoon, Shulamith had a clear sense of their comings and goings. Her fear dissipated. She did not call the exterminator, and for as long as she owned that house, she was never stung.

Joy

When we think of the spiritual way, we may think of the darkness that often brings us to it, the effort that it takes to stay on it, and the trials that we seem to encounter as we press forward. These are all dimensions of our journey, but we acknowledge too rarely the release of tremendous joy, which is also a central aspect of the way. Joy is greater than pleasure or happiness; it is a total expansion of self and a release from any sense of limit and constraint.

————— o —————

What seekers learn through spiritual guidance is how to become people
who are being shaped by the posture of listening. This is the posture of
the servant of God (in Hebrew, *eved Adonai*). It is not an attitude of cring-
ing compliance. Rather, it is a mark of human life lived ever more fully in
the spirit of love.

> To You, enthroned in heaven,
>   I turn my eyes.
> As the eyes of [male] servants follow their
>   master's hand,
> as the eyes of a slave-girl follow the hand
>   of her mistress,
> so our eyes turn toward Adonai our God,
>   awaiting God's favor.
>   —Ps. 123:1–2

Today we reject entirely the notion of a slave, and we have trouble, too,
with the concept of servant. We see servitude as demeaning—and it is, if it
is to anyone less than God. But in the Hebrew term *eved Adonai*—one
who does God's work in the world—the word *servant* becomes the highest accolade the Bible can bestow. Abraham is called God's servant, as is
Job, as is the central figure in the servant songs in Isaiah. Servitude to God
is our greatest freedom. It reflects the covenantal relationship that frees
us from all that is banal in this world. This is something we come to recognize over time. Still, the concept of servanthood is troubling. Old
images of someone manipulating a marionette come to mind. That is why
we need to explore our God-images and recall that Judaism is a religion
centered on sound rather than sight. Just as we can hear what is within
us as well as what is outside of us, we come to recognize that listening for
God's voice is not simply listening to external instruction but to our own
deepest voice. God is the immanent cause of our actions, so we can find
God in our most authentic desires.

> "A time is coming," declares Adonai our God,
> "when I will send a famine upon the land;
> not a hunger for bread, or a thirst for water,
> but for hearing the words of God."
>   —Amos 8:11

5

UNDERSTANDING OUR FEARS

Have no fear! Stand by, and witness the
deliverance which Adonai will work for you today.

—Exodus 14:13

THE BEGINNING OF WISDOM is the "fear of the Lord," but it is important
to realize that it is not the end. Fear can serve as a motivation, an indicator that there is something to which we should attend, something we
should approach with humility. We have to distinguish this sense of fear
and awe from fear in the sense of terror or aversion. Fear, in the sense of
reverence or respect, can serve as a wake-up call, but fear can also be an
obstacle to a deeper intimacy with God.

Fear takes many different forms. We are called on to recognize fear in
ourselves and in others. The spiritual guide must sometimes stand in the
place of the angel of *Adonai,* crying, "Do not be afraid," or like Joshua,
saying, "Be strong and of good courage." Sometimes the guide must simply be present so that the various fears can be explored. When fully
entered into, fear as terror can lead to gratitude and intimacy.

Fears That Hold Us Back from God

Fear can give way to gratitude and love, but it can be the single greatest
enemy of love—and of the spiritual way—if it is prolonged. To some
extent, fear reflects the animal aspect of our human nature.

Fear has had its uses in the evolutionary process, and it seems to constitute the whole of forethought in most animals; but that it should
remain any part of the mental equipment of human civilized life is an
absurdity [Horace Fletcher, quoted in William James, *Varieties of Religious Experience,* p. 90].

When we were children, our desires were explicit. We wanted that red
truck, that piece of candy, a dog for a pet. But as we grew older, our
desires became less specific. No one particular thing seemed to be the
object of our yearning. Something similar happens with fear. Our earliest
fears can be named: bigger children, witches, monsters. Later we can not
only name them, but frequently deal with them. But on the spiritual way,
fear takes the form of radical amazement before being and the terror of
being itself. We cannot be terrified of death or the pathetic vulnerability
of life until we are self-consciously aware that we are alive. But with self-
consciousness comes fear.

What is it we really fear? We fear our unworthiness. Perhaps we fear
our claim on knowledge or our own giftedness. We may fear expressing
anger. We fear being wrong, or our inadequacy considering the enormity
of the task at hand. We fear the loss of autonomy as we work to make
our will accord with the will of God. The unknown may present a whole
set of fears for us as well.

We are also afraid of approaching God, because we believe that God
sees and judges us and may therefore find cause to reject us. It seems easier
and safer not to bother trying to develop such a relationship. In the context of developing an intimate relationship with God, we may fear that we
will *really* see ourselves—and find ourselves unacceptable. In our day, there
seems to be a general fear of intimacy. That fear is particularly evident
when we speak about the possibility of developing an intimate relationship with God. Nevertheless, there is a growing feeling that a relationship
with God is the source of an infinite and incomprehensible blessing.

Though we may delay, God is patient and calls to us in unique and
individual ways, even in the context of our own fears. Tentatively, we
begin to respond. But unlike the biblical poet, we do not go leaping over
mountains to join our beloved (Song of Songs 2:8), even though this is the
love of our life. Many of our fears are tenacious. They are also quite natural. In an old movie scene, a nurse says to a patient in the recovery room,
"You're out of danger," to which the patient responds, "You mean I
died?" To be alive is to be at risk. On the spiritual way, we are coming
alive in more and more aspects of our being. Along with our increasing
aliveness comes the loss of the protective numbness most of us have main-

tained prior to embarking on the way. The fears involved in the spiritual way are complex, but if we wish to persist and want to be able to guide others who are making the same journey, we need to understand them.

Fear of Looking Foolish

Once we were adolescents, and our feelings were perpetually on the surface. We may have blushed, we cried easily, we were so enthusiastic that we caused older people to smile at us in amusement. Now that we count ourselves among those older people, our feelings are not as accessible. We've exchanged enthusiasm for caution. But we now recognize that all of our skillful maturing has come at a high price: the passion we had in our teenage years—and even the capacity to feel that passion—no longer seems available to us.

Do we really want to return to adolescence? Of course not. Nor is remembering those feelings part of a midlife crisis that may result in the purchase of a sports car or the dissolution of a long-term relationship or marriage. We are certainly not interested in reliving our adolescence. Instead, we seek to rekindle that indescribable feeling of being alive that is usually associated with adolescence. Consequently, we should not expect our tastes in music and fashion to change suddenly, but our depth of commitment and intensity of feeling very likely will.

One fear we have about recapturing the ardors of adolescence is that of looking and feeling foolish. It would be bad enough, we might think, to revert to a state of being "in love," but to fall in love with and feel passionate about *God*—such a stance is one we expect from our peers and most especially (though with some notable exceptions) from the Jewish mainstream in America. We may even think that our intellectual orientation as "The People of the Book" precludes us from such unabashed sensuousness. Whatever the reasons, we fear a loss of respect by those with a more scientific bent and a loss of self-respect if we try to recapture a youthful—and therefore seemingly more regressive—outlook on love.

Fear of Not Knowing the Future

On the spiritual way, another aspect of adolescence also returns: a sense of adventure, of not really knowing what will come next, which raises the fear that perhaps something bad will happen or, at the very least, something will happen that we have no control over. It's true that no one really *does* know what is coming next, but we lead our lives as if we did. We make retirement plans, take out thirty-year mortgages, set up pension funds, and act as if the future will resemble the past. Yet when we were teenagers, we knew that our closest high-school friend might go off to a different school the following year, and we ourselves would keep moving on. Still, we threw ourselves into friendships and confidences. We had dreams but generally could make no long-range plans. Many of us had no idea what we would study in college, even as we applied. Some of us thought we knew, but then we just as radically rethought our plans a short time later. We got interested in new subjects as we became exposed to them. The rare few among us seemed to know from early on (some as far back as first grade) exactly how they wanted to fashion their lives, but for most of us, the way was unknown.

Our fear of not knowing what the future will hold is both understandable and realistic. In our youth, we had the built-in insurance that if we faltered badly, our parents and extended family would always be there to help us regain our footing. As adults, however, we feel we must be self-reliant and therefore cautious about every undertaking. We have also learned to consider much more fully the potential consequences of our actions—indeed, doing so is the hallmark of having shed our earlier impulse to let our feelings take us wherever they will. It is the task of the spiritual guide to help us overcome the fear of not Knowing the future by helping us grow in trust. It is scary to feel so strongly, for everything to be so significant. It's also wonderful.

Fear of Love

We remember when the words of the popular song finally first made sense to us: "They say that falling in love is wonderful . . ." when we began to understand the imagery of the Song of Songs, when the love poetry of the Bible spoke to us, when we knew that love was wonderful. But love can also be terrible and everything else in between. We had no conception of everything that love would entail when we first fell in love. In those days, love simply meant spending as much time together as possible. We didn't really understand how it would shape every other decision we would make, but we were happy to let it become the fount out of which all other decisions flow. So here we were having learned to love as a child, friend, spouse, and parent, being invited into the love that lifts up and binds all our other loves. It is a little like reaching the top of the hill on the roller coaster, where our heart leaps into our mouth, and we want to scream "Stop!"

How do we overcome the fear and get ourselves from "Stop" to a triumphant "Yes"? Laurie came into spiritual guidance aware that something more was being asked of her life but not certain whether she wanted to evade the demands or learn how to respond to them. After several months, she became very clear about her own deep love. She still had questions about her courage, strength, and even her worthiness, but now she was determined to hear what was being asked. What amazed her was that although she was ready to sacrifice anything for this love, her "Yes" required not a sacrifice but a willingness to accept a great gift. Responding to God, which at first seems so frightening, is a gift we must learn to accept. With help and reassurance from her spiritual guide, Laurie freed herself to loving God.

Fear of Joy

The notion may be baffling to many, but some of us do indeed fear joy. Intellectually we may ask ourselves, How can anyone be afraid of being happy? Yet that fear is a reality: many of us are afraid of experiencing sheer joy. Perhaps we are afraid that if we become so happy and everything is so "perfect," something terrible will then happen. And behind such a fear is a strong suspicion that we are not worthy enough to enjoy happiness, not worthy to be loved. We fear being loved even more than we fear loving, because being loved means being known by someone else. Too many among us really don't like ourselves, so we can't believe that someone else might like us—let alone love us—if they really "knew" what we were like. Such Knowing implies honest intimacy. We fear that intimacy and therefore avoid relationships that would demand it.

Sandra described her experience of contentment, of waves of joy passing over her. When asked how she felt, she replied, "Terrified." Why was terror associated with joy? She felt unworthy, believed that the earth would open up and take her, that there were no unconditional gifts. In well-worn phrases, she conveyed her beliefs that there were "strings attached" and that joy was merely "the calm before the storm."

People who are afraid of joy are a bit like those who reject the possibility of heaven because hell seems so much more familiar to life on earth.*

The fear of joy and of feeling alive is one of the central topics Freud discusses in *Beyond the Pleasure Principle*. In this highly speculative and

---

* Some people think that the concepts of heaven and hell are foreign to Judaism. That's just not true. Though heaven and hell are not part of mainstream Jewish thought, and no clear description of either appears in the Bible, *Gan Eden* [paradise, heaven] and *Gehinnom* [the approximation of hell] figure prominently in rabbinic texts.

provocative work, Freud suggests that the ego instincts exercise pressure toward death and are countered only by eros, love, the instinct that leads us to join into ever larger unions. In simpler terms, we don't like to be disturbed. We avoid change. We don't even like changes in our routine. We prefer the known, the familiar, the status quo. Love draws us outside ourselves. As the cost of resisting love, we are caught between wanting and not wanting to experience the feeling of being alive. Freud's teachings on these issues resemble some of the insights brought to bear by mystics of many faiths, who hold that the self (or ego) is constricting, and release comes only by being in love with Love itself.

> And all of a sudden, God stepped in my soul. Talk about hollerin and rejoicin. I just caught fire. My mind cleared up. I got so happy— I didn't realize where I was. I lost sight of this world to a great extent [Nate Shaw, *All God's Dangers: The Life of Nate Shaw*].

We are afraid of the very same things we desire. We fear loving and being loved, knowing and being known. Above all, we fear the rejection that potentially permeates all dimensions of love. Love is what makes us alive, but it is also what makes us vulnerable.

Ambivalence about being known is expressed by the psalmist:

> Adonai, You have examined me and know me,
> When I sit down or stand up You know it;
> You discern my thoughts from afar.
> You observe my walking and reclining,
> and are familiar with all my ways.
> There is not a word on my tongue
> but that You, Adonai, know it well. . . .
> Where can I escape from Your spirit,
> Where can I flee from Your presence?
> If I ascend to heaven, You are there;
> If I descend to Sheol, You are there too.
> If I take wing with the dawn
> to come to rest on the western horizon
> even there Your hand will be guiding me,
> Your right hand will be holding me fast.
> If I say, "Surely darkness will conceal me,
> night will provide me with cover,"
> darkness is not dark for You;
> night is light as day;
> darkness and light are the same. . . .

Examine me, O God, and know my mind;
probe me and know my thoughts.
See if I have vexatious ways,
and guide me in ways everlasting.

—Ps. 139:1–4, 7–12, 23–24

Fear of Our Own Unreadiness

We don't feel ready. We feel unprepared. But such a mistrust of our own preparedness is not unique. The great prophet Jeremiah exhibited the same fear:

The word of Adonai came to me:
Before I created you in the womb, I selected you;
Before you were born, I consecrated you;
I appointed you a prophet concerning the nations.
I replied:
Ah, Adonai, God!
I don't know how to speak,
For I am still a boy.
And Adonai said to me:
Do not say, "I am still a boy,"
But go wherever I send you. . . .
Have no fear of them,
For I am with you to deliver you
declares Adonai.

—Jer. 1:4–8

Spiritual guidance helps the seeker first to recognize the feeling of being unready and unprepared and then to understand it. The seeker may not be conscious of the fear, or the fear may be disguised. We aren't always aware that we are afraid or why we are afraid. Instead, we think that because of our busy lives, we are merely unable to find time to pray, to be with God, to seek solitude. But what are we hiding from in the protective confines of busyness? When we look inward, we realize that we may be hiding from the intensity that comes from a relationship with the divine. As we approach God, we can expect to have experiences of great intensity, some purely spiritual, some emotional, some even physical. We may not be sure that we are strong enough to take them.

In some interpretations, the "darkness" that the Israelites experienced at Sinai did not result from a dark cloud that covered the mountain. Instead, the cloud was so bright that it appeared to the people as darkness.

Because we are imperfect and fragile vessels, we cannot contain such light. Human encounters are difficult enough for us. But an encounter with God, although it may present us with unimaginable joy, is so powerful that it could overwhelm us. This may be one of the many reasons why people involved in the spiritual way sometimes choose an ascetic setting. It is hard to think about anything else when in God's proximity, so they prefer the starkness of the desert or the utter simplicity of a bare room in order to focus on the overwhelming intensity of God's presence. For the same reason, as we recite the *Shema* and proclaim God's incomprehensible uniqueness, we close our eyes so that we may focus on God alone.

Although *Shekhinah* is all around us, the encounter with God's presence is rarely casual. It is electrifying. No matter how often we experience it and try to embrace it, there is a real need to be prepared for it. This is what *Shabbat* (the Sabbath) is all about. We spend the day opening to an encounter with God.

Isaac Luria (known also as the Ari), a mystic of Safed, Palestine, began the iteration of his theology with a story about the original light of creation. This light was so powerful, he believed, that the vessels built to contain it shattered. For Luria, this shattering of the sacred vessels explains the presence of the divine sparks in all things, but it also suggests that it takes strong and properly prepared vessels to hold the divine light. If the vessels can shatter, so can we. We rightly feel fear in the anticipation of intense joy; we sense the power in any experience of the divine. Our fear is not unwarranted; the vessels can shatter. The fear is really bound up with the idea that shattering means the dissolution of boundaries. Eventually, we discover that this breakdown is for the sake of reformation around a different center (a theory expressed in a secular formulation in Jerome Kegan's *The Evolving Self*). The terror of passion and intensity is not imagined; it is something we experience en route to ecstasy.

Fear of the Dark

Why do lovers enjoy the dark? Because in darkness we can forget about our dependence on the sense of sight; we call instead on our other senses. For the intimate relationship between lovers, vision is not the most significant sense. Sight dwells on externals and depends on distance. It does not pierce the inner self, the soul. In darkness, the senses of touch, smell, and hearing become much more important. "Hark! my beloved knocks" (Song of Songs 5:2). The lover's experience, however, counters a very natural fear of the dark, which often masks other terrors: fear of being alone, of losing control, of aging, of dying. All of them reflect our mortal selves and the finitude of our lives. Fear of the dark is fear of the night and of everything the night may contain. Our fear is not unique to us. The same fear is exhibited by the Israelites at Sinai.

> All the people witnessed the thunder and the lightning, the blast of the horn and the mountain smoking, and when the people saw it, they fell back and stood at a distance. "You speak to us," they said to Moses, "and we will obey; but let not God speak to us, lest we die." Moses answered the people, "Be not afraid, for God has come only in order to test you, and in order that the fear of God may be ever with you, so that you do not go astray." So the people remained at a distance, while Moses approached the thick cloud where God was [Exod. 20:15–18].

Like Abraham, Moses persisted in the relationship. He entered into the dark cloud that the Israelites feared. It was said of him: "Never again did there arise in Israel a prophet like Moses—whom Adonai knew face to face" (Deut. 34:10). So Moses' choice against terror led to the deepening of an intimate relationship with God.

Although there are points of resonance with Freud, spiritual guidance differs from psychotherapy in many respects—especially as it deals with fear. Unlike psychotherapy, spiritual guidance does not require us to examine all our fears but merely that we turn from the dark and move toward the light. Ultimately, we will examine our fears, but it will be in the context of a deepened relationship with God. The deepening of the relationship precedes and enables the safe exploration of fear.

Fear of the Unknown and of Death

Fear of the unknown is really part of our fear of death. The unknown life is seen as the end of life as we know it. Felicia went to her dentist for root canal work. She anticipated some pain and discomfort but was anticipating nothing out of the ordinary for such a dental procedure. Shortly after an anesthetic was injected into her gum, she went into shock. The dentist, also shaken by the experience, quickly opened an ampule of spirits of ammonia and brought her around. Within a few minutes, she passed out again. He opened another ampule. Finally, when she seemed stabilized, he let her go home. She managed to make it home but soon discovered that she couldn't stop shaking. She thought to herself, "How close did I come to death?" She really wasn't sure.

As she lay on her bed, chilled and trembling, she suddenly became aware of how little she knew about the functioning of her own body. Her

fear was transformed into a sense of wonder. She didn't know what sig-
nals her nerves sent to the rest of her body or the full route that her blood
took when circulating. But she recognized that just because she didn't
control her own circulation, it didn't mean it was out of control or not
controlled, only that it didn't all depend on her. Like the psalmist, she
soon declared, "I praise You, for I am awesomely, wondrously made"
(Ps. 139:14). Her fear had given way to awe and gratitude.

Many of us have felt the angel of death hovering in our midst. We feel
this especially when we go to sleep at night. We can really never know if
we will wake up in the morning, so we entrust our spirit to God. Unlike
the physical things that we may lend to a neighbor, which get returned in
not quite as good a condition as before they were borrowed, our souls are
usually returned to us by God in the morning fully renewed and restored.
It is this experience that leads our tradition to suggest that we are reborn
each day. When we awake in the morning, our formal prayer includes
thanks to God for providing us with the intricate system of our bodies.

Regardless of the life path we have chosen, death awaits us. Changing
paths does not forestall death, though it may distract us from reality. We
cannot escape our fear of death by refusing to commit to the spiritual path
or to a relationship with God. On the contrary, such a commitment will
lessen that fear, and in our capacity as spiritual guides, we must help seekers confront it. Yet people do attempt to deceive themselves, and we have
come to understand that their fear of death is at base a fear of life. In
order to transcend this fear, a person has to distinguish, first, between the
fear of death and the fear of dying, and second, between the fear of death
and the fear that loss of life includes a loss of self. Leaving behind life and
self as we know them leads us into a new life and a new self.

Fear of Union and Transformation

> One question that inevitably arises in connection with rivers, estuar-
> ies, and the open sea has to do with the fear that individual identity
> will be lost, as if it will "drown." We should relate this notion with
> the opportunity of joining a larger life and relinquishing earlier feel-
> ings of being cut off from the "mainstream of life" [Murray Cox and
> Alice Theilgaard, *Mutative Metaphors in Psychotherapy*, p. 108].

Fear of union is related to a fear of ecstasy. Freud was right—sex has a
lot to do with it. Sex and the spiritual way give rise to the same fear and
the same joy. We fear being overwhelmed. Instead, we choose the defen-
sive stance of guarding our boundaries. In a sense, we guard the borders
of our own prison. We are so much more than the roles that have been

assigned to us. For so long, we have been identified according to birth order in our family, our relationship to another person, the way we earn our living. Gently, life removes many of these constricting identities, but usually not without struggle on our part to retain them.

Emily was a woman in her late sixties who was still understanding herself as the youngest member of her family. When her husband retired, he wanted her to retire as well. She found the idea painful and wasn't sure who she would be if she were not going to work daily. Her children had long been out of the home, and she had adjusted fairly well to that change, but she could not imagine an identity that was not based on work or function. She hadn't understood that her present discomfort was related to a religious concern until she talked with me. When she did, some of her unease became tinged with a sense of excitement. Was it really possible that there were further adventures ahead that would allow her to think of herself very differently from the way she had been named all her life? I interpreted the issue of changed roles and status in later life as a religious call, largely because Emily chose to speak with me and not with a vocational counselor or some other type of counselor.

Fear of the Holy

> Our Rabbis taught: Four entered *pardes* [Paradise], namely: Ben Azzai, Ben Zoma, Acher, and Rabbi Akiva. Ben Azzai gazed and died. . . . Ben Zoma gazed and was stricken. . . . Acher cut down the shoots. [Only] Rabbi Akiva departed in peace [Babylonian Talmud, Ḥagigah, 14b].

This passage stresses the danger of powerful mystical experiences for the unprepared. Although the rabbis use this text to express many things about life, it is generally accepted to mean that Ben Azzai died, Ben Zoma went mad, and Acher (Elisha ben Abuyah, literally, the "other") became a heretic, that is, he destroyed his life-giving connection to the roots of tradition, a fate worse than death in Talmudic times. Only Rabbi Akiva emerged unscathed. To open the door to wonder is to open the door to terror; they live in the same house. The spiritual guide has to warn the seeker that the search for a "high" or the ecstatic in the spiritual life, which so closely resembles the use of hallucinogens in the secular life, carries the same attendant risk. One can be destroyed in all the ways that occurred for three of the rabbis who went into the garden. But the guide must also stress the teaching of the psalmist: "Nearness to God is my good." There is no danger in the natural development of a relationship with God. The danger comes in forcing the issue, in looking for the immediate, constant high, the quick spiritual "fix." Danger arises from trying to bypass the patient development of trust and openness. Spirituality itself is not dangerous, but the quest for ecstasy can be. The distinction is a critical one.

The real quest is for self-transcendence. The danger of storming the heavens must be contrasted with the bliss of the individual who shyly and patiently opens to the Other. To some extent, we can overcome fear by shifting our focus. It is not about "me" having this experience—which would foster acute self-consciousness and unease—but about God, whose works and words we revere. Gratitude and love can take us safely where curiosity and greed for this or that experience cannot. Our approaching the Holy One of Blessing is like meeting an important person. Rabbinic midrash is filled with such metaphor. If we seek out someone important because of our admiration, respect, and gratitude, we might be welcomed into a relationship with that person. But if we insinuate ourselves into that individual's company because we "collect" famous people, we are likely to be rebuffed.

We also must acknowledge the fear of the holy in the sense of the wholly other—that which is totally beyond our comprehension, what may even be considered uncanny. A curious passage follows the account in the Torah of Moses' encounter with God at the burning bush:

> At a night encampment on the way, Adonai encountered him and sought to kill him. So Zipporah took a flint and cut off her son's foreskin, and touched his legs with it, saying "You are truly a bridegroom of blood to me." And when God let him alone, she added, "A bridegroom of blood because of the circumcision" [Exod. 4:24–26].

This incident is never again referred to in the Bible. Coming right after the light and luminous vision at the burning bush, the night attack is haunting and puzzling. (See Buber, *Moses,* p. 58). The rabbis teach us that every aspect of the sacred text has its meaning, including the ordering of the narrative, especially when it seems out of place. This is not the work of a sloppy editor. The interjection is placed here to teach us something. As interesting as it may be to try to understand the meaning of this event in the life of Moses, our more urgent concern is to find out what it means to any of us on the spiritual way. So we need to ask, Are we in danger? Might we be attacked?

Commenting on this passage, Buber suggests that there are such things as "incidents of the night" in the life of any great leader. These unanticipated, surprising incidents follow moments of great exaltation and vision. There are real dangers along the spiritual way, but we can choose to proceed even in the face of terror, or, at least, we can be helped to face danger with the encouragement of a spiritual guide.

> What are the virtues of the spell . . . that allows one to go down
> unharmed and arise in peace [that is, to go down to see the glory and
> go up to leave]?

This text from *merkavah* (literally, chariot) literature, from the earliest
stage of Jewish mysticism, is part of a discussion concerning those who
would be spiritual leaders. The leaders are required to fulfill many pre-
conditions: they have to be of high religious, moral, and intellectual cal-
iber; they must fast for many days; and they had to assume a certain
posture—sitting with their heads between their knees. The text suggests
that danger threatens a secular person who approaches the Holy of
Holies. The prophet Isaiah gives voice to a similar thought and associates
it with a sense of uncleanness:

> In the year that King Uzziah died, I beheld my God seated on a high
> and lofty throne; and the skirts of God's robe filled the Temple. Ser-
> aphs stood in attendance on God. Each of them had six wings: with
> two he covered his face, with two he covered his legs, and with two he
> would fly. . . .
> The doorposts would shake at the sound of the one who called, and
> the House kept filling with smoke. I cried,
> "Woe is me; I am lost!
> For I am a person of unclean lips
> And I live among a people
> Of unclean lips;
> Yet my own eyes have beheld
> The Sovereign, Adonai Tzevaot."
>
> —Isa. 6:1–2, 4–5

This passage from Isaiah suggests both the power associated with the
notion of divinity and the need for purity before approaching it.

The third book of Enoch (the first is the Ethiopian, the second is the
Slavonic) is part of the Jewish pseudoepigraphical literature and describes
the visions of Rabbi Ishmael:

> Threatened by angels I drew back and trembled. I fell from my stand-
> ing posture and became numb and fell into a slumber before the splen-
> dor of the appearance of their eyes. Until God rebuked them and had
> them cover their eyes before "Ishmael my beloved son that he may not
> have to tremble and be afraid." And he restored me to my feet.

Here we are introduced to a psychological aspect of a complex type of
danger to which the seeker is exposed. Angels in the esoteric tradition are

not wholly benign. Before such splendor and holiness we are terrified. Mainstream Judaism did not focus on intermediary forces and found safety with God.

How can we see God and live? It is written:

> But if you search there for Adonai your God you will find God, if you only seek God with all your heart and soul [Deut. 4:29].

Fear of God represents our human ambivalence to the nearness of the holy. We have an impulse to withdraw from God's displeasure even as we are drawn to be near God's loving kindness.

The call to the spiritual way is a call to transformation, but it is foremost a call to intimacy. When we fall in love, we will, of course, be changed by that love, but we don't fall in love in order to be changed. We fall in love because that's just the way it is. Falling in love with God will change us; but we fall in love because of God's allure, not because we have an agenda for change.

Fear of Judgment and Challenge

We fear being judged, but we want to be judged. We want to be loved, forgiven, and comforted; but we also want to be known, valued, and tested. Acceptance is insufficient. We want to be challenged and strengthened. We want to grow because *we* want to grow, not simply to win love (which cannot be won anyway) or approval. We challenge ourselves on many levels. We desire to transcend ourselves. On the other hand, we are always tempted to settle or, in the words of the Song of Songs (5:2), not to get out of bed. God calls us to get up, to leap over mountains, to follow. Dostoevsky wrote, "Perhaps you should have respected us less and loved us more," but it is our experience that respect is a most profound form of love and that, ultimately, we do *not* want to take the easiest way. There are times when we are tired or impatient, or really afraid. But we know when we haven't been sufficiently challenged.

Work is related to both our desire for challenge and our fear of being obliterated. We use work as a way of challenging, transforming, and finally, transcending ourselves. Freud wrote that work is one of the three aspects of mature human life, together with love and communal life. We fear not working and leaving no trace. We need to add our mark, our pebble to the great monument being created by our people. We want the world to be somehow different as a result of our having been here. The Gerer Rebbe said that as a young man, he sought to change the world. When he reached what he thought was maturity (middle age), he desired only to influence his community and those around him. In his old age, he realized that all along he was wrong. Throughout his life, he had been looking in the wrong places, at the wrong things. All along, all he needed to do was change himself. That's when the world around him seemed to change.

There is a prayer in the High Holy Day *maḥzor* (festival prayer book) about how we want to be corrected and to learn, but we prefer not to do so through suffering. All of us who have experienced life know that suffering is a teacher, but none of us would voluntarily choose that route for learning. Nevertheless, we are drawn to the "true Judge." We want to live more authentically in God's image. Fear of judgment and fear of challenge remain positive, because in eventually choosing both judgment and challenge, we come to transcend ourselves.

The Need to Trust in God

The Torah portion *Shelaḥ Lekha* (Num. 13:1–15:41) describes another fear. God commands Moses to send leaders of each of the ancestral tribes to scout out the Promised Land. As noted earlier, the "spies" return to the Israelites with a generally poor report. To them, the inhabitants of the land had looked like giants. Only Caleb and Joshua dissent, saying that they saw "an exceeding good land. . . . If the Lord is pleased with us, He will bring us into that land, a land that flows with milk and honey, and give it to us." (14:89). Accepting the alarmist description, the Israelites refuse to move forward. God then informs Moses that all the people over the age of twenty, with the exception of Caleb and Joshua, will die in the wilderness.

This story raises a question of central concern to our own spiritual quest: How, contrary to the rest of the spies, were Caleb and Joshua able to see the goodness of the land? How is it that ten spies go forth and see the menacing strength of the inhabitants of the land and, as a result, bring back an unfavorable report, while two others see only the goodness of the land? And how is it that these two, Caleb and Joshua, fully trust God to bring them safely to that land? The answer is clear: Caleb and Joshua reached beyond their fear and looked with the eyes of love. They surely saw the same things that the other scouts saw. They too were afraid. But they realized that God would not ask anything of them that was not within their power. When we admit the same truth, we will, with God's help, be able to see. Our faith, our commitment, will transform our seeing.

When we think of what it feels like to be afraid, we think of a dry mouth, sweaty palms, a bodily posture of defense. We have seen cats with their fur raised in terror or dogs in the attack position. But we have also seen cats and dogs postured for surrender. For many, the term *surrender* is troubling. It may even feel "un-Jewish." (Rabbinic law expressly forbids kneeling at any time except during one specific prayer on Yom Kippur.) When we think of surrender to an opposing force, we see an image of ourselves kneeling, bowed down, turned in on ourselves. But we are not surrendering to a hostile force, we are surrendering to God. We need to be continually brought back to the awareness that there are two parties to a covenant. As we grow in our relationship with God, the image changes. The posture of surrender, once we have gotten beyond fear, is not turned in but rooted in the earth, with arms open wide. Surrender is the largest of all embraces. Giving of ourselves to another, to the most significant Other, turns out to be a great gift *to* ourselves. The most important characteristic of surrender is that we don't have to worry any more. The effort is still great, but the anxiety is gone.

Our answers to these many fears are also many, but there is one fundamental answer that we bring to all of them: we remind ourselves, and those we help, that we cannot envision the future. That doesn't mean we won't be ready for it when it comes. The inadequacy of Jacob's prayer as he fled Esau is an excellent illustration of not knowing what we most want or need. We do not know what to pray for, because we don't know who we will be or what we will value. In the old fairy tales, the protagonist is sometimes given three wishes. These wishes invariably fail—usually because of greed, anger, or thoughtlessness. But the biblical story of Jacob is more profound. Jacob, en route to Haran, is not being rushed; he is not accommodating someone else; he is not restricted to three wishes—and he still doesn't know what to pray for:

> If God remains with me, if God protects me on this journey that I am making, and gives me bread to eat and clothing to wear, and if I return safe to my father's house—then Adonai shall be my God [Gen. 28:20–21].

The inadequacy of Jacob's prayer comforts us because our own prayers are so inadequate. In time his consciousness will grow and his prayers will see beyond his present perspective (as it does so magnificently in "The Testament of Jacob," Gen. 49). But it is instructive to see in the figure who would later name our whole people, the beginnings of what eventually becomes a magnificent spirituality.

He cannot desire preservation of those he loves, because he cannot yet imagine love. The things that will matter to him do not as yet enter his consciousness. He prays to be brought back to his father's house. However, when he finally does return twenty years later, he buries his father and moves on. At the time he originally makes his prayer, he cannot imagine a sense of home deeper than the home he is leaving. He doesn't know that he will love, and that love will create a home wherever he settles: in the house of Laban, in the towns through which he will travel with Leah and Rachel, and in Egypt. Finally, in Egypt, he longs for Canaan, where his ancestors are buried. He is not only gathered to his ancestors, he is buried with them—but by then his most genuine place is with God. We often do not know our own deepest good.

Our inadequate knowledge about the future is symbolized by the lesson of the manna. In the wilderness, after the Israelites had fled Egypt, survival depended on having enough to eat. They were fed with manna. But manna could not be stored, even for one day. Whether the Israelites worked hard or little, they always found the same amount. It was outrageous. It was transformative. The essential need for food, whose quantity they could not control, taught them the first lesson of the desert: we are finite and vulnerable. Normally we keep that knowledge well concealed by our daily busyness. But in the wilderness, our tasks were limited to fulfilling our daily needs (for food and protection) and thereby emphasized our vulnerability. And we, like the Israelites, must touch on our own vulnerability and finitude. We cannot control the future, we can only trust.

It is a new stance for us to trust, to stop planning and manipulating. We keep thinking that outcomes in the future depend on us, but gradually we learn that what we do not control is nevertheless very well controlled.

> Too much is made of choice:
> we merely came the way we could
> being what we were, and we were changed
> by the terrain we came by. Nor could we
> see around a single bend
> until we'd turned it. And it was wind
> and not a course we'd charted
> that brought us to a pebbled shore
> whose stones the sea had shaped and
> polished, and gave us food we'd never
> tasted. Of this we had no premonition
> nor even, quite, desire.
> —Eleanor Wilner, "It's Not Cold Here," in *Sarah's Choice*

This poem speaks to us, perhaps about Exodus, but certainly about our contemporary lives.

All choices are made in ignorance—but thank God, there is grace. We cannot know how we'll feel about the choices we are now making, because we cannot know who we'll be when those choices bear fruit. Our lives transform us. We are changed by what we encounter. Yet we plan and plan, trying to lock the future into a facsimile of the past, even though the world is created anew daily, and so are we. Our desires grow, and trying to shape our future in terms of our present consciousness restricts our desires. Inchoate longings are probably better guides than full-blown desires, because these desires draw from a base of presumed knowledge arising from our *present* level of consciousness.

Trust and Resistance

Even in the loving pastoral imagery of the Song of Songs there are instances of resistance.

> I was asleep,
> But my heart was wakeful.
> Hark, my beloved knocks!
> "Let me in, my own,
> My darling, my faultless dove!
> For my head is drenched with dew,
> My locks with the damp of night."
> I had taken off my robe—
> Was I to don it again?
> I had bathed my feet—
> Was I to soil them again?
> My beloved took his hand off the latch,
> And my heart was stirred for him.
> I rose to let in my beloved;
> My hands dripped myrrh—
> My fingers, flowing with myrrh—
> Upon the handles of the bolt.
> I opened the door for my beloved,
> But my beloved had turned and gone.
> —Song of Songs 5:2–6

Resistance has real consequences. There may be fear involved in responding, but there is also a danger in not responding. The consequences continue:

> I sought, but did not find him;
> I called, but he did not answer.
> I met the watchmen

> Who patrol the town;
> They struck me, they bruised me.
> The guards of the walls
> Stripped me of my mantle.
>   —Song of Songs 5:6–7

But the guide can strengthen the fearful. The Song of Songs does not end with the incident of resistance. Resistance and fear are part of the rhythm of the spiritual way; God is infinitely patient.

> Let me be a seal upon your heart
> Like the seal upon your hand.
> For love is fierce as death,
> Passion is mighty as Sheol;
> Its darts are darts of fire,
> A blazing flame.
> Vast floods cannot quench love,
> Nor rivers drown it.
>   —Song of Songs 8:6–7

Trust, Love, and Freedom

Rabbi Levi Yitzchak of Berditchev taught that there is a difference between fear and love in the service of God. Those who serve from fear never forget their own existence but fear the Mighty One. On the other hand, those who serve from love forget about themselves entirely.

The transformative power of responding to God's love is illustrated in a postcard that Etty Hillesum threw out of a train on its way to Auschwitz. It was found by farmers outside Westerbork camp and posted by them.

> Opening the Bible at random I find this: "The Lord is my high tower."
> I am sitting on my rucksack in the middle of a full freight car. Father,
> Mother, and Mischa are a few cars away. In the end, the departure
> came without warning. On sudden special orders from the Hague. We
> left the camp singing [*Letters from Westerbork*, p. 146].

How could Etty Hillesum sing en route to the death camp? How could she have achieved the inner freedom that allowed her to think nothing of death and to meditate only on life? Hillesum's liberation from fear of death was the end of a long journey that began with less dramatic concerns:

> We have to fight them daily, like fleas, those many small worries about
> the morrow, for they sap our energies. We make mental provisions for

the day to come and everything turns out differently, quite differently. . . . The things that have to be done must be done, and for the
rest, we must not allow ourselves to become infested with thousands
of petty fears and worries, so many motions of no confidence in God
[Etty Hillesum, *An Interrupted Life,* p. 229].

When we read accounts like the life and letters of Etty Hillesum, we are
tempted to say, "She was a *tzaddik* [righteous one]; this is not applicable
in our life." No one else's specific experiences are applicable to the unique
life we are given to lead. And we pray that no one again will ever be
rounded up into a freight train en route to a death camp. But Hillesum's
story is significant for us because she was so human—just like us. She was
a very gifted twenty-seven-year-old who, in the course of the two years
covered by the diary that has been preserved, grows from a person
enslaved to her own ego to one who has learned to love God.

For once you have begun to walk with God, you need only keep on
walking with Him and all of life becomes one long stroll—such a mar-
vellous feeling [p. 189].

She isn't trying to be righteous; she is merely trying to lead a meaningful,
fulfilling life. That turns out to be a life in relationship with God.

Healing Fear Through Our Relationship with God

What we have discovered is that the primary way to heal fear is through
a deepening relationship with God. As seekers we need a supportive guide
and sacred texts that show us that others have safely traveled where we
now go in order to achieve this relationship. We also need to examine
which fears require further exploration and which simply need to be
avoided so that we might gain distance from them.

Lucia, who worked with me, wrote extensively about her experiences
with fear. The following "dialogue" personifies fear and the self she was
trying to become:

FEAR: You idiot, what makes you think you can do it? We both know
you can't.

SELF: Don't listen to fear. Fear is trying to paralyze you, stop you from
doing what you really want. Beware of fear, recognize it as a powerful
enemy that needs to be battled. Fear will put stumbling blocks in your
path, as many as you will allow.

FEAR: Don't listen. You don't know what you're talking about. Haven't I protected you all these years? Nothing bad happened because you listened to me.

SELF: God protected you, not fear. If you listen once again to fear you will not sense and use the strength you have to do whatever you want to do. I told you fear is a powerful enemy. All you have to do is listen to your heart. Fear will not just go away, fear will always be around, lurking in unexpected corners, waiting to pounce on you. However, as you become stronger, fear will occur less and less and you'll be able to recognize and deal with it.

Much of this chapter has dealt with the relationship of fear to love. Experiencing the presence of one we love expands freedom and melts away fear. We see this in the toddler who is fearless as long as the parent is within view but as soon as the parent is out of sight, reverts to dependency, shyness, and fear. Likewise, as we experience the presence of God, the *Shekhinah,* our freedom is expanded and we can move from a fearful, dependent relationship with God to that of lovers and friends.

6

REVISITING OUR IMAGES OF GOD

God created humans in God's image,
in the image of God did God create them,
male and female did God create them.

—Genesis 1:27

SPIRITUAL GUIDANCE has as its central focus growth in relationship with God. As seekers we accomplish this growth in several ways. First, we have to overcome some of our fears. Next, spiritual guidance helps us notice and thereby acknowledge God's presence and caring concern. Finally, we begin the process of developing language to ponder and express the reality of our personal experience of God. Because our images of God can facilitate (or obstruct) this experience, we must concern ourselves with these images.

Opening up the seeker's language and imaging powers is a primary goal of the spiritual guide. A second, related goal is to get seekers to take their own experiences seriously. Too often we are quick to censor other people's experiences or try to make them conform to some idea of "orthodoxy." Instead, guides must encourage seekers to be authentic and let their experiences educate them.

Our God Image and How It Evolves

As spiritual guides, the starting point in our relationship with seekers is our own relationship with God and the personal image of God that we have developed. Following the biblical notion, some people suppose that if we are made in God's image, then God is much like us—but on a grander scale, one perhaps even beyond human comprehension. Knowing the self, therefore, would lead a person to know God. The tenth-century philosopher Rabbi Bachya ibn Pakudah backs this view, suggesting that "through the evidence of the divine wisdom that is manifest within oneself, the individual will come to recognize the Creator" (*Duties of the Heart,* pp. 71, 72), and he quotes Job to support this assertion: "In my flesh I see God" (Job 19:26). Others reject any similarity between God and humans. But long before we become involved in such theological debate, we have images of God. They are not quite ideas or theories but some pastiche of experiences we have had with adults we revere or love, who we find have power over us—or who have even frightened us. We are also taught songs and told stories, all of which are usually absorbed uncritically in the early formulation of our God image.

Most people are unlikely to reflect on this image when they are older and to modify it in terms of their mature consciousness. More common is the experience that we formulate an image of God in our early years and do not look at it again until a crisis hits (usually the death of a loved one). At such times we may feel embarrassed, as we remarked earlier, by its resemblance to the moth-eaten teddy bear we embraced at the same age as we formed this image. As a result of the crisis, we may be tempted to discard the very notion of God rather than the inadequate God image.

The Self-Correcting God Image

The God image of a seeker, if it is sufficiently encompassing, actually corrects itself. It can evolve and grow as the seeker grows. Given a sincere desire for a relationship with God, the developing experience of God's presence will transform whatever image we initially have. This expanding or self-correcting aspect of God images is one reason spiritual guides can feel so comfortable allowing those they direct to start from their own position, regardless of how unorthodox their initial image of God may be.

By the time people seek spiritual guidance, they usually know on some level that they want their relationship with God to grow. They have found some aspect of this relationship enticing. What they don't know—and can't really know in advance—is how their experience of God (once they open themselves up to the possibility of such experiences) is likely to transform their ideas and images of the holy. As spiritual guides, we have no agenda to modify their views or bring them more into conformity with some acceptable notion. Our goal is to help them develop a relationship with God, which can grow only out of their own authentic experiences. Like a precious stone with many facets, God is experienced in a variety of ways. Yet it is still the same God with whom we relate, regardless of our experience.

People can start from radically different positions and all arrive at a similar sense of love, trust, and caring concern. Jonathan started out with the very rationalistic position that the universe needed an explanation and the hypothesis of God made sense. There was seemingly little room for a personal encounter in this image. Yet a deeply felt commitment evolved over time.

Mark, the highly cerebral systems analyst we met in Chapter One, was comfortable only if he had a written text to study, though he was not quite ready to work from a sacred text. I gave him a copy of Ana-Maria Rizzuto's "God Questionnaire" (see Appendix), which consists of forty-five questions that help the seeker probe deeply into the self, but I provided no instructions on what to do with them. When I next saw him, he said he had spent the entire intervening time considering just one question. He had found *his* issue and really allowed it to play out in his life:

The time in my life when I felt closest to or most distant from God was _____.

For Mark, the answer to the question about closeness was identical to the answer concerning distance: the time of his father's death. At the same time, he was relinquishing one image of God while, painfully and with great struggle, another was emerging. This became clear when Mark spoke of his decision to become a rabbi and described the role of rabbi as a builder of community among educated lay people. He did not seek a parental role.

Dorothy, too, lost her father. As she mourned, she recognized that she had previously held an image of God as a strong, firm, but loving father, much like the image she held of her own father. During the *shiva* (the traditional first week of mourning following the death of one's closest relatives), she had a profound experience in which, for the first time, she discovered God as mother. She described this image both in the classical terms of the *Shekhinah*—the loving, motherly, suffering, mourning aspect of divinity, who went into exile with the people of Israel and would remain with them until their ultimate redemption—and in terms of her own experience of having mothered her children. The feminine image validated the divine in herself and the feminine as well. She had been mothered and she had mothered. This change in her God image was not something she chose; it simply occurred.

People who describe themselves as atheists may not really have rejected God; rather, they may have rejected an inadequate image they formulated at an earlier stage in their development. What needs to be explored with them is just who the God is in which they don't believe. Frequently it turns out to be a "God" they have done well to leave behind. We should be prepared to see atheism as a provisional stage on a journey—a spiritual cleaning of the Augean stable before something new can enter. Even for the believer, there are "atheistic moments," times when the existence of God is doubted.

Psychologists have done significant studies of God images—how they are formed, how they affect self-esteem, how they are transformed. But these studies deal with only half the picture. As spiritual guides, we are also interested in the original God image, but unlike the clinicians, we believe that a covenant has two parties to it. People do not simply form a mature God image; instead, they open themselves to a relationship with God. That experience will transform any received image or images formed out of our childhood needs. We do not need to form our God image or deliberately transform it. We only need to become aware of the image we hold and be open to holding it lightly so that it can be reshaped by our experiences.

God Image and Self-Image

We have already discussed some of the fears that assail a seeker. Central to our fear of relating to God is our sense of unworthiness. Many biblical characters express this feeling. At one point in his spiritual journey, Jacob says, "I am unworthy of all the kindness that You have so steadfastly shown Your servant" (Gen. 32:11). This feeling of unworthiness is deeply interconnected with our image of God. It plays a part in the delicate balance between our image of God and our image of self. Both are equally mysterious. We pay lip service to our being "in the image of God" (b'tzelem Elohim) but rarely take advantage of the implicit invitation to explore our own nature. If God can know us and still care for us, then maybe we are not so undeserving.

If we cannot examine and accept our own unworthiness we run the risk of projecting aspects of what we deem our less acceptable attributes onto another. What the psalmist calls the wicked, others call Satan. Psychologist David Bakan suggests that the effort of separating ourselves from evil stems from the same source in the psyche as does the image of the devil. He finds in the Jewish mystical tradition a midrash that counters this radical projection of evil. It tells of the holy vessel that was shattered at the time of creation and of the dispersal of the holy sparks. "Hope lies in the possibility of the ingathering of these holy sparks. Implicit in this counter-myth is the notion that holiness may be anywhere, in both what appears good or evil; and it tends to overcome the sharp distinction between them" (*The Duality of Human Existence*, p. 43).

Ultimately we know that we want *shalem*, a sense of wholeness, but it is far from our experience. We do not know how to integrate our murderous thoughts and our anger into our personality, so we deny them and project them onto the world. We even project our self-hatred onto God, as an image of divine wrath and judgment. It is only the *experience* of God that can correct this misguided theology. Our experience of being loved and accepted can accomplish what all the logical arguments of philosophers and theologians cannot do. We begin to sense our own value and see ourselves as the recipients of God's loving concern.

The Mystics' Description of God

Jewish mystics, over the course of time, have developed myriad descriptions of what they call the ten *sefirot*, the emanations or attributes of God. These at first appear to be descriptions of the divine reality (which differ considerably from the biblical descriptions of God), but they really describe our own experiences as we come closer to God. So while some people view the *sefirot* as describing aspects of reality, others see them as offering different ways of imaging the holy. For now, let's regard them as ways of imaging God.

Above the ten *sefirot* is the *Ein-Sof* (literally, that which is without end), that which is beyond all imagining. This is the God beyond God, or God outside the mediation of human categories. The ten *sefirot* are usually represented by a shape that resembles the human body (thus giving new meaning to the verse in Job cited earlier, "In my flesh, I see God" [19:26]). There is a right side and a left; there are right and left arms and legs. In addition, there is both a *sefirah* (singular) representing womb or compassion (*rahamim*, derived from the word re-*hem* [womb]) and a *sefirah* representing phallus or foundation—the divine attribute signified by *yesod*. For the mystics, prayer must be directed through the correct *sefirah*. They argue that we have been presented with a series of attributes or images through which to enter into relationship with God. The profound insight in this system is that it is out of our own human experience of the flesh that we come to imagine God.

The kabbalist (Jewish mystic) moves from what is directly physical to the relational and more abstract principles of understanding and wisdom, to the Nothingness of *keter* (divine crown) and finally to the wordless mystery of the *Ein-Sof.* The journey up the sefirotic tree (another name for the ten *sefirot*) resembles the journey of the seeker in Plato's *Symposium,* who travels from love of the beauties of the body to the love of beauties of the soul, from the soul to the beauties of laws and institutions and from institutions to the sciences and, "thus, by scanning beauty's wide horizon . . . will be saved from a slavish and illiberal devotion to the individual loveliness of a single boy, a single man, or a single institution. And turning his eyes toward the open sea of beauty, he will find in such contemplation the seed of the most fruitful discourse and the loftiest thought, and reap a golden harvest of philosophy, until, confirmed and strengthened, he will come upon one single form of knowledge. . . . It will be neither words, nor knowledge, nor something that exists in something else, such as a living creature, nor the earth, or the heavens, or anything that is—but subsisting of itself and by itself in an eternal oneness . . . the same inviolable whole" (Plato, *Complete Works,* p. 562).

This glance at the sefirotic system suggests that there are many different ways to think about God and our approach to God through beings, ideas, and institutions.

Correcting the Patriarchal Image of God

Irene reluctantly admitted that her sense of the holy took an exclusively feminine form. Even with all the openness that liberal Judaism has shown toward feminist theology, she was hesitant to confess this tendency, because she feared that her experience would be considered heretical. I reassured her by talking about the recent history of Jewish theology. I pointed out that a major aspect of God images that has been explored in the past twenty years is gender. Now, it has to be said that acknowledging God to be no more male than female has not been as helpful as we might have wished. We are not operating in the field of systematic theology, where reason is a primary tool, but in the area of our personal relationship with God, which is more affective or emotional. The language of formal prayer affects us deeply, and it has the capacity to control and limit our experience. Wrong or limited language can make God unapproachable. Irene concluded that she could best be true to herself by helping others accept their own feminist view of God and by joining in the effort toward gender-neutral prayer books.

A friend of hers who is a theologian felt that the status quo was simply unacceptable. She told me that she can no longer participate in a worship service that limits her to words that address a masculine God. This has become a barrier that she is no longer able or willing to transcend. Many women have had experiences for which the language of the historical tradition is inadequate. They are making an important contribution toward expanding our tradition, although they realize that changing the gender of pronouns is only a starting point.

In correcting for the patriarchal formulation in Judaism, we are not entirely without resources. The Song of Songs has equal descriptions of the desirability of the male and the female. Both woo, and both are wooed. But throughout the Bible, God is described in predominantly male terms. Only two explicitly female images of God find their way into the Bible and postbiblical literature. One is God as *Shekhinah*, or presence, from the Hebrew word *shaken*, which originally meant "to sojourn in a tent." Later it signified "to dwell" and led in the rabbinic period to the Aramaic notion of *Shekhinah*. The other is God as *Sophia*, or wisdom (Proverbs 8:22–26). The issue of the gender image of God is not a theoretical one. It raises questions with practical import that can only be resolved experientially. When the image of God is solely male, we are tempted to devalue and even discard feminine aspects of ourselves, whether we are male or female. When the image of God includes the feminine, we include and embrace those characteristics of ourselves—individually and as a culture. The gender image also determines how comfortable we feel approaching God and self.

Although the explicit biblical representations of God as female are limited to the two images just mentioned, God is portrayed performing activities uniquely or traditionally attributed to women: experiencing labor (Isa. 42:14; Deut. 32:18; Job 38:8, 28–29) and serving as a comforting mother (Isa. 66:13–14).

In the midrash, we even have examples of men performing some of the functions reserved for women. Mordecai, for example, who is charged with raising his infant niece Esther, is unable to find a woman to suckle the young child. Thus, he is forced (and able) to do so himself.

Psalm 131 expresses the response of the soul to God's maternal nursing:

> Adonai, my heart is not proud
> nor my look haughty;
> I do not aspire to great things
> or to what is beyond me;
> but I have taught myself to be contented
> like a weaned child with its mother;
> like a weaned child am I in my mind.
> O Israel, wait for Adonai
> now and forever.
>
> —Ps. 131:1–3

Women reading this text understand what it is to give nurse as well as to receive. One woman, Greta, described to us the wonder of being able to feed her infant son from her own body. She recalled how frantically he turned his head until he finally found her breast. With his hand gently holding the breast, he sucked furiously until he fell asleep, his color remaining a rosy red. Her dismay at her son's desperate struggle to find food may suggest what God feels as we blindly stumble after everything but what would really nourish us. The baby was frantic for something that was right in front of him but couldn't recognize that it was what he needed for his comfort and nourishment.

O taste and see that Adonai is good [Ps. 34:9].

Not all women are able or desire to give birth to children, and among those who are, many are unable to suckle their own infants. But such limitations should not keep us from exploring and valuing this role.

Another way of discovering feminine images of God in the Bible is to examine the stories of women. Because we are all made in the image of God, the women in the Bible offer clues to thinking about the feminine aspects of God. It is therefore doubly impoverishing that women are represented so perfunctorily, mostly in relationship to men as wives, daughters, or mothers. Who they are in themselves and in their relationship with God is rarely expressed. But as classic rabbinic midrash has filled in some gaps, we can begin to fill in these.

Hidden in the spaces between Genesis 24:59 and Genesis 35:8 is the life of Deborah (not to be confused with Deborah the prophetess, who appears in the book of Judges). We are told in the first of these verses that when Rebecca, the intended wife of Isaac, was sent off by her family with Abraham's servant and his men, she was accompanied by her nurse. We do not hear of this nurse again until Genesis 35:8, when we learn her name:

> Deborah, Rebecca's nurse, died, and was buried under the oak below
> Beit-el; so it was named *Alon-bakut* [the oak of weeping].

We can make two inferences about her, each based on what little we are told. First, since Isaac, alone among the patriarchs, was monogamous, Deborah (unlike Sarah's, Leah's, or Rachel's handmaids) was probably celibate. Second, because we are told that the place of her burial was given a name that indicates grief (by contrast, we don't even know Rebecca's burial place), she must have touched someone's life sufficiently to have this information recorded. Hers is an interesting life about which to speculate, because whatever sense it made, it did so on its own merits, and not in terms of its usefulness to someone else's structures. The hiddenness of her life provides us with an image of the hiddenness of God. Sometimes we find God not through flaming cherubim or earth-shattering moments but in the awareness of God's silent, invisible presence in all of Creation. We take the time to be attentive to Deborah's hidden life, and, analogously, we take the time to be attentive to God's hiddenness in and through our experiences of sky, dawn, night, new growth, energy, friends, and strangers.

Images as Tools for Approaching Reality

These pointers may be helpful, but more fundamental is the reminder to seekers that we are speaking here of God images, not of God. God is always mediated to us through images, and there is no way to stand outside of images. Although God is beyond all conceptualization (God as male is no more true than God as female), in order to gain human understanding of what is beyond human comprehension, we need to conceptualize. We recognize that our images are tools, not absolutes. We merely try to find the images that authentically express our experience of the holy.

Our ways of imaging God are our ways of perceiving reality. They are not just mental pictures but perspectives and judgments about values and choices. Our use of images is not restricted to God. We use images also to try to understand other people. We never fully know another person; rather, we come to know others through their relation to us. All of our relationships are mediated through our own understanding. When the image we have been given and have developed of God is too forbidding, we may find ourselves relying on luck or nature rather than on God. Or, something small and homey may become the focus of our trust. We may be uncomfortable with such "superstition" or with what seems like polytheism, but what is really going on is a correction of our God image. With a little help and guidance, we can be shown that the things we revere and love as sources of life power are really intermediaries through which God is speaking and relating to us. We need to find a way to embrace them rather than reject them.

The same is true of sacred texts we may have read one way as children and now another way as adults. The God we meet in the experience of our lives transforms the way we read our received texts and expands our tradition in positive ways.

Naomi had become very aware of God in and through her pregnancy with her first child and his birth. She felt she could understand God's delight in Creation through her own delight with her infant son. As he grew through childhood and teens, so did the ways in which Naomi came to understand God's relationship with Creation. But when he got his driver's license, she knew that he now had a tool with which he could kill himself and others. She also knew that she had to allow him to drive.

The first time he took the car out at night, she sat at home listening for his return, yet trying to be both unintrusive and unanxious. The hours passed slowly. At last she heard the key in the lock. He had returned safely, and she pretended to be preoccupied with a book she was reading. If God loves as a parent, then God's love includes all those times when, like us, God relinquishes control but not caring concern. The texts tend to emphasize the image of God parenting infants or toddlers, but Naomi's most challenging experiences of parenting came during her son's adolescent years, and she began to explore the image of God as parent to adolescent Israelites. So much of what we are doing in our childrens' adolescence is a form of *not* doing: refraining from expressing an opinion, allowing them to make mistakes and then figure out how to rectify them, trusting that all the previous years of love and teaching have left their message, even if it is now disguised by their rebelliousness. We are preparing them to take responsibility for their own lives. God's interaction with the Israelites includes providing a supply of manna and water daily, regularly correcting both the physical path and the spiritual way— and giving a sense of a constant, protective presence. But this changes. Once the Israelites leave the wilderness they become responsible for finding their own food and drink. Even the law, which was once "in Heaven," is now with them, and they are responsible for making judgments.

The story is told of three rabbis disputing a point of the law, with each one trying to bolster the truth of his position by invoking a miracle. The prophet Elijah comes by, and the disputing rabbis turn to ask him if God is aware of their disagreement. Elijah says, "Yes, God is," so they ask God's opinion. Elijah responds, "My children are winning."

The image that Naomi was developing, based on the relationship of parent to adolescent, is only one of many images based on relationship, function, and action.

In a liturgical poem called *Shir Hakavod,* "Song of Glory," (also known as *Anim Zemirot* [I Sing Hymns]), an entire theology can be discerned. Here are just a few relevant verses.

> They imaged You, not as you are really,
> They described You only by Your acts.

> They depicted You in countless visions;
> Despite all comparisons You are One.

They saw in You both old age and young age,
With the hair of Your head now gray, now black:

Age in judgment day, youth in time of war,
His holy right arm bringing victory.

While this prayer has the advantage of illustrating the flexibility of images, it is restricted to predominantly male images and masculine activities. (God is addressed as male, and all the verbs take the male form.) We could imagine a prayer that described actions of healing and comfort, of birthing and nurturing, rather than war and judgment.

"Thou shalt not make a graven image," the second of the Ten Commandments (or utterances), is one of the central teachings in Judaism. Freud thought that it was the most important and singular teaching and that it served to explain what he found unique and valuable in Jewish consciousness.

> Among the precepts of the Mosaic religion there is one that is of greater importance than appears to begin with. This is the prohibition against making an image of God—the compulsion to worship a God whom one cannot see. . . . But if this prohibition were accepted, it must have a profound effect. For it meant that a sensory perception was given second place to what may be called an abstract idea—a triumph of intellectuality over sensuality, or strictly speaking, an instinctual renunciation with all its necessary consequences [*Moses and Monotheism*, vol. 23, p. 112].

Freud's opinion rests on a literal understanding of "graven image" that emphasizes the visual. A rejection of visual images of God is one aspect of what is known as the *apophatic* way. But contrary to Freud, those who have followed that way have described it not as an abstract idea or a triumph of intellectuality over sensuality, but as a profoundly intimate experience. They explain its intimacy by reminding us that what we see is always external to us, but the experience of being touched or spoken to can be more intimate. The God we cannot see invites us into Nothingness, into that which is greater than any form can contain.

The second commandment is indeed of great importance, but Freud's interpretation is too literal. A graven image is one that is long-lasting, that cannot be easily erased or changed. The commandment is not so much opposed to images themselves as to *inflexible* images. What we need are images that grow with us as our life experiences transform us. What was appropriate at one time will need to be modified at another.

Followers of the apophatic way claim to have no image of God. (Their way is contrasted with the *cataphatic* way, which professes positive affirmations of God's nature.) Maimonides was famous for his negative theology. All terms applied to God were said to be negative, thus "God is good" means "It is not the case that God is evil." But the statement does not tell us what the goodness of God, in a positive sense, might express. Baruch of Medziboz (1757–1810), grandson of the Baal Shem Tov, said that God is called the God of Gods (Deut. 10:17) in order to demonstrate to us that God is beyond any comprehension we may have—in other words, higher than any conception of which humanity is capable.

However, we are not really concerned, as spiritual guides, with apophatic and cataphatic *theology* but with the images of God that we experience. We may believe that we have no image of God. But when we find ourselves resisting intimacy, we may discover that although we have no visual image, we have an emotional image that can be obstructive. Our notion of *image* has to expand to include experiences of comfort, disapproval, imperiousness, patience, and compassion. Nevertheless, visual images remain central in our ways of thinking about God images.

The following liturgical poem from the Rosh Hashanah service (Philip Birnbaum, ed., *High Holyday Prayer Book*, p. 538) shows the intimate relationship between self-images and images of God:

> As clay in the hand of the potter
> Who expands or contracts it at will,
> So are we in your hand, gracious God;
> Heed your pact, heed not the accuser.
>
> As stone in the hand of the mason,
> Who preserves or smashes it at will,
> As iron in the hand of the welder,
> Who welds or detaches it at will,
>
> As helm in the hand of the seaman,
> Who handles or abandons it at will,
> As glass in the hand of the glazier,
> Who shapes it or dissolves it at will,
>
> As cloth in the hand of the draper,
> Who drapes it even or uneven at will
> As silver in the hand of the smith,
> Who makes it pure or impure at will.
> —Anonymous twelfth-century author, based on Jer. 18:6 and Isa. 64:7

If we are iron, God is a welder; if we are silver, then God is the silver-smith. It is important to recognize such correspondences. However, all the poem's images are inanimate, almost overlooking the fact that unlike clay or glass or cloth, we are people relating to the source of our personhood. The following Yom Kippur prayer (Philip Birnbaum, ed., *High Holyday Prayer Book,* p. 676) comes much closer to that reality:

> We are thy people, and thou art our God.
> We are thy children, and thou art our Father.
> We are thy servants, and thou art our Lord.
> We are thy community, and thou art our Heritage.
> We are thy possession, and thou art our Destiny.
> We are thy flock, and thou art our Shepherd.
> We are thy vineyard, and thou art our Keeper.
> We are thy work, and thou art our Creator.
> We are thy faithful, and thou art our Beloved.
> We are thy chosen, and thou art our Friend.
> We are thy subjects, and thou art our King;
> We are thy worshipers, and thou art our exalted One.

Here all of our human relationships inform our relationship with God. (Each relationship is drawn from expressions in Exodus, Deuteronomy, Leviticus, Ezekiel, Isaiah, Jeremiah, and the Song of Songs.)

The image of ourselves as children and God as the loving parent is particularly comforting:

> Is Ephraim, then, so dear a son to me,
> a child so favored,
> that after each threat of mine
> I must still remember him,
> and still be deeply moved for him,
> and let my tenderness yearn over him?
> —Jer. 31:20

It is still a long journey to the image of ourselves as faithful lover and God as beloved. At the heart of Judaism is the notion of *brit,* or covenant. Before we can even try to define *covenant,* we need to look at how it is portrayed in the Bible. The human covenant that is used to convey our relationship to God is marriage. Marriage has changed somewhat in modern times, but much that was central to marriage in the biblical era remains true. Marriage was essentially a lifelong commitment. At its best, it was built on a love relationship. The celebrated book of love, the Song of Songs, is a text simultaneously showing human love and the love between the Israelites and God. If we take seriously the analogy between marital love and our relationship with God, we will recognize that there is a great distance for us still to travel. A committed love relationship requires openness, vulnerability, honesty, time spent (and "wasted") together, and a living out of all the vicissitudes of life.

It would not be surprising if a great shyness overcame us as we contemplated the idea that we might actually enter into a love relationship with God. The reassurance of texts throughout the Bible may help us on the cognitive level, but all the terror we once felt as we approached the one we loved seems infinitesimal compared to what we feel as we turn in love toward God.

> And you shall love Adonai your God with all your heart, with all your
> soul and with all your might [Deut. 6:5].

We have taken this passage to mean that we should recognize God's greatness, or should be awed and filled with wonder. We haven't really related it to the love expressed in the Song of Songs and echoed in the prayer book.

> With a great love have you loved us Adonai our God;
> Great and abundant mercy have you bestowed upon us

We tend to rush to the second sentence, focusing on God's gifts, unable to absorb the statement that God loves us.

Esther recognized God's presence and love but was not yet able to achieve a full image of herself. She tried to convey her growing love of and trust in God in terms of her cat's growing confidence in her. She gave me the following poem:

THE CAT GOES TO THE COUNTRY
Why are you taking me
to places I've never been?
The ride makes me sick.
I thought you loved me—
How can you so disrupt my life?
The Country!
I never dreamt of such splendor!
Was that really me who meowed and scratched?
Sorry. I should have known better.
I never imagined the country.
It was worth the ride.

The poem conveyed her experience that God was offering her riches she had previously been incapable of imagining. But it was many months before she could move from the relationship between pet and faithful owner to that between lover and beloved, as expressed in another poem:

> You come to me with quiet steps
> in the comfort of my friends.
> You delight and guide me
> in the words of the books I read.
> In moments of sorrow
> a bird calls out.
> All of Creation is your love letter.
> And now, filled with your Creation,
> I turn to You.

My goal with Esther, as with all those who come to me for spiritual guidance, was to open her to a deepening intimacy with God. I had no idea what form that relationship would take or what final image of God Esther would arrive at. I knew only that the relationship itself would instruct her. My job was to encourage her, to "give her permission" to use whatever preliminary images were necessary to allow her to continue on the way. Esther's journey surprised me (and surprised her) because it was emotional, almost sentimental, and she had always understood herself as a hard-headed analytic thinker. Had I thought about it (and I make it a point not to think about it or plan in advance, but to be open to the ways I am led to direct seekers), I would have appealed to Esther's cognitive abilities and suggested some philosophical texts for her to read. Esther's growth was facilitated by my noninterference, and incidentally, her growth transformed my own God image. I now believe that God has a sense of humor. Texts do help us on our journey, and in Judaism, study is considered a form of worship.

7

ENGAGING GOD THROUGH THE STUDY OF SACRED TEXTS

Inspire us to understand and discern,
to perceive, learn and teach, to observe, do,
and fulfill gladly all the teachings of your Torah.

—Philip Birnbaum, ed., *Daily Prayer Book,* p. 74

STUDY HELPS US GROW in our relationship with God. As spiritual guides, we are often called on to find texts that will stretch people's God image, help them understand themselves, and aid them in finding language through which to express their journey. Very often we find a way to discuss some of the most intimate aspects of the seeker's life through the "safe" context of studying a biblical story together. We also discuss ways of engaging sacred texts, because study can become an important occasion for an encounter with God.

The Commandment of Sacred Study

The commandment to study is one of the many gifts we have from God. Each time we study, we recite a blessing that summarizes our attitude toward the enterprise: "Praised are You, *Adonai* our God, Sovereign Guide of the Universe, who has made us holy with *mitzvot* and instructed us to occupy ourselves with the words and works of Torah." Study is particularly important, say the rabbis, because it is the only *mitzvah* that leads us to all other *mitzvot.* That is why, in contrast to other *mitzvot,* there are no limiting parameters placed on study. The midrash states it this way: "Heaven and earth have limits of time and space, but the Torah has none" (Genesis *Rabbah,* 10, 1).

As those of us who are involved in the discipline of regular study well know, sacred study is indispensable to the life of the spirit. It nourishes us when we feel dry; it accompanies us along the paths we travel; it shapes and challenges us. Study anchors us in this world while helping us transcend it at the same time. "The road to heaven," say the mystics, "bears supports based on the Torah. Those who study the Torah, therefore, will be able to find their way to heaven" (*Zohar,* i, 175b). Whether we read this as myth or as metaphor, we discover that if we immerse ourselves in study, that it is intrinsically valuable and delightful in itself. It also unleashes passionate and inspired creativity that brings us closer to the spiritual gift of freedom. Through study we come to know the self and develop a relationship with God. That is our ultimate goal. The rabbis put it this way in *Pirkei Avot:* "When two sit and study, the *Shekhinah* dwells in their midst" (3:1).

Jews are called the People of the Book. But even before there was a book, there was a scroll, and before that there was a story. That story, told from one to another, can serve as a map that helps us locate ourselves in the universe of meaning. By applying the two spiritual maps of Exodus and the Song of Songs, we have seen how we are able to locate ourselves on the spiritual way (Chapter One), how we are able to place ourselves within the context of the ongoing story of our people. We encounter the story in a variety of places. One rabbi wrote in the midrash:

> Let no one tell you that the Psalms are not Torah, for they are indeed Torah and the prophets are also Torah . . . as are the riddles and parables [Midrash to Ps. 78:1].

Sacred Text and the Text of Our Experience

As we use the maps found in the Torah, we learn to apply to our lives the language of the Torah and the story of our people. We may examine our own lives and find that we want to begin thinking about our spiritual journey in terms of the call. We may have already heard the call, which we have seen expressed in the summons first to Abraham and then to the Israelites. And as we take the first steps of our spiritual journey, we may become aware of our enslavement without yet knowing the full promise of freedom. Like our ancestors, we too may have witnessed signs and wonders. Then suddenly we find ourselves at the Red Sea, and it is here (as we saw in Chapter Five) that the spiritual guide serves as an angel, crying, "Do not fear!" But we are afraid. Ahead of us lies the long desert sojourn. We grumble and complain. We desperately want to return to Egypt, even though we remember the bitter pain of our enslavement. Then we begin to experience the richness of the desert and the experience of God's caring presence throughout our odyssey.

In the desert, the Israelites learned the fundamental spiritual categories of sacred and profane, of Sabbath and secular; they were being prepared for revelation. But revelation did not occur immediately after the Israelites fled Egypt. They needed seven weeks in the desert before they could approach Mount Sinai. Revelation can come only to the prepared mind. For the unready, the unprepared, revelation goes unnoticed.

In addition to telling of the liberation of the slaves from Egypt and the revelation at Sinai, Exodus recounts the creation of the Jewish people. The horde that came out of Egypt was a mixed multitude. The decisive moment on the opposite shore of the Red Sea has been represented as the physical birth of the people, but the spiritual birth required entering into the covenant at Sinai. So liberation becomes creation as the fleeing slaves are born into a world of new possibilities.

Using the map of Exodus, then, we note three fundamental signposts: Redemption (from slavery), Creation (of the Jewish people), and Revelation (at Sinai). We find these signs in our formal prayer too. Each time we pray, we move through the same signposts, although not in the same order. In the major call to prayer, *Bar'chu* (Blessed are You), we bless God for creating light and darkness and renewing the work of creation daily. After the *Shema,* which follows the *Bar'chu,* God is thanked for redeeming the Israelites from Egypt and the house of slavery and for dividing the Red Sea. This leads into the *amidah,* in which we thank God for bestowing knowledge, understanding, and insight and ask that we be returned to the Torah (Revelation). Even in the shortest of worship services, we rehearse the journey of our ancient past. At every moment, God renews Creation; we are constantly drawn out of narrow places (the Egypts that form the darker phases of our lives); and repeatedly we receive revelation.

There is another sense in which we may speak of two texts: that of the Bible and that of our own experiences. Through study, the two texts become fused into one. We can no longer even see where one ends and the other begins. The text of our lives has become the sacred text of our people's journey through history as they struggled in relationship with the holy. We use our own experience as a prism to understand what the Bible is teaching us. At the same time, we use the Bible to illuminate our experiences. As a result, we see things, both in the text and in our lives, that we might not otherwise have seen. We could say, for example, that the way we understood the Bible was forever changed after the Holocaust and the birth of the state of Israel.

As we study sacred text—the touchstone of Jewish spirituality—we become conscious of every dimension of what is written; we also become insightfully aware of its silence. The rabbis understood this phenomenon. They drew meaning out of every aspect of the text. We should do the same.

We stand in a privileged place at the dawn of the twenty-first century. Many commentators on the text have preceded us, and we have learned both from their techniques and from their insights. We must also realize that their readiness for a significant spiritual experience was no greater than ours is today. The commentaries they left alert us to questions that address the specific context of our own lives. Although we treat our past with respect, we do not revere it as an artifact. Instead, we want to engage a living tradition that is strong enough to withstand the challenges of the present. And when we confront the text and tradition, we may be surprised at their flexibility and their capacity to meet the needs of people of our time. The message of Torah transcends time and the vagaries of societal change.

Consider some of the major changes. Our view of slavery has, thankfully, changed. We have become critical of economic systems that create the inequality of rich and poor. We have lived through the Industrial Revolution, which completely changed the way work is understood. And now technology is quickly changing what we thought was the foundation of labor in our society. An urgent issue in our day involves our relationship with nature. We can now bring the perspective of women to this issue and others. In addition, advances in science have raised a variety of questions, particularly about the capability of humanity for destruction and creation; the findings of astronomy have raised questions about our place in cosmology; and the fundamental categories of scientific understanding themselves have been challenged by perspectives of feminism and the introduction of non-Western views. Discoveries in archeology have broadened our understanding of the world in which our ancestors lived.

Study is at the center of Jewish spirituality. We can serve our love of God and our people by being aware of the salient issues of our time and by acquiring the intellectual background and capacity to critique the positions of others. When we speak, we want to speak passionately and thoughtfully. Disciplined study provides us with the tools necessary for making responsible moral decisions. Study increases our understanding of our own lives as well as lives detailed in the stories of our people. And above all, study opens us to an encounter with the holy.

Participating in the Text

The Bible, particularly the Torah, is the sacred text that shaped our people. But what is our individual relationship to this text? In the Greek world, a distinction is made between two types of relationship to the Platonic forms or archetypes: *mimesis,* imitation, and *methexis,* participation. *Mimesis* supposes that our lives are imitations (and faulty ones at that) of the great archetypal lives that fill the scriptures. In *methexis,* on the other hand, we do not mimic those lives but actually participate in the text. This means that although the text shapes us, we also shape the text. We actually begin to change the text as we see the many different ways of reading it. Our individual lives form part of the ongoing story of our people.

The early mystics wrote: "The one who toils in Torah and discovers in it new meanings that are true contributes new Torah, which is treasured by the congregation of Israel" (*Zohar,* iv, 152a). The Torah tells the story of our people, but it also tells the story of each one of us individually. We find in Exodus the stories of bondage, liberation, revelation, and creation; we also find them scripted in our lives.

It should come as no surprise that we find the same signposts echoed in the Song of Songs. The bondage of physical slavery in Egypt is paralleled by the bondage to the narrowness of self-love. In both Exodus and the Song of Songs, liberation from slavery takes the form of an awakening to love and commitment. Revelation in both texts appears in terms of a covenant that tells us that life is meaningful and we are cared about. Creation in Exodus is the rebirth of a people through God's love; in the Song of Songs, it is love that allows us to experience the world as new. So because the two biblical texts mirror one another, either one can serve as a spiritual map for plotting our lives.

Ongoing study disciplines us to become involved with the text on a regular basis. We are presented with a variety of methods for engaging the text. The mystics of the eleventh and twelfth centuries believed that the Torah spells out the name of God in different ways and that the divine name includes all the mysteries of the spirit, so they focused on each letter. They found in the Torah confirmation of their own system of *sefirot.* For example, one construction of the opening of Genesis reads:

IN THE BEGINNING *(Be-reshit):* The letter *bet* is the most elevated Crown *(keter)* and therefore this *bet* is larger than all other *bet*s. The word "beginning" *(reshit)* is in fact Wisdom *(ḥokhmah).* In truth, then, two *sefirot* are encompassed in one word [Rabbi Isaac the Blind, quoted in Joseph Dan, *Early Kabbalah,* p. 80].

An earlier Rabbi Isaac constructed a system for interpreting the text that later interpreters adopted as the foundation for all interpretation. Some of his thirteen rules are complicated and require a detailed knowledge of the entire Bible. Although they appear to be logical principles whose purpose is to protect the sanctity of the text and the authority of former generations, they are really more about encouraging the student of the text to spend more time with it, to engage it. Increasing familiarity creates a comfort with the text. Only through such intimacy can genuine encounter can take place. We don't "tame" the text so that it comes under our control; we want a dynamic, living relationship with it. So whether we come to it daily or weekly, we come quietly, gently, yet passionately and let it reveal itself to us. We work with the text in the expectation of meeting an aspect of the divine.

The text is more than just a scripture of ink on parchment. It is, as the rabbis suggest, black fire written on white fire. The text is the medium of our relationship. This love letter of Torah is a reflection of our love of God. We do not love the letters of our beloved; we love the person and are engaged in that love through the correspondence. Real love letters are not artifacts that we tie with a favorite ribbon and put into cold storage. Instead, they are part of an ongoing conversation of love. They are not merely part of a historical record of relationship. They are present. So we bring all we know and all we are to our engagement with Torah.

What Is Sacred in Sacred Study?

What makes study *sacred?* Part of the answer is the content of what we study. Sacred study generally focuses on a sacred text, but it doesn't have to. Nature is also a text. Although we may study it for purely secular purposes—including use and control—we also study nature to discover the Creator behind the creation. And we study it in such a way that we are led to awe, wonder, and a sense of God's presence. Albert Einstein understood this distinction when he wrote about his wonder at the orderliness of the physical world:

> But, on the other hand, everyone who is seriously involved in the pursuit of science becomes convinced that a spirit is manifest in the laws of the Universe—a spirit vastly superior to that of man, and one in the face of which we with our modest powers must feel humble. In this way the pursuit of science leads to a religious feeling of a special sort,

which is indeed quite different from the religiosity of someone more naive [Helen Dukas and Banesh Hoffman, eds., *Albert Einstein*, p. 33].

An Evolving Relationship with the Text

The fact that our text is the Bible does not, by definition, make our study of it sacred. Both the content and the method of study must be sacred. We could spend our time immersed in Scripture and yet never become open to being "radically amazed" by it, as the modern philosopher Abraham Joshua Heschel might have said, or open to an encounter with it. Too often, we study "at a distance," trying to force our structure on the text. That kind of study leaves us outside the story—which is really our own story—and renders it opaque to us. Genuine sacred study sees the life force of the text as a reflection of our own life force.

As we approach the text, we are invited to adopt a special world view:

> To see a text as making sense for me is to see not just the history behind it, but also the world in front of it which opens for my commitment [Kathleen Fischer, *The Inner Rainbow*, p. 32].

We anticipate meeting the text just the way we might anticipate any new encounter. In the case of people, we inquire about many things, trying to gather as much information as possible: How old are they? What are their interests or concerns? Who are their relatives (maybe we know them)? But the information we gather to help us prepare for this first encounter recedes in importance as we become acquainted and as subsequent encounters take place. No longer do we want to *know about* the person; instead, we want to *know* the person. So it is with Torah. Too often, we read *about* the text, perhaps in an anthology or summary or selection of what someone deems appropriate for us. We learn when a particular text became part of the canon. We learn what other texts are related to it. We do so in the belief that such knowledge will be helpful to us, as it is, say, to a scholar in the field of Hebrew literature. But as our distance from the text diminishes, we begin to realize that we are no longer studying the text as an outsider. We find ourselves actually inside the text, using it as a prism through which to see the world. Put another way, our eyes are now open to a world that has been transformed by the assumptions and values of the text. How, we can now ask, does the world look through the eyes of Ruth or Job?

But even these questions fade as we move deeper and deeper into the text, and a point is reached where we no longer ask the text for answers. That is when we become aware that the text is questioning us! Now it is us under study. The text has become a place of encounter. And we are addressed by its message. We are able to experience the power of the text—a power to transform our lives.

Daniel, a fourth-year rabbinical student, had been coming for spiritual guidance for several months. I suggested that he read the *Tanakh* straight through. Daniel thought this was a strange suggestion, but I reminded him that he rarely had a chance to see how the parts related to one another. I also pointed out that there were undoubtedly parts of the *Tanakh* that Daniel had never read. However skeptical Daniel may have been, he did read the *Tanakh* and animatedly pointed out the parts that attracted him, those he found boring, and those he considered far from holy. Over the course of the next year, Daniel kept returning to issues arising from this reading. He found himself repeatedly drawn to Genesis and frequently used its narratives to illustrate some of his own conflicts. He was also drawn to Exodus. At first he found Numbers boring but came in one day reporting that "boring is good"! It made sense to him that day-to-day life in the desert was full of details he found tedious. His challenge was to find the holy in the everyday.

However, he couldn't suppress his dislike for Leviticus. Over the next few months, he would bring up various prophets and would invariably toss in the comment that he hated Leviticus. Challenged to explain why, he began to respond in terms of specific laws when he stopped himself and then blurted out, "Because I hate priests." His words surprised him, and me as well. Could he be a rabbi with that attitude? Wasn't he about to enter a form of the priestly tradition he claimed to despise? Or was he moving to a new model of the rabbinate—one that has less to do with authority and ritual and more to do with care-giving? I suggested that he pray about his vocation and that he use the *Tanakh* itself as a source of prayer. Daniel wasn't sure what I meant. He was told, "Read the Bible, and let its words speak to you." What I had in mind was that Daniel's engagement with the text, although it couldn't cause an encounter with God, might make it more likely by helping him to be open, alert, and welcoming of such an encounter, and by preparing him to take any direction from God seriously.

I was not surprised when Daniel returned to say that he had found a text that had spoken to him. Though a little embarrassed by it, Daniel couldn't deny that it had definitely felt as if it were addressed to him personally:

> Before I created you in the womb, I selected you;
> Before you were born, I consecrated you;
> I appointed you a prophet concerning the nations. . . .
> Do not say "I am still a boy,"

But go where I send you
And speak whatever I command you.
Have no fear of them,
For I am with you to deliver you—declares the Lord.
—Jer. 1:5, 7

To understand more fully the progression from reading about a text to studying it to finally being engaged by it, we should return to the book of Genesis. There are two very different kinds of knowing that we encounter in our study of Genesis. First, there is the knowledge promised as a result of eating the fruit of the tree of the knowledge of good and evil. Eating that fruit was the cause of the expulsion of Adam and Eve from the Garden of Eden, according to Genesis 3. More specifically, there is a species of knowledge that is estranging and deadening, and that can thrust us out of Paradise: it is the knowledge that gives us the power to predict and control. The result of such power seems odd when we consider that Paradise is characterized by the closeness of God:

They heard the sound of Adonai God moving about in the garden at the cool of the day [Gen. 3:8].

The knowledge they gained as a result of eating the forbidden fruit precludes or obstructs this easy sense of God's presence. On the other hand, Genesis also offers us insight into a different kind of knowledge—one that is intimate, life-giving, and transformative:

Now the man knew his wife Eve, and she conceived and bore Cain [Gen. 4:1].

In this case, "knowledge" is *experienced;* it is life-giving and transformative. There is an important distinction between these two types of knowing. In the first, we act and are in control. In the second, we do not act but are acted upon, so we must be open and receptive. Moreover, in order to bring the act to a satisfactory conclusion, we must willingly yield control. Here, letting go and allowing ourselves to be acted upon is what enables us to meet with what is alive, independent, and has the ability to surprise and transform us. This type of aliveness, independence, and otherness of something beyond ourselves—like our sacred text—is precisely what leads us—as artists, scientists, and spiritual seekers—to speak of inspiration. Something breathes into us:

Adonai God formed Adam from the dust of the earth. God blew into Adam's nostrils the breath of life, and Adam became a living being [Gen. 2:7].

When we are inspired, we become alive and renewed. Everything becomes alive: our art, our scientific ideas, our study of sacred texts. It would be much easier—and certainly less scary—to recite a monologue, to address an inanimate object rather than a person who might answer back and lead the conversation in directions we had never imagined. Although such one-way talk may initially feel safer and more comfortable, we recognize that in the end, this approach is also sterile and deadening. What is alive, by contrast, is frightening, but it is also renewing. We are led—we know not where—and so can discover things we never imagined possible.

Before she studies, Elizabeth prays:

> Let the text be a place where I can come to You and You can come to me. Let it be our rendezvous. And let it be a place where I can love and serve You, and a time when I can encounter You.

We should approach study in the same way we undertake to solve a problem. We first prepare for study by seeking to understand the text on a literal level, using the commentaries that are available. We do this because we have learned that revelation occurs to the prepared mind. We learn the basic assumptions of the text and the questions that have been raised about it. When the text, as presented to us with all the commentaries, no longer satisfies us, we must be willing to let go of accepted interpretations, even if it means entering darkness and chaos. It is difficult to release these commentaries that have nurtured us without feeling a sense of guilt. Must we really challenge them? This stage of questioning is painful, but it makes it possible for a new perspective to grow. Revelation, as it usually occurs in creative endeavors, is characterized by its suddenness. It may come in the face of all consciously held beliefs. Our breakthrough is characterized by vividness, brevity, conciseness of thought, and immediate certainty. Although we may not consider it as such at first, Torah study at its best is a form of learned creativity.

Torah Study and Creativity

Torah study may not generally be associated with creativity. However, not only is study of sacred text a powerful example of creativity, but creativity itself can be understood in terms of the two maps we find in the Bible. The creative process starts within a contained world or "kingdom"—the world of science, say, or the world of a particular art form. We experience bondage in this kingdom—the limitations of its world view. And then, after a struggle for autonomy, we experience liberation—the breakdown of old ways of viewing things. Liberation also has a frightening aspect, represented by the Israelites' initially futile wandering in the wilderness. This is a time of despair. But it is followed by revelation—a whole new way of seeing. And after revelation comes the long process of integrating the new perception, which is analogous to the forty years following Sinai that the Israelites spent in the wilderness. The Song of Songs states the same thing in different language. We begin in the narrowness of self-love. We are led out through attraction. But although we are attracted, we also experience fear and resistance, and the recognition of impending loss. So we need to risk letting go of constraints and opening up to what can surprise and transform us.

Creativity is based on the process of emptying the self, abdicating the ego, and giving oneself over for the sake of one's creation. It takes courage to face the void out of which creation emerges. The discipline of a devoted routine can provide the individual with a foundation for creativity out of which a profound sense of spirituality emerges.

Transcending the Sexism in Biblical Texts

Over the past generation, we have all been made aware that the Bible presents an overwhelmingly male-dominated view of the world. Not only is the biblical text restricted almost entirely to the history of *men*, it records that history from what we would describe today as a male point of view. Women, when they are mentioned at all, are typically cast as bit players in the larger drama. In recent years, theologians and scholars have striven to identify the various obscuring layers that hide the role of women in the biblical narrative. There is now an extensive and growing literature that brings the invisible women of the Jewish tradition into the spotlight and puts their stories into a broader perspective.

The contemporary theologian Kathleen Fischer has outlined the steps that must be taken order to engage Scripture in light of this new awareness and make the text representative of both sexes. She suggests that all of us, women and men alike, attempt to discover ourselves in the stories of biblical women. We can find hope in "liberating" scriptural passages by showing that the voices of these women can often be recovered and can model for us the faith to which we aspire. We must recall and mourn women's pain, and we must learn how to listen to their silence (Fischer, *Women at the Well,* chap. 5). Even those stories that are familiar to us must be studied anew in order to uncover the significance of the women who appear in them, to take cognizance of their contributions.

Recent feminist scholarship has helped restore Miriam to a central role in the Passover story and in the celebration of the seder. Although

Miriam is called a prophet and is one of the three leaders of the Exodus, only five references to her appear in the entire Torah. If Miriam's story were told simply to add a female name to the list of people involved in the Exodus, it would not constitute a major step forward for seekers. What is being offered, however, is the view that Miriam gave a different teaching, one that complements the traditional understanding of the holy. Holy (*kadosh* in Hebrew) is traditionally defined in opposition to the ordinary (*ḥol*). Miriam, it is suggested, locates the holy in and through the ordinary. Where Moses must climb Mount Sinai to receive revelation, Miriam finds it in and through the ongoing tasks of feeding her family, nurturing and raising children, and caring for the sick.*

Thinking about Miriam's contribution to Judaism has inspired many Jewish women artists to create "Miriam's cups" for use in the Passover seder. A collection of one hundred of these cups formed a moving exhibition (sponsored by *Ma'yan*, 1997). New midrashim are being developed on, for example, the daughters of Zelophed, the first women to argue for and win a property inheritance in the Promised Land (Num. 26:33); the wife of the prophet Hosea; and Elisheba (wife of Aaron and mother of Nadab and Abihu), who serves as a prototype of the female Job—that is, the just woman who suffers. With the anticipated appearance of a women's commentary on the Torah (under the aegis of Women of Reform Judaism), there is reason to expect much more exciting work that will be of use to future spiritual seekers.

Stages of Discovery

How do we actually read the text? The Jewish process of study turns up in the Middle Ages as the monastic contemplative practice of *lectio divina* (divine reading): we read under the eye of God until the heart is touched and leaps to flame. The crucial point is that textual study in both religious traditions is meant to challenge the mind *and* the heart. We begin with the slow, receptive engagement with the text. Drawn into meditation—reflection on what we have been reading—a response may arise from within. A feeling of prayerfulness is one possible expression of that response. A sense develops that we are not engaged in a mere monologue with the text, that is, projecting our self onto it, but that we are in genuine dia-

---

* This fundamental teaching that our daily tasks and ongoing commitments constitute one way to the holy is explored more fully by Carol Ochs in "Miriam's Way" [*Cross Currents*, Winter 1995–96] and Ellen Frankel in *The Five Books of Miriam* [New York: Putnam, 1996].

logue with it. Finally, once we are fully engaged with the text, open to what it may teach us, our heart is touched, and we are moved to respond. We feel a silent resting in God's presence. The text has moved us from the head to the heart.

We read the weekly Torah portion as we have read it every year for as long as we can remember. We also read the commentary that accompanies it. At some point, we even read commentaries on commentaries. We think about the portion and perhaps go so far as to write *divrei Torah* (mini-discourses) on it. We are not anticipating any surprises. We expect, instead, to follow along with the text, thoughtfully reviewing our previous conclusions as to its meaning and building up our expertise. But suddenly this text with which we have great familiarity breaks free of all our categorizing. All of our knowledge about it and our reflections on it feel like so many dry, dead words. What happens now is experiential, transformative, fruitful. This in no way is meant to denigrate all the study that has gone before. Our earlier familiarity with the text in the usual modes of knowing helped precondition us for this new way of knowing. But now study has become prayer—an encounter with God. The difference is the same as that between studying a guide book and finally standing before the scene we have long read about.

In this fresh encounter with the text, revelation is experienced as ongoing and twofold: something is revealed to us, and we ourselves are increasingly unveiled, as layer after layer of defense and disguise drop away. Because, as noted in Chapter One, Exodus and the Song of Songs map the same journey, we can understand revelation in terms of the terror and wonder at Sinai *and* in terms of the terror and wonder of intimacy. Revelation in love is no less earth-shattering than the revelation at Sinai. Never again will the world look the same. And just as we were fearful as we stood at Sinai ("You speak to us and we will obey; but let not God speak to us, lest we die" [Exod. 20:16]), we are fearful in intimate situations too ("I had bathed my feet, was I to soil them again?" [Song of Songs 5:3]).

We read and reread the Torah because *we* are always different. The same story speaks to different aspects of ourselves at different points in our lives. We read together in community so that we have the balance and perspective offered by millennia of reflection on the story. That doesn't make the story less personal, but it does give us some guidance as we begin to reflect on the text. Just as communal prayer keeps our prayer from being too egocentric, so communal reading reminds us that this text speaks to all of our people. Perhaps that is why tradition has it that the Torah was revealed in seventy languages. And the prayer book has grown throughout our history, marking the collective theological growth of our people. As individuals, we add to the prayer book with the spontaneous words and the silences that spring up in the midst of our prayers—and as we open our hearts to the prayers. Publicly, we add to the interpretation of the text by what we write, teach, and discuss. Privately, we begin to adopt the text as a map to make sense of our own faith journey.

The account in Genesis focuses on two forms of knowledge: that given by the tree of the knowledge of good and evil, and the knowing that leads to the birth of Cain. In our contemporary usage, we focus on three forms of knowledge. The first is *cognitive knowing*—we know that such and such is the case. For example, we know that there are five books of the Torah. The second is *methodological knowing*—we know how to read Hebrew (or we would like to learn how to read Hebrew). These two forms of knowledge can both be accessed quite easily, and they are usually addressed by institutions of learning. But the third form of knowledge, *spiritual knowing,* offers the greatest challenge. Such knowledge engages all of our being, and it can transform us. It is this kind of knowledge that religious study is designed to transmit.

Often it is a question, a "cognitive concern," that first stimulates someone to become a seeker. For many of us, this is the only way we have been taught to gain information, to inquire into the world. We even deceive ourselves into believing that we are interested in an intellectual pursuit. We enroll in courses and leave disappointed, thinking that the instructor has failed us by being ill-equipped to transmit the information we seek. But our questioning is more than an abstract intellectual concern. It is the starting point of the inquiry that leads us to wonder about our origin and our ultimate destiny. These are the essential questions of finitude, of purpose, of ultimate meaning. Why am I here? What have I been placed on earth to do? Why me and not others? And in the context of our tradition, why do the lives of our biblical ancestors move from dependence to self-reliance and then back to dependence once again? What meaning can that pattern of the past have for our lives? Why were we born into the family of Abraham and Sarah? What does Israel's perennial engagement with this family mean to teach us?

These ever-present questions nag at us. Too often, we ignore them or simply dismiss them as unanswerable. But when such a question seizes us, we are energized by it. As a result, it becomes more than an abstract intellectual concern, more than mental exercise. If we keep "worrying" about the question, we will find that we remain in the desert. The question leads to a psychological impasse, and finally we understand that it cannot be answered in the usual rational/analytical way. So we search in deeper recesses of our spiritual consciousness. Zen Buddhists call such riddles *koans* and carefully select certain questions for their capacity to bring rational processes to a halt. And the Torah presents its own riddles to trigger this response.

The spiritual guide is at pains to remind the seeker that sacred study is not intended simply to produce answers to life's riddles. We study for the purpose of an encounter. When we realize the profound spiritual depth of that encounter, the text becomes sacred. Such study unites the head and the heart. As we come to understand the implications of the encounter, we are endowed with a living heart (in contradistinction to the hardened heart of a Pharaoh). Sacred study has an *intrinsic* value, because we study what we love. Through the text, we are brought into the world we love, surrounded by the characters, issues, and values that nourish and delight us. We don't study in order to complete the task of study; we do so because it moves us to study more, to probe more deeply. It is the process that we come to enjoy, in the fullness of the world as it has been bequeathed to us—expanded and enriched by the perspective of the Scriptures and the rest of the Jewish tradition. That is the joy of study and also its reward.

We become what is bound up in our questioning, what we seek to learn from our study. Study returns us to those thoughts that occupied us during our youthful questioning of the world—thoughts that enlarged our heart and mind, and that we feared could never be recaptured. Study is a gift we receive. Just as through other *mitzvot*, God has provided in the study of sacred text a way by which we can nourish ourselves and add richness to our lives. There, in the pages of our text, we meet God.

Study provides us with a language whereby we can name and think about our experiences. It gives us a way to enter into an engaged relationship with God. Through study, we come to learn that the text shapes our world and our way of relating to that world.

As Rabbenu Nissim wrote, "Every person is obligated to study constantly, day and night, in accordance with his [or her] ability" (commenting on Babylonian Talmud, *Nedarim*, 8a). Study is related to all that we do in this world (as discussed in Chapter Ten), because our lives depend not just on our prayers and emotional responses but also on our thinking. And as we open ourselves to new ideas and the intellectual challenges of others, we grow in wisdom. The path of sacred study has no end, for our understanding of Scripture can always be deeper than it is. "The one who loves Torah is never satisfied with it" (Deut. *Rabbah*, 2:23).

With this introduction to the dimensions of study, we are led to ponder temptation and sin (see the discussion in Chapter Eight), because our engaged relationship with the text brings us to the people we encounter in the world. Soon we realize that the text transcends the written page. Each person is a sacred text, existing in the image of God. We encounter God in our relationships with others, so each person must be approached with reverence, with quiet and patient waiting, and with an openness to surprise and transformation. And just as each person must be approached with this care and openness, so must God. Underlying many of the temptations and sins to be explored in Chapter Eight is the underlying sin of closing ourselves off to this developing relationship.

8

ENCOUNTERING
TEMPTATION AND SIN

Why are you distressed
And why is your face fallen?
Surely, if you do right,
There is inspiration.
But if you do not do right
Sin crouches at the door;
Its urge is toward you,
Yet you can be its master.

—Genesis 4:6–7

IT IS CLOSE TO THE BEGINNING of the *Tanakh,* close to the story describing the creation of the entire world and the human species, that we encounter sin for the first time. In this earliest use of the word *sin* in the *Tanakh,* the biblical text suggests two important insights that are applicable to us as seekers and as guides. First, our distress and our feeling of being downcast mark our vulnerability to temptation. But second, we can master the urge to sin, we can be uplifted to overcome it. As spiritual guides, we can help the seeker see this truth and must provide encouragement not to succumb to despair and depression. We should not think of ourselves as judges, "confessors," or pastoral counselors. Our primary concern must always be to nurture the seeker's relationship with God. Whatever issue is raised or behavior is discussed by the seeker must be viewed in the context of that relationship.

Our obligation as spiritual guide is to look beyond the specific behavior to the meaning and motivation of sin. The behavior is an indicator of the state of the relationship with God. But before we can be helpful, certain assumptions have to be made about what it means to live a spiritually based life. Among these are: our lives are serious and significant; our decisions are of profound importance; and the fundamental ordering principle is our love of God. In addition, we must examine how the relationship with God helps to keep our *yetzer tov* (good instinct) and *yetzer hara* (evil instinct, including our lustful drive) in balance, and how it transforms our passions and urges so that morally correct behavior naturally follows.

On a practical level, the rabbis were right: the only way to really know whether we have mastered sin is to reencounter the same temptation to which we once succumbed by sinning and not to sin again. I shared this rabbinic perspective with Andy, a married father of two who came for spiritual guidance just before Yom Kippur a few years ago, and he decided to experiment with it. To test his capacity for spiritual transformation and repentance, he intentionally placed himself in a situation in which he had sinned before.

He went back to a sports club he had been avoiding since meeting a woman there to whom he had felt attracted. He had frequented the club ostensibly to increase his exercise regimen, but his real purpose was to further his relationship with the woman. Indeed, he had never come close to initiating an affair with her. Through his discussions with me, he became much more aware of what he had been doing. He had allowed a certain boredom and dissatisfaction with himself to lead him to seek an external remedy through excitement, even though doing so could jeopardize his family commitments. He realized that he had to face the boredom as an invitation to grow more deeply in his covenants with God and with his family, not to flee to the drama of an affair. This time, he sought her out once again and realized that he had overcome his temptation to sin.

In spiritual guidance, sin, or just the thought of it, is often revealed as a cover for deeper needs. Margaret came to me distraught. She was having fantasies about Robert, a friend of hers and her husband's. She was happily married—"really," she emphasized—and couldn't understand why she was having these fantasies. She was working hard to stop thinking about Robert: every time he entered her thoughts, she pushed him out of her mind, because she regarded fantasizing about sinning as being close to sinning itself. I asked her to deliberately think about Robert. She was confused, upset—she had been working so hard not to think about him. I explained that this was a safe setting in which to really examine what was going on.

She began to describe a fantasy—one that she had never allowed herself to complete. She and her husband are walking with Robert and his wife in the woods. Her husband and Robert's wife walk on ahead. She is alone with Robert. He turns to her. Here, she stopped abruptly, obviously feeling very uncomfortable. I urged her to continue. "He turns to me and says . . ." Suddenly tears began running down Margaret's cheeks. She laughed and managed to say, "He says, 'How has this year been for you?'" When she could finally talk again, she explained: "You know what a difficult year this has been with my daughter's illness. My husband and I have been so worried. And everyone we've spoken to has wanted to know how she is, but no one has asked me how I am. So I imagined someone who would recognize that I was in pain and ask me how this year had been for me. That was what my attraction was all about. I can imagine Robert now and feel no attraction. I just needed to know that someone cared about how I was feeling and how I was faring."

These stories may suggest that people coming for spiritual guidance never actually sin but only fantasize about doing so. That is not the case, although it has been my experience that they tend to be very thoughtful and careful in their actions. Their sins tend to be inadvertent and usually very subtle. They have already felt sufficient concern about their relationship with God to be in spiritual guidance, so the temptations that come are not the more obvious ones.

Characterizations of Sin

There have been attempts in many cultures to define sin. And once you even begin to capture the sense of the Hebrew word *ḥeit* (sin), you are forced to attempt renderings of the word in English. As we know, all translation is interpretation. Sin is understood variously as the arrow that misses the mark, a transgression of a God-given commandment, a disregard for the standards of behavior established by the rabbis. Each interpretation considers sin in terms of a wrong action that we perform or an expected action that we fail to perform.

Let us take a look at twelve characterizations of sin out of the many that have been put forth.

1. Sin as Pride

Pride, or egotism, puts the self in place of God. One of the advantages the Israelites had in the wilderness was that the poverty of the barren terrain allowed them to recognize that *everything* is a gift. We tend to forget that

God is the source underlying all that we are, have, and accomplish and fall into the mistaken notion that we are self-made, or that we do it ourselves. This mistaken belief is what lies behind the sin of pride. As it is with most sins, we are the first to suffer from committing it, because to recognize something as a gift is to be in touch with the love that supports us. When through pride we insist on our individual isolation, we feel alone and defenseless.

Sam, a colleague, had informally mentioned that he thought people had come to religious services to hear him preach. After all, he always drew crowds numbering in the hundreds. But as we talked, he began to realize that people came to hear God speak. Sam was only a mouthpiece. As he shrunk in his own mind, an inner understanding was able to grow, and he was brought closer to God.

From this characterization of sin as pride, the next definition of sin logically follows.

2.   Sin as Distance from God

This is a difficult notion for many people. If God is omnipresent, how can we ever be distant from God? As recounted in Chapter Two, when the Hasidic teacher Menachem Mendl of Kotzk was asked by his students, "Where is God?" he replied, "Wherever you let God in." God may be ever-present, but we aren't always open to this divine presence. If we shut the door, even God may not be able to open it.

Shoshana told me that she had closed that door ever since her father's death at an early age. She felt that God had betrayed her father and abandoned her—as well as her mother. It was not until after the birth of her first child—a difficult birth that came after years of struggling with infertility—that she was finally ready to open the door once again. She said it was for her children; eventually she admitted that it was really for her. She had discovered, like the psalmist, that "nearness to God is my good." It is not only what is healthy for our very being, it is also what helps us to be good.

3.   Sin as Missing the Mark

We tend to miss the mark through inattention. We get lost in our own concerns, unable to perceive the needs of others. This inattention can lead to much of the hurt we cause others. Our lives are all sacred texts. We can all be living Torah. Thus sin as missing the mark is failure to be open to the text of others. Blinding ourselves to the text of someone else's life paves the path for us to hurt them. Other people don't exist simply to serve us. Their lives are valuable in their own right. The highest form of love manifests itself when we love others for who they are and not for who we want them to be. We can't fashion others through the prism of our relationship with them. The attempt to do so causes pain—both to the other person and to ourselves. We must learn to be less angry, less swept around by the winds of passion, less voracious in our appetite for things or covetous of what others have. Our lives are not to be lived exclusively for the sake of our own selves. Instead, we need to remember who we essentially are and to constantly remind ourselves about our evolving relationship with God, for forgetfulness is exile.

4. Sin as Alienation

We are able to be in community and accept our fullest self only when we feel the love and support provided by God's presence. Consequently, when we sin, we alienate ourselves from our community, from God, and from our deepest selves. In such circumstances, spiritual growth is not possible. Instead, we experience spiritual decay.

Wendy, like so many other people I have met, shared with me that she had felt distant from God since childhood and therefore felt free to behave as she pleased—drinking and using drugs much of her adult life. It was the lack of meaning in her life that led her to anesthetize herself with chemical abuse. The gradual return to a relationship with God allowed her to move away from chemical dependency.

5. Sin as Inauthenticity

Who are we really? When we sin, we live the life of someone who is not really us. We become estranged from our essential selves and no longer know who we are. We have taken on the labels our behaviors have given us or the roles that others have come to expect of us because of those behaviors. Yet we were created to be ourselves. That's what Martin Buber meant when he wrote:

> It is the duty of every person in Israel to know and consider that he is unique in the world in his particular character and that there has never been anyone like him in the world, for if there had been someone like him, there would have been no need for him to be in the world. . . . The wise Rabbi Bunam once said in old age, when he had already grown blind: "I should not like to change places with our father Abraham! What good would it do God if Abraham became like blind Bunam, and blind Bunam became like Abraham? Rather than

have this happen, I think I shall try to become a little more myself"
[Martin Buber, *The Way of Man*].

6. Sin as Division

We are called on to be whole. We long to feel that sense of wholeness. The
need for integration of the self follows from the deceptively simple concept that God is one (as distinguished from the idea that there is one God,
a quantitative statement that denies a plurality of gods). Although we cannot fully grasp the principle of God's unity, we can take it as an imperative that we ourselves become one, because we are created in God's image.
The fundamental dualisms and oppositions have to be brought together.
The secular and the sacred must each permeate the other so that we can
learn to find God in every dimension of our daily routine. The spiritual
models of the journey and the relationship should no longer be in conflict
but should be drawn into one focus. Male and female should not be
opposed to one another; they should be two complementary lenses that
give depth to our view of humanity.

7. Sin as Disordered Love

Dante wrote, "Set love in order thou that lovest me." Right relation is tri-
partite: with God, with ourselves, and with others. It is our relationship
with God that allows us to order and correct our relationships with ourselves and others.

Freud wrote that the three tasks of maturity are love, work, and communal life. In naming these tasks, he also named an implicit ordering: our
first obligation is to our covenantal partner; the next is to our work; and
our third obligation is to the community of which we are a part.

Bernard's wife was gentle and soft-spoken. Because she didn't assert her
needs, he found it all too easy to let the demands of his work and of many
civic organizations intrude on the time he would normally have spent with
his wife and family. His workday eventually expanded to fill all his time.
As his children grew older, they complained, and his wife finally added her
voice, but still Bernard did not change the pattern that had been set early
on in his marriage. The precipitating event that made him aware of his dis-
ordered priorities was a heart attack. He promised himself in the hospital
that if he survived, he would remember to set love in order. The hospital
chaplain who visited Bernard reminded him that the model of God in the
Tanakh is not that of Divine Laborer in relation to God's work or Divine
Artist vis à vis God's aesthetic creation, but Lover to the Beloved. Although

Bernard could not automatically institute his new priorities, they were in the forefront of his consciousness, and over the course of the next year, he was able to modify his work, resign from some organizations, and really implement the values he now recognized as his own deepest good.

8. Sin as Impatience

Impatience is based on lack of trust and a need to control. We have seen (in Chapter Four) how patience is at the heart of discernment. Without patience, we can't develop a substantial relationship with others or with God. Such relationships take time.

Lois was acutely uncomfortable with the ambiguity of her situation, which she steadfastly refused to specify other than to say it was not "an affair of the heart." She had no idea what was going to happen next. She prayed for guidance, and when the lack of clarity persisted, she grew irritated and angry. I was able to point out that she *had* been receiving guidance—but only enough for each day. When she asked, "But what about tomorrow?" I assured her she would have as much guidance as she would need for that day too. I reminded her of the manna in the wilderness that would be sufficient for each day but could not be stored. The example of this phenomenon, which was so central to the formation of trust in the newly liberated Israelites, calmed Lois, and she decided to look for the guidance that was being given each day. Over the course of the next four months, she was able to handle uncertainty much better, although she still had periods of discomfort. But in addition to emerging clarity about her own direction, she was discovering emerging trust. She never did say specifically what had led her to seek spiritual guidance, but whatever the problem was, it seemed to recede in importance as her trust grew.

9. Sin as Refusal to Love

When we refuse to love, we reject one of the gifts that God has given us. Perhaps we do so out of a fear of being vulnerable or even rebuffed. Instead of taking such risks, we try to shelter ourselves, but as a result we soon become cold and distant, the precise characteristics from which we had been seeking protection. With all of its attendant risks, love can be a primary force for transformation in our lives. Among those to whom we express love will be those who are depressed or ill or who have suffered injustice. It is tempting to retreat, to close ourselves off from and avoid the pain of the other. When we love, we do share that pain. But if we keep praying—maintaining an evolving relationship with God rather than requesting specific outcomes—the pain of others will not overwhelm us. Instead, our capacity to love and to be present for those in need will be our way of responding to the charge given to Abraham—to be a blessing to a sorrowing world.

Certain professions have high "burnout" rates. These include medicine, nursing, and hospice work, where the professional is involved with terminally ill patients. What such patients most need is health care professionals who can genuinely love them, not those who, out of fear of the pain they will experience when the patient dies, are cold, formal, distant. A spiritual guide who worked with nurses recognized the importance of helping them stay open to loving the patients even in the face of their imminent demise. She helped the nurses articulate their theologies (theologies that developed more out of their actual experiences in nursing than out of any specific denominational background) and helped them find people to mourn with when a patient died. This group of nurses really became a blessing to the hospice center where they worked.

10. Sin as a Refusal to Recognize That We Are Loved

Many of us feel unloved, a feeling that may have grown over time, perhaps as a result of rejection or of loving relationships that failed. Most of us have many such experiences in our lives. In the end, we even fear discovering that we have been loved all along.

Anne told me that she had gone through life feeling unwanted and unloved. It was only after she developed a relationship with God and could feel loved that she was prepared to risk a relationship with a man, something she had avoided for many of her adult years. Whenever she withdrew from a relationship, or it began to fall apart, she would find herself retreating to a former state of feeling unloved. Once I helped her understand that withdrawing from love emanated from the same motivation as did sin—in her case, a lack of trust—she began to open herself up to opportunities for love.

Often we feel insecure about being loved, and so we compete or try to give ourselves tokens of love instead of waiting to see what will come on its own. This is why people pursue one partner after another. They do not know how deeply loved they are, and so they think that they have to keep proving that they are lovable. They do not understand the extent to which we create the beloved by our own projections.

11. Sin as Jealousy in Love

One of the wonders of loving God is that God's love is inexhaustible. God's love for the rest of Creation in no way diminishes God's love for any of us.

Mandy, a mother pregnant with her second child, wondered if she would be able to love her new child as much as she loved her first. And if she could, would her love for her firstborn suffer? Months later, after her second child was born, she was amazed at her own capacity for love. With the birth of Michael, her love for her first child increased rather than diminished.

The tenth-century Sufi mystic Al-Hallaj claimed that the root of all sin is jealousy in love. The centrality he gave to jealousy makes sense if we look at how jealousy deforms us and distorts our world. We become possessive of love when love cannot be possessed but can only be welcomed as a freely offered gift. When we suffer from jealousy, we do not see things as they are in themselves but only as they appear to us as we compete for the attention and time of our beloved. The world becomes constricted, and instead of love expanding our world and the world of our beloved, our jealousy reduces both.

12. Sin as Refusal to Grow

Growth requires change. Such change may begin as dislocation and discomfort. Growth requires substantial effort on our part. It does not usually come on its own. The opposite of growing is "settling" for something. Settling does not get us anywhere—and certainly not where we need to go. In the Torah, settling usually leads to disaster. We must not settle for—and settle—a land that may be close but is not the Promised Land. And it is love that convinces us not to just settle, for love waters our growing edge and opens us up to new worlds, many of which are initially frightening.

The spiritual person recognizes the time to act. What worked effectively yesterday may not be an appropriate response for the situation we confront today. Pharaoh was unable to adjust to the changing situation of the Israelites when Moses was emerging as a leader. He certainly could not read what was going on. We must be able to perceive the changes in our world and respond to them with a freshness that calls out for God's attention.

It is common to get tired of changing, of following the pillars of cloud and fire as we wander in the desert. At every turn, the Israelites were ready to go back to Egypt rather than risk moving forward into the unknown. Sometimes when we see the pillar of cloud beckoning us forward, we just close our eyes. We no longer want to follow. Again, the basic teaching is to conquer fear. When we refuse to grow, a kind of stiffness sets in, a prelude to spiritual rigor mortis. The sin is to stay asleep—to refuse the call and not open to the beloved, as the Song of Songs might express it.

God calls out to us to be holy. Note that nothing is said about being good—it's not the main teaching here. The relationship between the good and the holy has long been debated. One of the most exciting formulations of that debate may be found in Plato's *Euthyphro*. In this dialogue, Socrates asks if the holy is that part of the good having to do with our relationship to the gods (the rest dealing with our relationships to other people, institutions, animals) or if the good is a subset of the holy, where being holy transcends correct behavior (acting justly). As in most of the Platonic writings, no final answer is reached, and the value of the dialogue rests in posing the questions. The prophet Micah relates the good and holy in this way:

> What does Adonai require of you but to do justice, to love mercy, and
> to walk humbly with your God? [Micah 6:8.]

Here, the good is part of holiness, and holiness includes a relationship with God. The call to holiness means opening ourselves to the movement of the pillar of cloud, opening ourselves to the possibility of transformation, opening ourselves to see others as sacred text, and deepening our relationship with others. Some might call this living a truly surrendered life, a concept not often articulated in Jewish circles. But when we are prepared to commit to the evolving covenantal relationship established on the fiery mountaintop of Sinai, then we are, in the most positive sense, surrendering our life to the covenant.

The Sin of Growing Weary

When all is said and done, perhaps the real sin is that of growing weary. It is certainly not the traditional notion of sin, of transgressing God-given commandments that are clearly articulated by the Torah or elucidated by the rabbis. It matters not. Weariness with change is an affront to our Creator, a near blasphemy. We ask, Do we really have to move yet again? Are we capable of any more change? Can't we just stay put? (This topic will be discussed more fully in Chapter Nine.) We must strive to remain fully alive spiritually until life has given out.

Sin in the Jacob Narrative

Each of these dimensions of sin can be found in the biblical story of Jacob in his relationship with his brother, Esau. Jacob deceived his father (with the assistance of his mother, Rebecca) in order to receive a blessing originally intended for Esau. Implied in the narrative is the assumption that there is only a single blessing. The biblical text implies, then, that jealousy in love is not a sin but a logical necessity. The narrative also depicts Esau the way Jacob saw him—as an obstacle—allowing Jacob to be callous in his relationship with his brother.

We see how far Jacob has to go when we examine the words of the prayer he uttered when he fled to Haran. As noted in Chapter Five, he did not pray for those he would come to love and the children he would have; he didn't even pray for forgiveness for what he had already done to his brother. Jacob did not pray to be healed—to be made whole—because he didn't know that he was wounded. It would be twenty years before he would wrestle with the angel at Jabbok. Some commentators suggest that he was really wrestling with his feelings toward his brother. That's why he was able to say, on seeing Esau, "Seeing you is like seeing the face of God." He could not see that face in Esau until he had confronted his sins.

Distancing from God and Returning

As spiritual guides, we must learn to shift the focus of discussions about sin from some notion of external punishment to the effect it has on the sinner's spiritual life. Just as virtue is its own reward, sin is its own punishment. The punishment of sin is to feel cut off—from our deepest self, from community, and, ultimately, from the sense that we can approach God. The spiritual guide must remind the seeker that the cure for sin is a deepening relationship to God, that the sinner must not compound the sin by becoming distant from God.

Rabbi Nachman of Bratzlav (1772–1810) illustrates this estrangement in a story that he often told. A king, wishing to punish his son, sent him into exile. After three years, he deeply missed his son and sent his emissary after him to find out what the prince wanted and to give it to him. The messenger located the young prince, threadbare and starving, and asked what he wanted. The son replied, "A warm cape." The messenger immediately gave it to him.

The prince, not remembering who he was, could not ask that he be restored to his father's house. Forgetfulness is exile. We, too, have forgotten that we are children of the Most High, and instead of asking that we be brought close to God, we fill our prayers with our most immediate needs when all our needs would be met if we could only remember who we are. Instead of asking for *teshuvah*—repentance, renewal, a return to God's ways—and working toward it, we ask for some trivial, often material, thing.

All Sin as Idolatry

As children growing up, we develop a concept of sin in a context of right versus wrong action. As we mature, our concept of sin also matures, as we realize that sins "against God" and "against other people" are just as much sins against ourselves. Our concept of sin develops further as we discover how wonderful life is, how deeply God loves us, and how blessed we are. Now sin is less a matter of cruel deeds and more a disposition toward ingratitude, lack of trust, impatience, and depression. All these states are symptoms of one overriding sin: idolatry.

What is idolatry? Surely few, if any, people reading this book have, like Abraham's father, physical idols that they worship. And while the concept of idolatry is now often applied to the worship of money, power, and the like, that's only part of the story. We can think of idolatry as acting without an awareness that we are in God's presence. We try to grasp what can only be offered freely and can only be free to come and go. We think that happiness depends on something that is in fact transitory and irrelevant. We compete for love when there is love enough for all. We see others through a prism of self and subject them to the laceration of our sharp tongue (*lashon hara*). We may not realize it, but when we lessen the worth of others, we diminish our own concept of God and of the holy. We cannot opt out of the responsibility we bear in the context of our freedom. Put rather grandly, idolatry means turning in the opposite direction on the spiritual way to God.

The Yom Kippur Confession of Sins

Beyond this generalized notion of sin, there are, of course, specific sins, many of which find their way into the confessions pronounced on Yom Kippur. Some of them are very clear; we know them all too well. But along the spiritual way, the sins grow more subtle—as if, in the words of a centuries-old saying, "When the light grows brighter the dirt becomes more apparent." Of the forty-four sins listed in one of the long confessions, sixteen have to do with sins of speech or thought. The sin of *lashon hara* (the evil tongue) is really the sin of failure to see the image of God in others, of having a view of people as inferior.

The list of sins confessed during the Yom Kippur service begins with the distinction between what is done under coercion and what is done of our own free will. One question raised by this distinction is where weakness of will comes from. Spiritual guidance helps us recognize the extent to which we are responsible for the weakening of our own wills (see also the discussion of lust that follows).

Among the first things we confess is that we have acted callously. Callousness brings us back to the whole issue of learning to pay attention, of recognizing the image of God in all people.

We then name the first of many sins related to speech or thought: the sin we commit through idle talk. Further sins in this category are offensive speech, evil thoughts, defaming God's name, unclean lips, foolish talk, scoffing, slander, our manner of speech, passing judgment, levity of mind, talebearing, falsehood, swearing falsely, and plotting against others. In the midst of this litany of sins, we might pause and ask what makes speech so significant. The old childhood taunt comes to mind: "Sticks and stones may break my bones but words can never hurt me." That's simply not true. It is not our experience of the world. Bones can frequently be mended more easily than psyches, or worlds of trust and meaning. In Genesis 1, God creates by means of word. "God *said,* 'Let there be light,' and there was light" (1:3). We, in the image of God, create worlds of meaning by our acts of speech, and we have the potential to destroy them in just the same way.

Lustful behavior is among the next group of sins for which we repent on Yom Kippur. What is really at stake in lust (as well as in sins of eating and drinking) is incontinence—loss of restraint over our will. The act is initially a free choice, but gradually we become bound by what we lust after. We become entangled in a web of self-deceit that carries within it the potential for self-destruction.

The list of sins continues. We need not rehearse them all here, but the inventory ends with the sin of "a confused heart." This is climax, essence, and summary. It is here that we understand why the spiritual guide can be helpful to those facing the difficult reality of the confession.

One seeker came to speak to me for the first time, saying that her heart was confused. It struck me as an odd construction, until I remembered the Yom Kippur confessional. Whatever sins we are guilty of lead us to a confused heart. They are burdens we carry as we wait, yearn, to be cleansed.

The Temptation of Despair

The spiritual guide never forgets that as seekers we may be tempted to despair, that is, give up on ourselves and our relationship with God. Temptations are real. We know that. We all constantly confront them. But we need not approach temptation unprepared. One task of spiritual guidance is to help us learn how to prepare and then stay prepared. So there is no need to despair or lose hope. With God, no situation is hopeless. But what is the nature of our hope? We do not pray that the situation we confront will be different. That, we know, may never happen as long as the world remains the same. We only pray that the situation will be *meaningful* and that we may derive meaning from confronting it.

It may seem surprising to think that moral scrupulousness can be a temptation, but all temptation is really a variation on the temptation to turn back, to not continue on the spiritual way. Some seekers give up because their continued sinning deadens them to the subtlety of God's presence in their lives. But others who may rarely sin give up because they have unrealistic standards.

Tamara, a student teacher, came to see me between Rosh Hashanah and Yom Kippur. She had been preparing for Yom Kippur by going over the confession and doing a spiritual inventory *(heshbon hanefesh)*. She was despondent because she felt she was guilty of *lashon hara*. Of whom had she spoken evilly? She hadn't actually said anything bad, but she had thought it. I persisted. What had she thought, about whom? Reluctantly, she told me that her master teacher had taken Tamara's lesson plans and submitted them to his supervisor as his own work. Where was *lashon hara*? Well, she had thought that was dishonest. Did she now think that it wasn't dishonest? Well, not exactly, but it was thinking ill of someone.

Here we come upon a problem that arises with some highly conscientious people—the problem of scrupulousness. Tamara had experienced an injustice, had named it an injustice, but now was trying to be so "perfect" that she was condemning herself for her own righteous anger. This problem, in many forms, is more common than may be imagined. If we set ourselves impossible standards, we will fail, and in the process undermine our own progress toward spiritual intimacy with God. In the book of Habakkuk we read,

> Though the fig tree does not bud
> And no yield is on the vine,
> Though the olive crop has failed
> And the fields produce no grain,
> Though sheep have vanished from the fold
> And no cattle are in the pen,
> Yet will I rejoice in Adonai
> Exult in the God who delivers me.
> Adonai, my God, is my strength:
> You make my feet like the deer's
> And let me stride upon the heights.
> —Habakkuk 3:17–19

The prophet Habakkuk lived through destruction without losing faith. We sense it in the words he has left for us. Rather than yielding to despair, he came to an understanding and an experience of God that allowed him to rejoice in God. Although he lost his crop and his livelihood, he embraced God as one who was present in all the vicissitudes of his life.

The Temptation of Comparison

There is a strong temptation for us to compare ourselves with others. We draw conclusions based on the "outside" of a person, assuming it reflects the "inside." Then we estimate how far they have traveled on their spiritual journey. We never know what they have really been through—even if we have traveled part of the way with them. Julie, a very serious rabbinic student, had been studying the literature from medieval Safed, which contains rules of daily life to foster Jewish piety. For Janice, this literature led to a feeling of personal inferiority and self-loathing. I reminded her of the truth that God calls each of us in our own way and that our job is to take our own way and know that it contains all good ways. I reminded her also of Rabbi Zusya's statement, "In the world to come I shall not be asked: 'Why were you not Moses?' I shall be asked: 'Why were you not Zusya?'"

This same point illustrates one reason Exodus is so important. The journey to the Promised Land had little to do with miles covered each day. The Israelites could have gotten there much sooner and covered much less territory. But they frequently circled back on areas already traveled because remaining in the desert was necessary for their spiritual growth. We cannot measure, we cannot compare. We cannot live the lives of others, nor can we really know another person's struggle and pain. We might think we know how it would feel to us if we suffered their loss, but in fact we could approach such a tragedy only from our own depth of being, our own history, associations, and ways of making sense of experiences. The other person's life is really a mystery to us. And we have to learn to revere that mystery, to be open to the other's story. We do not ever know how God works in another person's life. We can only live the life given to us and try, in the time allotted to us, to be faithful and to grow in deeper intimacy with God. So, like Moses, we approach with our sandals off, knowing indeed that the ground on which we stand is holy ground.

Repentance

Teshuvah is not about punishment but about return—coming back into right relationship with God. Whatever the form of evil we have been guilty of—and we've all done evil—it is time to turn from evil and do good. The major problem is not sin; rather, it is the way sin convinces us that we can no longer come to God. (As the fevered patient said, "I'm too sick to see the doctor.") We need a way to return, to be forgiven, to forgive ourselves.

So what is *teshuvah?* If sin implies that we have ceased to follow the pillar of cloud, *teshuvah* is a decision to look beyond the effects of that error and to seek the cloud again. If sin is regarded as falling asleep, *teshuvah* is waking up. If sin is failure to see and esteem the sacred text of the other, *teshuvah* is a heightened sense of the other. If sin is weariness, *teshuvah* is a shaking off of weariness. *Teshuvah* is renewal of our covenant with God.

The spiritual guide should be aware that sin, and the seeker's awareness of it, can serve as a wake-up call. Such awareness can get the person back on the spiritual way. Of course, it can be terrifying to be awake, to have to confront the dark side of one's nature in its totality. This dark side may be the seeker's central concern, but for the guide it is significant primarily in terms of the individual's relationship with God.

Scripture provides us with an invaluable map for the exploration of sin and repentance. It is not abstract; it talks about people and events. It talks about us. Those who inhabit the pages of sacred text are people first and foremost; only secondarily do they illustrate characteristics or ideas. This is important to remember, because sin is about a failure in relationship, and repentance is about the ways relationships can be healed. Jacob's deepening relationship with God is made apparent by his transformed relationship with Esau.

Sin and the Ten Commandments

As we saw in the *Euthyphro,* Plato tries to determine whether the good is a subset of the holy or the holy a specific form of the good dealing with right relationship to the gods. Plato leaves the question unresolved. However, we have discovered for ourselves that ethics is indeed a subset of the holy. We could not have understood the fundamental issues of the *Euthyphro* until we had lived our way into the experience of having ethical flaws healed by the posture of listening and waiting on God. Waiting, as discussed in Chapter Four, is central to the process of becoming ethical.

When we stop trying to control and just live in openness and trust, what needs to happen seems to happen. Ethics is the blueprint of the life of freedom, the exposition of a way of thinking, the recommendation of a way of living that will help free us from our unruly wills and affections that are the cause of our misery. This is the liberating gift of *mitzvot.*

The real transformation comes, of course, from loving God. We cannot become less judgmental by our will power. We cannot make ourselves more trusting, more serene. On the other hand, such changes set the stage for ethical behavior. As the philosopher Baruch Spinoza (1632–1677) wrote:

> Blessedness is not the reward of virtue, but is virtue itself; nor do we delight in blessedness because we restrain our lusts, but, on the contrary, because we delight in it therefore we are able to restrain them [*Ethics*, V, prop. 42].

Sin is the result of distance from God. Virtue is made possible by openness to God's love. The relationship between nearness to God—piety—and ethics can be shown if we examine the instructions of Exodus 20, which in the original Hebrew are called the Ten Words but are better known as the Ten Commandments.

1. The first statement, and the essential point of the revelation at Sinai, is *I am Adonai your God* (Exod. 20:2). The whole experience is transformed once we name it, "I am *Adonai* your God." This sets the foundation for what follows, bringing us into relationship with God by first declaring God's presence in our midst. It is the task of spiritual guidance to help the seeker to discern God's presence in and through all that happens. Once the first of these ten words is truly internalized, the others follow with a certain inevitability. We become free from the fears that lead us to strike out in anger, envy, and inauthenticity. By naming all we experience within the framework of "I am *Adonai* your God," we evoke the realities of miracle and revelation, of courtship and commitment, of unfaithfulness and forgiveness. All of the central categories of our faith become available to enrich and sustain our lives once we accept the first of the Ten Words.

But the statement doesn't end there. It continues, "who brought you out of the land of Egypt, out of the house of bondage." If revelation is really addressed to us, then the first of the Ten Words demands that we admit that we have been slaves.

2. *You shall have no other gods before me. You shall not make a graven image* (20:3–4). As already discussed in Chapter Six, the crucial word here is *graven*, meaning inflexible. The spiritual guide, in working with the seeker on issues of sin, is attempting above all to keep the relationship with God growing. Thus the issue of openness to flexible, changing, or expanding images of God is crucial to the deepening intimacy that spiritual guidance fosters.

3. *You are not to take the name of Adonai your God in vain* (20:7). None of us has a book of life's problems with the answers at the back. The spiritual guide does not know what God wants. All the guide knows is how to foster openness and attentiveness to God's guidance. The highest

form of hubris is to speak in the name of God or presume to know what God wants. We all try to be open, but that requires knowing the limits of our knowledge and not speaking with God's authority on any subject.

4.   The fourth of the Ten Words tells us to *remember the Sabbath day, to keep it holy* (20:8). Built into the Ten Words is a statement of the need to rest, to grow in trust, and to recognize the things that we cannot control. In and through this weekly experience of rest, we grow aware that even when we don't control, things are not out of control. A lot of sin is really the by-product of fear. The practice of rest and love serves as an antidote.

5.   From that perspective, we then examine the first of the Ten Words specifically addressed to interpersonal relationships—the commandments that take their lead from the relationship God has established with us. *Honor your father and your mother* (20:12) is the fifth commandment. Most of Genesis is concerned with the working out of family relationships, and, indeed, that is one of our central human tasks. How we see "the other"—whether father, mother, or sibling—ultimately determines how we see ourselves. The self that sees the other simply as what opposes it or needs to be controlled by it is a constricted self. It brings us back to Egypt—*Mitzrayim,* the narrow places. A transformation in our view of the other transforms our view of the self. And, in turn, a change in our understanding of self will transform our relationships with others. Furthermore, behind the other who is our parent or sibling is the Other who is God. As our image of God expands, so does our image of self. As the Torah teaches us early in the book of Genesis, human beings are created in the image of God. Gradually, the power of God's love allows us to return to our most fundamental relationships and heal them. We can release our sense of the inadequacy of our parents by recognizing that God has loved us as a parent all along.

6.   Sixth on the list of divine words is *You shall not kill* (20:13). This follows fast on the heels of "Honor your father and your mother," for our most murderous thoughts attach themselves to those closest to us. From Cain and Abel onward, those nearest to us have seemed most threatening to our being. In acknowledging that the members of our family are people in their own right and not defined merely by their relationship to us, we expand our notion of them and release the need to control and strike out. Once we recognize God's presence in our lives, we can affirm the words of Joseph as recorded in Genesis: "You meant it for evil, but God meant it for good" (50:20). Our need for revenge is past, merged in our growing relationship with God.

7.   The seventh commandment is *You shall not commit adultery* (Exod. 20:13). The model of the covenant by which God's self is bound

to us is that of betrothal and marriage. It is the sacred prism through which we view all relationships. The prophet Hosea portrays God as saying to the Israelites:

> Assuredly, I will speak coaxingly to her
> And lead her through the wilderness
> And speak tenderly. . . .
> There she shall respond as in the days of her youth,
> When she came up from the land of Egypt. . . .
> And I will espouse you forever:
> I will espouse you with righteousness and justice,
> And with goodness and mercy,
> I will espouse you with faithfulness.
> —Hosea 2:16–17, 21–22

The patterns we bring to our human relationships are the same patterns we bring to our relationship with God. If we are insecure, demanding, and impatient with our spouse, we may well be insecure, demanding, and impatient with God. And if we are unfaithful in human love, how much more likely will we be unfaithful to the love that transcends humanity. At the heart of this gift of love is an image of the faithfulness that mutually binds us.

8.   *You shall not steal* (20:13) is the eighth of the Ten Words. The seeker learns through spiritual guidance that there is gift enough for our being and well-being. Stealing is motivated by a lack of trust—there won't be enough for us all. But when trust grows, we know that we do not have to steal, or even grasp. The Israelites' experience of receiving manna in the wilderness can serve as a model for us. It was freely given to us, and the people were shown that there would be enough; there would be no need to steal for our sustenance. Nor is there a need to steal or compete for love. We have already been given the love we need in order to thrive.

9.   The ninth word states: *You shall not bear false witness* (20:13). As seekers our experience in spiritual guidance should be one of going beyond perception to reality. We leave behind the assumptions of society, find that the labels society has used to name us really misname us. These misnomers ignore our deepest identity as someone who has been courted and wooed into the wilderness by God. The time in the wilderness is a time for us to get to the heart of everything.

10.   Finally, the tenth word: *You shall not covet* . . . (20:14). This is the essence of the challenge we face. Were these verses really *commandments,* this would be an impossible directive. We can no more *not* covet than we can *not* think of a white elephant if we are told we shouldn't. The

paradox here is that if we are told *not* to think of something, that is the very thing we think about. We cannot, by fiat, not covet, because our desires are not directly under our control. But the way we manifest these desires in behavior *is,* as is our growing openness to God, and it is that openness that changes the shape of our desires and allows us to be guided by the last of the Ten Words.

Exodus 20 can be seen as a map of the route we will travel on our way to liberation. We can read the Ten Words as guideposts that mark our growing trust in God, our deepening awareness of God's gifts to us, and our cognizance of God's presence and concern. The first four of the Ten Words open us to an awareness of God and our growing relationship with God. This relationship transforms our relationship to our parents (as expressed in the fifth word), and the most egregious behaviors (the next three words) no longer tempt us. Our sense of self grows in the warmth of God's love so that we cannot bear false witness (the ninth word). And as we continue on this route we discover that the shape of our hopes and dreams have been transformed. When we recognize these things, we have no choice—we cannot covet.

The Ten Words are a light that reveals a path out of sin and into relationship with God. As the spiritual guide continually reiterates, we were created to be in such relationship. Our gift is to be God's; yet God created us to be ourselves. Sin forces the loss of both those perspectives. We no longer know who we are, either in relationship with God or in relationship with our own deepest self.

It would be simpler if overcoming temptation were something we had to do once a year, or sin were something we focused on only on Yom Kippur. But relationships are built up over a lifetime of interactions. The spiritual guide should offer support and encouragement and help us keep aware that our determination to grow in deepening intimacy with God will require ongoing commitment. The guide helps the seeker find the strength to "endure the spiritual desert."

9

ENDURING THE SPIRITUAL DESERT

But they who trust in Adonai shall renew their strength
as eagles grow new plumes.
They shall run and not grow weary
They shall march and not grow faint.

—Isaiah 40:31

THE DESERT, SO FORMATIVE for the Jews as a people, is also the classic image used to describe our own transformation as individual Jewish believers. The desert symbolizes a move away from constriction, away from the civilization in which we've been formed.

Characteristics of the Desert

The characteristics of the physical desert serve as powerful analogies for our own spiritual geography. The desert means silence and large vistas; the unmeasured and unmarked; it means a return to chaos.

Nothing Gets Lost

Things do not disappear in the wilderness. They may be bleached by the sun or weathered by the wind and sand, but anything that was there just remains. The problems that beset us twenty years ago still sit there, seemingly unchanged, though they may be half-buried or smoothed by the years of sand blown against them. Nothing really gets lost. We will discover that it is possible in the desert to recover gifts and opportunities that we thought we might never see again.

Isolation

Nothing accompanies us in the wilderness. It may seem surprising to say that the Children of Israel were alone. They both were and were not. We each inhabit the desert of our own heart, and even acknowledgment of that shared reality does not heal our sense of isolation. Though the Children of Israel fled as a horde and were later transformed into a people, each step of the journey was individually experienced. Fearfulness of the wilderness drives each of us inward, and it may be just this sense of isolation that opens us to the experience of God's companionship.

Clarity

The same isolation also lets us see much more clearly, as we do in the wilderness. Nothing interferes with our vision, so we get to see patterns and structures that normally escape our eye. We don't come to this realization in the early stages of our journey, when we cannot stop long enough to see even the surface. But there comes a day when all is stripped bare and we get to view the essence of our surroundings. The capacity to see is helped if we understand that the journey is part of the goal. When the journey has taken on intrinsic value, we pause to look at the changes in the scenery and light. Before we do that, we are aware only of the distance traveled, the obstructions that block our way, and the many detours. Journeying time is wasted time that we refuse to enter into and therefore time that cannot enrich us. But despite our blindness and obstinate focus on some future goal, some of the features of the desert do register on our consciousness.

Extremes

Nothing is moderate in the desert. It is blazing hot or freezing cold. It is the domain of solitude and silence where we can perceive the essence of things away from cultural accretions. The desert is a land of starkness, fierceness, and the special beauty inherent in those qualities. As spiritual guides, we help the seeker focus on the lesson that the fierceness can be trusted. What appears as fierceness is, on closer acquaintance, really warm, loving, and nurturing. The desert is a difficult, lonely place. We have no choice but to endure it. However, we do have the option of embracing the journey, and it is important that the spiritual guide place great emphasis on this. Our ancestors traveled in the desert for forty years, enough for the passing of one generation and the birth of a second. The journey was not straightforward; it was full of twists and turns, just like ordinary life.

Clarissa experienced one of these strange twists when she was faced with life-threatening cancer. The experience changed her life and that of her family. But unlike some people who grow bitter when they fall ill, Clarissa learned, with the help of a spiritual guide, to ask, "What is the cancer trying to teach me?" She does not attribute her illness to God, but she has come to recognize that she can use anything that happens to her to fuel her spiritual journey.

When Elizabeth, whose prayer before study was mentioned in Chapter Seven, lost her seven-year old son, she glimpsed an aspect of reality that other people are at pains to disguise. We really don't want to know how much suffering there is and how vulnerable we are. But in mourning we know it firsthand. We can no longer accept easy, glib assurances. We see the fragility and—to some extent—artificiality of our society. The usual goals of life no longer attract us.

Elizabeth did not really know why her son had died. But she learned how wrong it is to blame the victim of suffering or to turn away from those in pain. God showed Elizabeth divine love, not by preventing the death of her child or providing an explanation for it but by giving her a powerful sense of God's presence, concern, and attention. God remained present through her silence and withdrawal, through her angry cries and accusations, and through all that followed. As a result, Elizabeth came to love God even in the absence of her son. She did not know what death might mean, but she learned, after a long struggle, to trust.

Like Elizabeth, we don't "get over it," we grow around it, and somehow a space is left for God's presence. We cannot give healing to others; we need to wait and let them come to their own insights. We know that in every desert there is or can be revelation. We don't know how healing takes place, but we don't have to know. We just need to be authentic, let the process unfold without hurry, and allow time and space for all that is in the heart to come out.

Lessons of the Desert

We don't merely endure the desert or even just experience it—we reflect on our experiences and so achieve insight into them. The desert becomes our teacher.

We Learn Not to Grow Weary

That Moses, our leader, never made it to the Promised Land may be one
of the greatest teachings we have received: we see a lifelong relationship
and not a single goal. We probably will not make it to the Promised Land
either; we never finish the process of *teshuvah,* of repentance, because we
are really not supposed to. Some journeys have no end, and so "the joy is
in the journey." Likewise, spiritual guidance does not end. As long as we
seekers remain on the spiritual path, we need continued guidance to make
sure that we are going in the right direction. However, there may be certain periods of time when we need it less frequently. For example, the
guidance we initially receive may serve for an extended period to keep us
sensitive and awake, helping us move away from the automatic responses
that previously governed our life.

Obviously, life brings changes. Things follow a certain path for a time,
then suddenly we're at a different place in life. As a result, whole new
questions arise. Not everything works out the way we originally planned,
whether in our career or our family. But the adventure does not stop: we
have an inherent potential to be repeatedly surprised and refreshed by the
newness of life. Sometimes the changes we face are large, challenging,
scary. These demand a quiet time for integration. And just when we
thought we had the answers to all the questions—or at least, the majority of them—new ones suddenly arise.

There are many models of heroic action that involve a single dramatic
encounter: climbing a mountain, facing the villain, rescuing a drowning
child. But spiritual guidance teaches the heroism of resiliency, "abiding-
ness," and what it means to be faithful daily to a lifelong covenant.

We Learn How to Fall

When we first learn to ride a bicycle without training wheels, the first
lesson is about how to fall. It is usually a lesson that we are forced to
learn, because we fall so often during our first few times out. Even the
thought of falling may scare us, keeping us from initially trying to ride.
We will fall; the question is how to fall with minimal damage and how
to get up again. The physical fall of the new bicycle rider has its spiritual analogue in our falls into doubt and discouragement. Here too, we
need to learn how to fall with minimal damage. The spiritual guide will
help us prepare for falls in times of comfort and fervor. We learn to
develop habits and structures of practice that will support us through
difficult times.

The spiritual guide reminds us about the gift of covenants. We can't always be at the moment of our greatest insight, but we can make covenants and retain the memory of those covenants. This is one of the reasons that as seekers we are encouraged to keep journals; if we do so, we will be able to read descriptions of our times of deepest intimacy with God. Such a practice is not about nostalgia; rather, it helps us to recapture a prior experience of God's presence.

When I met Jody for the first time, she brought some photographs to show me. She kept them in her purse, and they were dog-eared and dirty from so much handling. They were pictures of the place she frequented where she felt God's presence most. Because it was many miles from where she lived, and she couldn't travel there frequently, she would gaze at the picture for a few minutes and then close her eyes and be swept away by the memory of God's presence. We can live out the commitments made during our moments of deepest insight even when we can no longer feel the original fervor of those moments. As spiritual guides, we might share with seekers our own experience of, say, being able to close our eyes and breathe deeply the air of Jerusalem—swept across the miles in a matter of seconds. Many of us share the sense that our souls live in Jerusalem. And with our memories of divine encounter, we learn to fall and rise again:

> My father said to me once
> with sorrow that stunned me
> "I'm a mediocre man."
> I've argued with him silently
> long past his death, having seen him
> "rising to the occasion"
> like the ascending saints with their toes
> still pointing earthwards—
> phenomenal how they rise
> how we all rise.
> —Robert Winner, "Phenomenal Men and Women," in *The Sanity of Earth and Grass: Complete Poems by Robert Winner*, p. 128

Marriage counselors frequently help couples learn how to fight. It is apparent that couples *will* fight, but they can learn to do so in such a way that communication is increased, unforgivable things remain unsaid, and the focus remains on addressing the concern at hand rather than on dredging up issues from forty-two years of marriage. Likewise, spiritual guides help seekers learn how to complain, focus on what is really wrong, and fight within a context of faithfulness. Often the complaints are aired with the spiritual guide, and the guide then helps the seeker bring them before

God. Seekers must learn not to withdraw, grow silent, or become too busy to pray. Strong relationships can survive many harsh statements, but they can become cold and formal if we are less than authentic with ourselves and the other. During a time of numbness, dryness, or even a sense of meaninglessness, we can, as seekers, sustain ourselves by calling on the structure we have set in place during the fruitful times.

Why do we fall? Falling is not an indicator of any weakness. It is part of the normal systole and diastole of the spiritual way. Falls are inevitable—which is why we need to learn how to fall. It is hard to say with any certainty what is actually going on during these times of dryness, but a few possibilities among many suggest themselves.

One explanation is that deadness, lack of fervor, lack of a sense of faith all serve as a natural pause in our spiritual growth so that everything that has occurred before can be integrated into the developing self. Another explanation: although most of the self is unified around the developing relationship with God, the nonunified aspect is exposed and challenged during the time we experience as a "fall." This view suggests that falls are an important, indispensable part of growth. They are like battles for which we need to prepare, for which we must be strong, because unification and integration of the self are central to our journey. Falls can also be explained in terms of an organic model that focuses simply on the ordinary rhythm of blood pressure and breathing. (The Jewish tradition has never separated body from soul; it has always considered them to be part of the same undifferentiated self.) The intensity of joy in feeling God's presence is balanced by the desolation caused by the sensation of God's absence. The psalmist writes of both:

> In Your presence is perfect joy;
> delights are ever in Your right hand.
> —Ps. 16:11

> I say to God, my rock,
> "Why have you forgotten me,
> why must I walk in gloom,
> oppressed by my enemy?"
> —Ps. 42:10

Some people imagine falls as times of trial and testing. Whether or not that is their function, this model can lead us to prepare and can encourage us to endure. As seekers, whatever model we use to explain our experience, the guide's task is to encourage and reassure, to help us go beyond fear, and above all to keep us in the relationship. As Rabbi Nathan wrote of his teacher, Nachman of Bratzlav:

The Rebbe would thus fall and begin anew several times each day. He often told us how he continually began serving God anew. This is an important rule in devotion. Never let yourself fall completely. There are many ways you can fall. At times your prayer and devotion may seem utterly without meaning. Strengthen yourself and begin anew. Act as if you were just beginning to serve God. No matter how many times you fall, rise up and start again. Do this again and again, for otherwise you will never come close to God [Rabbi Zvi Aryeh Rosenfeld, ed., *Rabbi Nachman's Wisdom*, p. 152].

We Also Rise

Just as falls are inevitable, so are occasions of rising. They are what we all seek in our spiritual quest, yet we seem almost surprised when we experience them. Ironically, rising can be as dangerous as falling. Our highs present their own challenges. We may grow overconfident and become lax in our habits of faithfulness. Our focus may shift from the relationship to the phenomenological accompaniments of the relationship. We may become careless. Relationships are built up out of carefulness and attention.

At times of rising, we are instructed to establish habits and practices in anticipation of falling. In a sense, that is what the biblical Joseph did when he stored grain during the seven years of plenty in anticipation of the seven years of famine. When we fall, we look to habits of faithfulness to sustain us. We have to constantly remind ourselves that we are engaged in a lifelong relationship that must never become automatic. So in times of plenty, we rest and refresh ourselves, taking time to express our gratitude. We should not rush through this oasis. Though we may not feel in need of rest, we have no idea how long it will be until we encounter the next oasis.

We Prepare for Sandstorms

Sometimes sandstorms arise that obliterate the pillar of cloud guiding us through our desert journey. We must prepare for them on clear days. In the midst of a storm, we know we must trust worthy friends—people committed to their own faithfulness as well as ours. We return to the sacred texts and prayers that have carried us over rough terrain. We lean on the structure of our regular practice. We use our favorite songs or *nigunim,* wordless melodies that elevate the soul. Music makes a significant difference in our spiritual lives. The spiritual maps of Exodus and the Song of Songs help to remind us that other people have gone where we now wander. The journeys began with our ancient ancestors, but the same tracks have been followed by many generations since.

Facing fears in our journey becomes even more important as we explore our images of God. Study can water our roots. This is not a time to get caught up in exploring sin. Our objective is to move from darkness toward the light, not to get stuck exploring the dark. Preparing for sandstorms brings us back to all that we have been learning through spiritual guidance. We repeatedly discover that we are strengthened by habits of faithfulness—in practice, in relationships with friends—and strengthened as well by texts and music that can speak to our heart.

A favorite Hasidic story tells of a teacher who, near his death, brings his student into a dark forest. The teacher carries a lantern to guide them through the forest. Once they reach the heart of the forest, the teacher extinguishes the light. The student asks his teacher, "Will you leave me here in the darkness?" "No," came the teacher's response, "I will leave you searching for the light."

During a storm, we are very gentle with our body: we eat well, sleep adequately. We rely on memories and remembering. We tell and retell the stories of our deliverance.

> You, Adonai my God, have done many things;
> the wonders You have devised for us
> cannot be set out before You;
> I would rehearse the tale of them,
> but they are more than can be told.
> You gave me to understand that
> You do not desire sacrifice and meal offering;
> You do not ask for burnt offering and sin offering.
> Then I said,
> "See I will bring a scroll recounting what befell me."
> —Ps. 40:6–8

We Learn to Endure

We constantly expect the journey to come to an end; instead, we experience its continuity. This is a core issue in spiritual guidance, because people are used to things beginning and ending. But that's just not the case in this endeavor. The spiritual guide is not a coach who prepares athletes for a single race. The seeker's journey is not a single brave effort; rather, it is the ongoing reality of the routine tasks and challenges of daily living. Whatever we build, we will have to continue to build. Early on, we may see the desert experience as one requiring only endurance. Later, the vision changes, and we see that the desert is really where we spend our entire life. We don't just endure it; we find a way to live with gratitude.

After decades of living in the open desert expanse, a different kind of trial may arise: having to move into the cluttered confines of society. We've seen something in the desert, and we like it. In one of the most moving parts of the Sabbath and festival worship service—after the Torah is read in simulation of Sinaitic revelation—we humbly stand in front of the open ark to which the scrolls have been restored, pleading: "Return us to thee, God, and we shall return; renew our days as of old" (Lam. 5:21). This biblical verse expresses the wish for a return to Jerusalem and the days of the Temple. However, it can also be read as a wish to return to a time of closeness to God or, by extension, to life in the desert.

The Israelites had a single goal in the desert: getting to the Promised Land. Every day that they didn't get there was a disappointment, an unlived dream. But had they been able to focus on the moment, they could have entered a kind of Promised Land and tasted its goodness. As seekers and spiritual guides, we do not aim at large, single goals, such as winning the Nobel prize or even entering the Promised Land. We focus on the inherent potential of each day, the possibility of entering into God's presence and deepening our covenantal relationship with God. Each day's activities can be lifted into a larger pattern and have value in their own right.

When we raise a child, we want the child to grow into a mature, independent person, but even as the parents of screaming infants or rebellious adolescents, we might occasionally dream of short-circuiting the process but, in truth, we really don't want to give birth to an adult. We want the developing relationship with all its attendant daily challenges. We want to participate in all the steps that make for developing independence and maturity. The time we spend as a family moves quickly, so we want to savor one another's company. The journey *is* the goal. The Israelites left Egypt unformed, not ready for freedom. God delivered them from Egypt and could have directed them quickly into the Promised Land, but had them journey through the desert. They could not instantaneously have been transformed into free people.

As seekers, we too need time spent in loving relatedness and intimacy. From that beginning, transformation will follow; we will be shaped by a lifetime of listening for God's direction, the echoes of Torah still ringing from the mountaintop of Sinai. The journey is our goal. And just as we look back on our childhood with a certain nostalgia, even if those years had their difficulties, so Jews to this day look back with nostalgia to the forty years in the wilderness. Those were our people's formative years. Like the children we individually once were, the Children of Israel did not feed themselves, did not plot their own course, neither understood nor controlled most of what was going on in their lives. But these lacks were compensated for by the ongoing sense of God's presence. Beyond nostalgia, we find ourselves looking back at childhood because during that time there were things of genuine value that we now want to recover. Among them are spontaneity, a capacity for total involvement, or a sense of wonder. And we look back to the wilderness years for similar reasons. As difficult as those years were, they were filled with wonder, trust, and simplicity.

Enduring a spiritual desert requires patience and trust. For a long time we are tempted to look beyond the desert to a settlement (any settlement) as a way of structuring our lives. We fear the desert and avoid even thinking about it. Eventually, though, we begin to explore the terrain and find aspects we like: its silence, its vast expanse, the opportunity it offers us to explore ourselves. Finally, we can carry the desert within us, in the deep recesses of the soul.

We Learn to Find Meaning in Work

In the desert, all the efforts of the Israelites went toward meeting their immediate needs. They possessed only those things they could carry with them on their journey. Their lives were simple and focused. Simplicity is not emphasized as a value nowadays, but we know that it is one. We *experience* its value when we unclutter our mind, let go of convoluted schemes, and directly and unambiguously go after what we want. No plots or subplots; no mixed motives. A simple life. As the Zen master Yün-men wrote,

> In walking, just walk.
> In sitting, just sit.
> Above all, don't wobble.

Eat when you're hungry, sleep when you're tired. But we eat because it's dinner time and sleep because it's part of our established routine. We're not in the present and not alive to God's presence.

In the wilderness, a kind of simplicity prevailed. Work had not yet developed into countless areas of specialization. Only a few "occupations" were needed, among them priests to organize worship, artists and artisans to construct the Tabernacle, elders to adjudicate disputes, warriors, potters, weavers. For these Israelites, specialties represented one way to God. In today's world, such simple relationships between possessions, work, and immediate needs have largely been replaced. We have a complex society in which only religious "professionals" (theologians, clergy, members of reli-

gious orders—that is, those who regularly formulate their relationship with
God in words) are living lives centered in God. Judaism, it is true, is a religion of the word. But all serious practice requires the day-to-day discipline
and involvement with the mundane that make up the foundation of our
lives: the tastes of cooking, the hum of machinery, even the smell of cleaning. All of the early rabbis pursued primary vocations in addition to their
rabbinic functions. They were vintners or lens grinders or farmers who
labored for their livelihood. Likewise, we need to be in touch with physical
demands, rooted in real tasks that have to be accomplished.

The things that bind us to this material world are of great importance.
There are, as we have seen, innumerable paths to the center such as
prayer, text, and ritual. But we have also seen that we must take our daily
lives seriously, because all of life is part of our faith. The wilderness is a
perfect setting for learning that, because it is undomesticated. So plant-
ing a garden around a tent, creating structures of time and space, telling
stories, singing songs are all ways of being part of Creation. Anything
that is done with authenticity and devotion can become a way of worship. God's love does not want our love merely reflected back. We are
asked to bring that love to our relationship with the world entrusted to
us: the world of our partner, our children, our political/social order, and
our caring for the environment. We can see this mirrored most clearly in
our relationships with our children. Children are focused on their parents, but parents try to instill skills and values so that the children can
look out into the world.

Going into our wilderness, we need to recognize that all of our actions
find their ultimate grounding in God. Then we can turn to face the world
and all the areas in which we will make contributions.

We Learn to Find Meaning in Daily Life

It is so easy to lose heart. The beginning is new, exciting, filled with daily
challenges. But for a long time we are essentially in a holding operation.
We have made fundamental commitments, and now we have to live them
out. We are still filled with doubts, subject to anger. We constantly ask
ourselves, "Are we *really* on a spiritual way?" Courage lies in endurance
and in the daily routine. Anyone can gird up courage for a single act, but
this is a lifetime of repeated actions of faithfulness and commitment. We
try to shape ourselves to be faithful people. But day-to-day events can
wear us down. We begin to wonder whether or not there really *is* motion,
progress, discernible forward movement in our spiritual quest. Our task
remains to discern motion.

As we saw in Chapter Four, motion can be understood in six different ways: coming to be, passing away, increase, decrease, locomotion, and becoming other. As seekers, we look to the sensitive spiritual guide to help recognize changes that we might have overlooked because we are so close to them: well, yes, trust has grown, some anger has passed away, patience has increased, agitation has decreased, and a sense of peace prevails. We may deny that there has been any locomotion—change of place—in our life because we haven't moved or changed jobs, but the spiritual guide sees our place in relation to The Place (*Hamakom,* God). This is a time when, with caution, we may be directed to read our earlier journals. Looking back is risky. We may become frozen with tears, as Lot's wife was when she looked back at the burning Sodom and Gomorrah. Nevertheless, as painful as it may be to read earlier accounts of ourselves—a self we may not like very much—the process, if done correctly, will help us understand how far we have traveled.

Spiritual guidance goes on while life goes on. We do not enter spiritual guidance and withdraw from life. We make commitments, interact. We create, destroy, transform. And we pause to reflect on what we have experienced and where we have experienced the presence of God as all these things have happened.

Eventually, we abandon the attempt to cross the desert and come to understand that the desert is our spiritual home. We have been tempered by the desert experience and no longer expect any radical external change. If we now find ourselves in a "Promised Land," it turns our to be the actual world, which presents its own set of challenges or trials. These trials are part of life, or what James Joyce, in *Portrait of the Artist as a Young Man,* calls "the confusion and misrule of my father's house" (p. 162). The world (the path that takes us through the desert on our way to the Promised Land) is in great confusion. But because we have learned in the desert to perceive our surroundings, we can see the order that underlies the chaos. So we not only can accept the world, with all its trials, we can embrace it.

We are educated to view the material world in terms of the laws of cause and effect. After experiencing revelation, we find that in addition to the material world and its attendant laws, there are worlds of meaning, value, love, and commitment. Through all of these we strengthen our relationship with God.

As seekers, we look to the spiritual guide to help us perceive the divine manifestations in our world. We look for help in learning to see the Creator in all Creation and experience the Creator through the actual world. As we look at our own creative process, we begin to discern some of what makes the world so amazing: we see the wholeness or integrity of every-thing, its harmony and its radiance. This vision is not restricted to the unusual but applies to everything we make and do, including all the most commonplace: the coffee pot perking in the kitchen, the pen resting com-fortably in our hand as we write. Each object has its limits and bound-aries, and its uniqueness, a unity that is central to our spiritual vision. We find ourselves seeking unity in our art or in our scientific approach to the world, and also in our human relationships. Then we are struck that each single thing is made up of parts that work together harmoniously to form the whole. Unity does not preclude complexity—it can accommodate and even incorporate diversity. We come to value the individuality of each thing. It is what it is! We are who we are! The uniqueness and individu-ality of each aspect of Creation is cause for wonder and celebration.

In spiritual guidance we are learning a whole new way of making meaning. We all have been introduced to new categories at points in our lives; they both provide new structure for our experiences and also trans-form them. In the same way, ordinary life is transformed through the cat-egories discovered and assimilated over the course of spiritual guidance. We don't, of course, become overnight saints, as Tolstoy tells us:

> I shall still lose my temper with Ivan the coachman, I shall still embark
> on useless discussions and express my opinions inopportunely; there
> will still be the same wall between the sanctuary of my inmost soul and
> other people, even my wife; I shall probably go on scolding her in my
> anxiety and repenting of it afterwards; I shall still be as unable to
> understand with my reason why I pray, and I shall still go on praying—
> but my life now, my whole life, independently of anything that can hap-
> pen to me, every minute of it is no longer meaningless as it was before,
> but has a positive meaning of goodness with which I have the power to
> invest it [*Anna Karenina*, pp. 852–853].

In other words, spiritual guidance is not a method of changing our per-sonality; it is a call to be transformed so that we, in turn, transform the world. We will do this work one act and one relationship at a time. The bare, untamed desert now suddenly takes on structures of meaning and holiness. The gift we receive is the ability to see the underlying structures. And we try to retain this vision as we leave the desert.

Keeping the Vision

How shall we "sing *Adonai*'s song in a strange land"? How can we retain our vision, our maps, our values, in a world of alien values? What does the just person do in an unjust society? For Plato, in the *Republic,* the just huddle against the storm and try to keep clean hands; being just is its own end. By contrast, the prophet Amos, speaking perhaps for all Jews through the ages, said:

Seek good and not evil,
That you may live,
And that Adonai, the God of Hosts,
May truly be with you,
As you think.
Hate evil and love good,
And establish justice in the gate;
Perhaps Adonai, the God of Hosts
Will be gracious to the remnant of Joseph. . . .
I loathe, I spurn your festivals,
I am not appeased by your solemn assemblies.
If you offer Me burnt offerings—or your meal offerings—
I will not accept them;
I will pay no heed
To your gifts of fatlings.
Spare Me the sound of your hymns,
And let Me not hear the music of your lutes.
But let justice well up like water,
Righteousness like an unfailing stream.

—Amos 5:14–15, 21–24

Unlike the citizens of Plato's *Republic,* we are not the end, only the beginning. Our life takes on meaning because we are not the object of our own growth and transformation. Rather, we are part of something larger than our own lives and efforts—something to which we can make a significant contribution. It is as a part of family, of the People of Israel, of God's Creation, that our lives gain stature and magnificence. And that is the reality that we will explore in the next chapter.

10

DRAWING FROM AND GIVING TO COMMUNITY

Do justice, love mercy, and walk humbly with your God.

—Micah 6:8

MICAH'S WORDS PROVIDE US with a simple prescription for spiritual living. The challenge is to figure out how to make real in our lives the teaching that the prophet offers. Through spiritual guidance, we can learn to discern the meaning of the prophet's words. The objectives are all there: justice, mercy, and humility. Note the action that is required. Spirituality is not static. It doesn't just happen. We must *do* things that are just. We must *love* mercy. And we must *walk* in humility—in a relationship with the Almighty. So we certainly cannot afford to sit around waiting for something to happen. Part of commitment to the spiritual way, then, is our choices of action. As our ancestors journeyed in the desert, they were constantly presented with the choice of action or inaction. When the Israelites were ready to help themselves (and therefore act), they discovered that God was present to help them. Yet when the trials in the desert became too difficult, they were prepared to return to Egypt—knowing full well that that would mean a return to servitude and slavery. Inaction would cause them to be swept back into a past that they had struggled to leave behind.

We are individually responsible for going on the spiritual way, but we do not do it alone. We need someone else to guide us, a community that lifts us up and carries us when the way seems too difficult. We also require a tradition that furnishes us with a map and provides us with the tools for nourishing and supporting us along the way. And just as we do not do our spiritual work alone, we do not do it just for our own benefit. The spiritual way transforms us so that we can, finally, do some good in the world. When we get out of our own way and keep our egocentric tendencies (an aspect of our *yetzer hara*) in check, the results of our spiritual work are genuinely beneficial for all those with whom we come in contact.

> We suffer in so far as we are a part of Nature, which part cannot be conceived by itself nor without the other parts [Spinoza, *Ethics of Spinoza,* part IV, prop. 2].

We are a *part* of Nature, and our wholeness consists in discovering our relationship to the other parts and to the Whole, and making our contribution in this context. Relatedness and *mitzvot* are inextricably interconnected.

Oliver Sacks, in *The Island of the Colorblind,* shows how having too small a mass of people living in a society leads to genetic disorders. Freud, in *Beyond the Pleasure Principle,* demonstrates that a cell can drown in its own juices if it does not have contact with other cells. We have also come to know that developing only the self leaves us in urgent need of a community that can expand our vision and correct us.

As discussed in Chapter One, the origins of formal spiritual guidance lie in the history of the Christian Desert Fathers. Those men and women who fled to the desert in the fourth century of the Common Era led a largely eremitic existence, yet even they understood that to achieve full humanity, they required three circles of community.

The Three Circles of Community

The early Christian hermits had abandoned the cities of the ancient world in order to live in solitude. They believed that the values of the pagan world jeopardized their salvation (and salvation, they assumed, was individual and personal). They quickly learned that solitude was in itself a temptation. Although they sought solitude, they recognized their responsibilities, and so those who were older and more spiritually experienced aided newcomers to the desert. They functioned as "spiritual parents" to the younger hermits. In addition to this intense one-on-one relationship, the hermits gathered together regularly for liturgy. Finally, they were sustained by a community across time through their sacred writings and tradition. In the same way, we find these three circles of community nourishing and sustaining us as seeking Jews today.

Our Family or Covenant Community

For many of us, our principal community is our family. The family provides us, day in and day out, with a model of the covenant. How we live in relation to others in our family is a reflection of that covenant. And this is true not only in the family as traditionally understood. We now recognize that there are many ways to structure a family. Even in biblical times, where marriage was primarily centered on property and inheritance rights, familylike structures grew up around those who were servants in the same house and those who were mutually raising children. Some of these individuals were biological parents, and some had been assigned the task of nursemaid, a confusion that deepens when Moses' biological mother is asked by his adoptive mother, Pharoah's daughter, to nurse him. Although nontraditional family structures have always been with us, they have in recent years become experientially much more familiar. We all know one-parent families and blended families. Even in biblical times, we find that Jacob had children by two different wives and two different handmaidens and also adopted the children of his son Joseph—the primordial example of a blended family. We also know families where the covenantal partners are of the same sex, as in the biblical story of Ruth and Naomi, where Ruth makes a covenant with Naomi, "Wherever you go, I will go; wherever you lodge, I will lodge; your people shall be my people, and your God my God. Where you die, I will die, and there will I be buried. Thus and more may Adonai do to me if anything but death parts me from you" (Ruth 1:16).

Leslie lived alone for many years; she found it difficult to find someone with whom to share her life. She avoided the synagogue but sought out spiritual guidance. Through guidance, she became clearer about her spiritual journey and decided to create a community of others like herself: single adult men and women who were somewhat lonely but longing for God. In the midst of the community she formed, she also found God. Likewise, in reaching out for God, she was able to find community, which functioned for her like a family.

Our covenant with God will shape the way we relate to everyone and everything. It is the primary "stuff" out of which the life of a spiritual person is created. We acknowledge that we have not been created just to serve ourselves. We were brought onto this earth to build a human community that might bring perfection to the world through our own personal efforts at *tikun olam,* or repair. Relating to others, particularly the members of our family, is not easy—many spend a lifetime trying to get it right. That's why family should be regarded as a covenantal form of relationship, call-ing for a strong commitment on the part of all parties involved.

The biblical patriarch Jacob, after long years of separation from his brother, was moved toward reconciliation. He was afraid, to be sure. In order to protect himself, he divided his household and all that he owned into two camps so that at least half would escape an attack. He sent mes-sengers ahead to tell Esau of his desire to reconcile—and even sent gifts that might pave a path toward peace and rapprochement (Gen. 32:3–5). The Torah text suggests that Jacob came to his brother in peace, *shalom*. Perhaps the text wishes to imply that he came *shalem,* that is, whole. There were no longer the pretenses that had plagued them since child-hood, no more competition for parental favoritism. Jacob's life journey had brought him to this point—the place *(hamakom)* where he encoun-tered God *(Hamakom,* the Place*).* But it took struggling with a stranger (an angel? a messenger of God?) in the darkness of night to awaken in him the courage and the insight necessary for the climactic meeting with his brother (32:24–29). This time he would send no messengers (not even angels, as he had done previously, according to some commentators). This time he came himself—fully himself. If we are to build community and begin with our families, then we have to begin by building (or rebuilding) the self. In seeking the self we seek the other, and we may come to find God in the process.

Harry hadn't seen his brothers for years. They became estranged pri-marily because their spouses did not get along. Following the death of one brother, Harry sought out the other. He did not want to die disconnected from his only surviving sibling. He said that in the midst of community, he felt the presence of God beckoning him to renew his covenant with his brother. The process needed time, which they got when Harry himself fell ill, and his brother moved into his house for a month, in order to care for him. Afterwards, they still communicated as rarely as before, but both brothers felt that the rift had been healed.

Itzik, who lost his entire family in the Holocaust, bristles when he hears stories of family discord. He cries, "I have no family. And people who do have relatives no longer want to speak with them!" It's easy to be hurt, to get angry at the thoughtless acts of others. But neither are we blameless in all that we do. To build family and to build community, we have to reach beyond ourselves. When we do, we are able to see ourselves and others more clearly. Then together, as the contemporary Hebrew song lyric sug-gests, *Ani v'atah nishaneh et haolam,* "You and I will change the world."

Sometimes we become aware of family, our first covenant community, in unexpected situations. With Louis, it was when he was shaving in the early hours of the morning—not very unusual in its own right. The house was quiet, and he was getting ready for his daily commute to New York City. It was a familiar routine, one that he had followed methodically for many years. Suddenly, he saw his father staring back at him from the mirror. It was Louis's own face, but for the first time, he saw his father in it. As he looked further into the images that were bouncing from the mirrors in front and behind him, he could also see his grandfather and his great-grandfather. We carry our family within us.

Our Worshiping Community

Spiritual guides must help seekers realize the importance of the worshiping assembly. Moses was often told by God to "assemble the people," and they would come together to hear the word of God. The Torah may be studied in private, but in public it is always read aloud. And when it is read, revelation is re-enacted, simulated. Although we might think it would be easier and more powerful to discern the word of God privately, in a remote setting, the opposite seems true. Community provides the context for us to hear God's voice in the world. The philosopher Mordecai Kaplan (1881–1983), founder of the Reconstructionist movement within Judaism, believed that the folk was of utmost importance, that community was more important than anything else.

Although the traditional worship experience contains moments for private prayers, much of what takes place in a service is the movement of the private into the public. Throughout the entire worship service prescribed by Jewish tradition, we move back and forth between the need for private communion with the Almighty and the call for community. That's one of the reasons it takes so long to get to the core of the worship service. The service begins with a section called *pesukei d'zimra* (literally, "lines of song"), which is really a warm-up, a time for us to move from the comfort and security of our private selves into the public arena of community, where we gain strength for those selves. And at the end of worship, we typically sing a song that declares God as supreme in the world. The last lines, which are often overlooked as people rush out of the synagogue, read:

> Into God's hands I entrust my spirit, when I sleep and when I wake; and with my spirit my body also. As long as God is with me, I will not fear.

The central concept of *minyan,* ten individuals gathered for the purpose of communal prayer, is the basis of community for Jewish worship.

According to Jewish tradition, some prayers are not to be said privately; they can be recited only with this quorum of ten. Is there something more efficacious about prayers said by a group? Perhaps. In any case, the requirement reflects a profound understanding of the community's significance. Those in mourning, for example, are called to say the mourner's *Kaddish,* the memorial prayer, daily for a year following the death of a parent. But this *Kaddish* is to be recited in public, in community, obliging the mourner to attend worship services two or three times a day and others to reach out in support of those who suffer loss, to share the burden of bereavement.

Day by day, we may not recognize how sustaining a worshiping community can be. Gary relates that he could not understand how to listen for God's voice until he participated in his son's bar mitzvah (the ceremony marking a boy's passage to adult religious responsibility). Although neither very observant nor much of a synagogue-goer, when Gary handed the Torah to his son, instead of feeling freed from an obligation when reciting the required "blessing of release," he felt more bound to the Holy Scriptures. The bonds of the *shalshelet hakabalah* (chain of tradition) became stronger once the community forged another link in it through the celebration of this bar mitzvah. As a result, Gary felt more secure being bound to it, no longer afraid that he might fall.

Our Community Across Time

The new interest in Jewish adult education that is sweeping the country is not merely a quest for literacy, as some experts read the trend; it is really a longing for community. Together, through our shared tradition, we can pursue our past, contemplate our present, and consider our future. If we are to understand our part in the larger whole, we need a vision larger than our own narrow perspective. This is given to us through the study of our tradition. We go beyond today's headlines to concerns that have resonated through three millennia. Other generations have grappled with the issues that now confront us, have found their way, and left us useful teachings. Repeatedly, whether we are in the desert or simply in a suburb without a Jewish community, we discover that we are not alone. The texts accompany and comfort us. They connect us to a community across time—a community with a moral vision and a spiritual center. As we read the text we feel like Isaac, who dug anew the wells that had been dug in the days of his father, Abraham (Gen. 26:18). We find living water in our ancestors' wells.

The Charge in Each Circle

We cannot artificially construct communities for their own sake. Communities arise around shared concerns and obligations. There are serious covenantal obligations in the first circle of community, the family, and a call to really know one another and be there for one another at the second level, the worshiping community. Our tradition demands that we preserve it, transmit it, and live it. In the study of culture and its changes, we discover that a crucial transition is marked when religious artifacts move from the house of worship to the museum. The museum does preserve the artifact and try to transmit what it represents, but it does not place the viewer under a moral obligation to live up to what has been transmitted. Our faith must not become the material of museums. It must continue to live, grow, and challenge us.

Our Covenantal Obligations

Our covenantal obligations straddle the three divisions of time. They bind us to the present, in relation to spouse, colleagues, and peers; to the past, in relation to parents, predecessors, and tradition; and to the future, in relation to children and the coming generations. Our commitment to each of these three sets of relationships demands attention and action. We care for our loved ones, and that care is not simply a feeling but a way of ordering our priorities and our time. It should be noted that a spiritual guide also functions as part of a person's family as a "spiritual parent," not because of age or authority but because of the role given to the guide by the seeker. As seekers, we give the guide permission to accompany us, challenge us, and correct us.

Because of the demands of covenant, many contemporaries are running away from commitment. As Janet reported: "I spent much of my early adult life running away. I left my parents to go away to college. But then I left my friends in college and got a job in a new city. But that was not enough for me. I kept moving from city to city. I knew that I was searching, but I never quite knew what I was looking for. My spiritual guide helped me realize that I was running away from myself and that I kept running because while I thought that I had outdistanced myself, I knew each time that God was way ahead of me." Janet had to learn to be still. She was running both from herself and God (her low opinion of herself had a lot to do with this evasion). In time Janet stayed in one place and began the slow process of making commitments to a steady job, a neighborhood, friends, and colleagues. In and through these commitments she began to find both herself and God.

Obligations to Our Worshiping Community

Synagogues exist to provide a locus for worship. In that narrow sense, they serve only those members of their community who actually come to pray. Increasingly, members recognize that their synagogues should not only serve them but should give them the strength to serve a larger community. Where synagogue members gain such strength, they may, for example, establish several outreach programs: a soup kitchen, a drive to raise funds for the Ethiopian Jewish community, an adult literacy class.

When Jason first came for spiritual guidance, he was glad to learn how the map of Exodus could be used to explain his own journey. He was, he claimed, already in the Promised Land. He had lived through exactly what the text was teaching. He had been enslaved in a metaphorical Egypt, struggling with his dependency on drugs, before he could even enter the desert to find his way back home. And on his way, he found his first spiritual guide ready to help him on his path. But it was in the context of community that the path was laid out before him. And it was the stepping stones of *mitzvot* that set him in the right direction. Jason revealed that what really connected him to his new life was the feeling that he was needed. He appreciated being asked to attend *shivah minyanim* (quorums for worship in the homes of mourners)—it was hard to get enough people at a morning *minyan,* and he was available. He loved being asked to visit people in the Jewish Home for the Aged. Here he was not a recovering anything, he was a welcome visitor who took the time to listen to someone else. Every time he gave of himself, he felt generously rewarded by people's gratitude and by his own sense of belonging and growing commitment.

Each week, when Eric works in the synagogue's soup kitchen, he feels that he is participating in God's work by joining in this service with members of his community. Following the guidance of some of the Hasidic masters, he has discovered that such work is a necessary part of his spiritual journey.

Candice joined a women's group several years ago. They get together only on *Rosh Ḥodesh,* the new moon, in order to celebrate the lunar cycle, their personal cycles, and their community. They have lived through a great deal together—some of it happy, some sad. The time they share prepares them for the weeks when they are alone.

Jerry decided suddenly to skip regular worship services. When queried by a member of the community, he replied, "I just don't feel like going to the synagogue any longer. I can pray just as well on my own." Jerry's bewildered friend told the rabbi. The next day, on the way to synagogue, the rabbi stopped by Jerry's home. He went straight to the fireplace, where a fire was roaring. Wordlessly, he took the tongs and separated one of the burning embers, watching as it slowly lost its glow and burned itself out. The rabbi got up and was leaving when he turned around and asked, "Will I see you at the synagogue tomorrow?" And Jerry, who understood the rabbi's silent lesson, responded, "Of course you will, Rabbi. Thank you."

What does it mean to be a worshiping community? It means caring about each other. Pray? We can pray at home. We come together as a congregation in order to share in our life as Jews, to be part of the Community of Israel. The Gerer Rebbe decided to question one of his disciples: "How is Moshe Yakov doing?" The disciple didn't know. "What!" shouted the rebbe. "You don't know? You pray under the same roof, you study the same texts, you serve the same God, you sing the same songs, and yet you dare to tell me that you don't know whether Moshe Yakov is in good health, whether he needs help, advice, or comforting?" Here lies the very essence of our community way of life: every person must share in every other person's life. One must not be left alone, either in times of sorrow or in times of joy.

We have seen in Chapter Two that praying is more than reciting the words of a formal prayer or attending a worship service. Once we have opened up the concept of prayer, we analogously open up the notion of the worshiping community. And when we discover that work is one of the means by which we make our contribution to this world, our work becomes an arena where we can encounter God—and our coworkers become, by virtue of this extended definition, part of our worshiping community.

We all have work to do. One key aspect of the spiritual life is discovering what, in fact, our life's work is all about. We can discover this work only in the context of our relationships with the community and with God.

Work is co-creative. Some believe that God intentionally created an unfinished world so that humans could finish the work of creation. It is certainly a holy task. We work because the world is unfinished, and it is ours to develop. Work is our gift to the world. It ties us to our neighbor and binds us to the future. It saves us from total self-centeredness. It gives us a reason to exist that is larger than our self. Work leads to self-fulfillment. It uses the talents we are aware of possessing and calls on others that have been hidden from us. The Apter Rebbe taught that people should not choose the form of their service to God but should perform it in whatever manner opportunity affords. The individual should be like a vessel into which anything may be poured: wine, milk, or water.

Obligations to Our Tradition

Sacred texts are the touchstone of Jewish spirituality, but what we believe is only secondary to what we do with our lives. Our beliefs must be reflected in how we act. We study in order to find a lifescript for ourselves, crafted out of the spiritual struggles of our ancestors. We want their struggles to inform our own. Perhaps that is why Joe identified with his namesake Joseph in the Torah. He reminded me of the story of Joseph whenever we met. Each time, he would rehearse the part of the Joseph narrative that he felt reflected his own lifescript. He felt that he too had been "sold into slavery," forced against his will to take over the family business after his father-in-law died. He left his training as an attorney far behind him. Running the family business allowed him the opportunity to become president of the local synagogue (a position he could never have assumed in his demanding former life as an attorney). It was in his community work that he came to understand what it took Joseph nearly a lifetime to realize—that the journey he endured was not about himself. And the biblical Joseph discovered that only after he let go of his own ego. Joseph realized that his sojourn in Egypt was about building his community, doing God's work in the world, saving the Jewish people from famine. Joe realized that it was God who was directing his life—he was merely responding to the call, even if sometimes kicking and screaming. Joe was fulfilling his obligation to his Jewish tradition by drawing on it to inform his own life, thereby keeping the tradition alive.

The principle of *ein mukdam, ein muchar* (literally, there is no early or late [in the Torah]) allows us to bind our lives with our ancestors' as if they were contemporaneous with our own. The dimensions of time impose no barrier to us. We live in the same spiritual space as our ancestors. It is living in both these worlds that fosters the potential to make present time and present events sacred. We can learn from these spiritual ancestors as if they were teachers from whom we are learning this very day. Indeed, they are part of the spiritual lives of those who offer us guidance. And in this way, both seeker and guide contribute to the maintenance of the tradition.

The "texts" referred to here are not only the written books of our faith, but the tradition passed on orally and by custom. These texts remind us that there are *mitzvot* we should be taking on ourselves. Frances framed it this way: "Each week, I try to add to my *mitzvah* life and by the following week I have a better sense of the particular *mitzvah*. I know that the process is slow, that I may never achieve a life full of *mitzvot*. They don't all feel the same: some seem minor and insignificant, some are challenging and difficult, some come rather simply, and some I can't figure out at all. These are the ones that don't seem to do anything for me, so I don't bother with them. But doing *mitzvot* not only brings me close to the holy, it keeps me in mind of my Jewish tradition."

Our tradition consists of much more than our history, our texts, and our practices. Jewish tradition, like every other, includes a rich store of tales, especially those that teach some lesson. Passing these tales along is a delightful way of fulfilling our obligations to our tradition. One story is particularly apt for those aspiring to do spiritual guidance. A pupil once asked his teacher how he could become a spiritual guide for his study partner. "Listen," began the sage, holding up an admonishing finger. Then the sage stopped speaking. After a period of silence, in anxious anticipation of hearing the advice, the student said: "I am listening, teacher. Please continue." But the teacher replied, "There is no more to say."

The Spiritual Guide's Role in the Circles of Community

As spiritual guides we can play a role in every circle of community. We are part of the covenantal family of the first circle and can help seekers recognize that family is a major arena in which to learn how to live up to covenant. We encourage seekers to participate in a worshiping community, and we suggest texts that help them engage with their tradition. We point out that revelation is ongoing, that it didn't happen just "once upon a time" to our distant ancestors, and that the dedicated, obligated life didn't belong only to them but to all of us today as well. As seekers, our choices, too, are meaningful and fraught with significance. We are part of the ongoing struggle between dedication and meaninglessness. With the help of our spiritual guide, we carefully choose our allies—the communities of those who will stand with us against emptiness, selfishness, deadness in life. Our allies are the communities of our family, our co-worshipers, and the millennial tradition of the People of the Book.

Rabbi Hillel taught, "Do not separate yourself from the community" (*Pirke Avot,* 2:4). *Mitzvot* bring the individual into the context of community. As we have seen, performing *mitzvot* provides us with another prism through which the spiritual life can be evaluated. Through the fulfillment of *mitzvot,* particularly those *bein adam l'ḥaveiro* (between individuals), we are brought closer to God. That's one of the many reasons why Rabbi Joshua ben Korcha taught that "one should always be as alert as possible to perform a mitzvah" (Babylonian Talmud, *Nazir,* 23b).

Community and Mitzvah

The book of Exodus informs us, "You shall be a kingdom of priests and a holy nation" (19:6). This text confirms for us that there is a communal dimension to the covenant. Tradition has it that God revealed the Torah to the entire community of Israel, gathered around the foot of Mount Sinai, in order to emphasize that as much as the Torah was given to each individual, it was given—then and now—to the people as a community. And with that communal revelation comes responsibility, as Isaiah reminds us:

> I Adonai have called you to righteousness
> And have grasped you by the hand.
> I created you and appointed you
> A covenant people, a light of nations.
> —Isa. 42:6

And as the Talmud makes clear:

> Let respect for the community always be with you.
> —Babylonian Talmud, *Sota,* 40a

Community is what has given our people structure and strength throughout the vagaries of history. The Jewish community, and our relationship to one another within it, transcends time. Its historical past and its creative present nourish and support us. As we have seen in the lives of our ancestors and in the lives of our own families, our communal faith helps us endure all that we must face in life, all that comes into a life. The role of community is a constant.

11

CONTINUING THE
SPIRITUAL JOURNEY

I have strayed like a lost sheep;
search for Your servant.

—Psalms 119:176

BECAUSE THE SPIRITUAL LIFE implies an ongoing and continuously evolving relationship, the process of spiritual guidance never ends. It is like the reading of the Torah, which continues from week to week. Even when we seem to have concluded the reading, we celebrate (on the festival of Simḥat Torah) by beginning the reading once again. At the end of twenty-two stanzas of Psalm 119, the psalmist can still write: "I have strayed like a lost sheep; search for Your servant." We do not outgrow our need for discernment, for help along the spiritual way. However, having acquired some tools for offering direction to others, we can now recognize some of the stumbling blocks.

The Way We Have Come

This chapter summarizes many of the points made during our study of spiritual guidance and illustrates how a single text, Psalm 119, incorporates many of the most important elements of the spiritual way and illuminates various aspects of spiritual guidance.

David came to me for direction. His biblical namesake, King David, is credited in Jewish tradition with the authorship of the entire book of

Psalms, including Psalm 119. David *entered* into spiritual guidance, initiating a relationship with me without coercion or constraint—the only way that allows spiritual guidance to take place. The motive for entering guidance is a desire to draw closer to God, and the impetus *must* come from the seeker. When he first arrived, David claimed that he did not believe in God. It would have been counterproductive at this beginning stage to point out how paradoxical it was, under the circumstances, for him to be entering into a process whose very purpose was to deepen his relationship with God. He would recognize the spiritual tension of competing claims later in the relationship. I simply recognized his openness and trusted the potential of spiritual guidance to bring about personal spiritual transformation.

The seeker usually comes with some initial question, like that of the psalmist: "How can a young person keep to a pure way?" (Ps. 119:9). The question fundamentally functions as an invitation to the spiritual journey; frequently no answer will really suffice. However, it is noteworthy that the original question asked by the seeker persists throughout the process of guidance, even when the form of the question changes. For example, the question just quoted from Psalm 119 might change to "How can an overly busy adult keep to a good way?" and later to "How can an aged person keep to the right way?" There are different temptations at different ages, but they are temptations nonetheless. Perhaps for the young person, the temptation is hubris, excessive pride in one's physical strength and mental acumen. For people in mid-life, the temptation is their own busyness and need for mastery; middle-aged people, with their many responsibilities, have difficulty finding time for the silence and solitude that have helped nurture ongoing relationships with God. Old age has its own temptations. With the loss of personal strength and the deaths of so many friends, the great task is to fight off despair. However the specific question is formed, the seeker is looking for assurance that there is a way, that others have wrestled with the same questions.

We all want to know that although we must take responsibility for our own spiritual lives, we do not have to do so alone, without the guidance of another. Earlier in this book, Exodus and the Song of Songs were presented as two "spiritual maps." These maps reflect the journey of our people; they provide us with historical memory and help us participate *(methexus)* in our people's story. They chart the way others have traveled along the same path, providing us with reassurance: others have been there and survived. And these maps lift up our personal stories into the larger story of our people. (This sense of connection is a major support for the spiritual way.) The stories offer us a shared vocabulary so that we may talk about the spiritual way and reflect on it.

Early in spiritual guidance, even for David who claimed that he did not believe in God, the focus of discussion turns to prayer, the basic form of communication in the spiritual relationship. "I have called with my whole heart; answer me Adonai" (Ps. 119:145). I emphasize to David the central importance of prayer for spiritual living, and together we explore the many forms it takes. There are seekers who do not believe that God has a plan for us or controls or influences the world. With them, I speak in theological terms, suggesting that they broaden their concept of prayer beyond the categories of petition and traditional liturgical texts. I invite them to include all the moments when their hearts and minds are lifted up.

With most seekers, it is sufficient to reaffirm that prayer is a form of communication. They must learn to say what is most important to them, and they must also learn how to listen for any response. With David, the language had to be changed so that he could comfortably stay in the conversation. We discussed inspiration, and communication from the right hemisphere of the brain. My task was not to convince him of anything; the relationship itself would do so, as long as he simply remained open to the process.

Fears change, but they do not disappear along the way. For David, a lot of fear was associated with the possibility of "losing face," embarrassment, not "being cool." Ilana, seeing an increasing number of friends fall gravely ill or die, feared mortality and finitude. She could not put off addressing that fear any longer. Like all of us, she sought intimacy with God. It is a powerful attraction, but it is also very frightening. This fear is expressed throughout Psalm 119:

> My flesh shudders in fear of You;
> I am afraid of Your judgments.
> —Ps. 119:120

Our task as spiritual guides is to cry out, "Do not fear!"—and to encourage seekers to persist in their search for God.

David learned in spiritual guidance that the God he rejected was just one image of God advanced by certain teachers or books. In fact, God transcends all images. David's biblical counterpart uses different images of God throughout Psalm 119 to illustrate his progressively deeper understanding. In various places, God is portrayed as a judge, as one who is merciful, as a shelter and a shield, and in the tender image of one who looks for a lost sheep.

For our David, study was no problem. As a college student, he understood study as a major component of his life. He spent most of his days with his books. David understood the formative power of study, and he recognized that he was in a formative stage in his life. It was harder for Ilana, who was very busy, to find time for study; it was even harder to find a teacher (although she understood that she could study with a *chevruta*, or even by herself as long as she had a user-friendly commentary). But in working with Ilana, the primary task—always a major responsibility in spiritual guidance—was convincing her that formation does not end, that motion does not stop. We must continue to study and find in study a place of encounter. Study, for the biblical David, is one of the ways he comes near to God: "I reach out for Your commandments, which I love" (Ps. 119:48). In fact, we study not so much to learn more about the text but to provide ourselves with a context in which to encounter God. Faith is not about acquiescence to a certain set of propositions laid out in the text. Faith is about developing and maintaining a relationship with God. And study provides us with a context in which to explore and expand this relationship.

As we study, we learn about many things—including sin. For the psalmist, sin is a wake-up call:

> Before I was humbled, I went astray;
> But now I keep Your word. . . .
> It was good for me that I was humbled,
> So that I might learn Your laws.
> —Ps. 119:67, 71

The most serious aspect of sin is its capacity to rupture the relationship with God. Recognizing the possibility for *teshuvah* (the process of repairing this relationship through repentance) is central to ongoing development on the spiritual way.

The length of the spiritual path—reflected in the idea of "enduring the desert"—is also alluded to in verses 83 and 84:

> Though I have become like a water-skin in smoke,
> I have not neglected Your laws.
> How long has Your servant to live?
> —Ps. 119:83–84

To view our lives as analogous to a water-skin dried in smoke is to see it in terms of the many trials that dry us out and make us brittle. This sense of aridity is part of "enduring the desert." And yet life needs to be regarded not as a trial but as the blessing and gift of God. Whether we are blessed with a long life or an unfortunately short one, we can remain connected with meaning and value through faithfulness to our many spiritual practices. Each day, we can reaffirm our love and commitment; each day, we can reconnect to our people and our texts. These spiritual practices give shape and structure to our lives.

As seekers, we view the guide as a model to emulate in a form that makes sense for our own life. In some cases, the spiritual guide models the trust we need to grow into.

Mindy provides us with an excellent example. A spiritual guide with rare humor and warmth, she was suddenly diagnosed with a life-threatening illness. Sherman, one of the people for whom Mindy provided spiritual guidance, visited her in the hospital. Sherman did so out of genuine affection, as well as in fulfillment of the *mitzvah* of *bikur ḥolim* (visiting the sick). He felt the usual sense of discomfort that healthy people experience on encountering someone who is seriously ill. The sight of Mindy festooned with innumerable tubes was extremely difficult for him. But Mindy's spirit was strong and vital, and as it turned out, she gave far more energy to Sherman than he was able to give her. Healthy or ill—even on their death beds—those who are intimate with God often energize their visitors.

Mitzvot are intrinsically good; they are valuable in their own right even before they benefit someone else. When Judith was persuaded to work in a soup kitchen, she did so with the idea of "doing good," but she found herself deeply touched by the experience. She was particularly moved by the dignity and humanity of those who came to be fed. Suddenly Judith realized that it was *she* who had been served. The rabbis who said they had learned even more from their students than from their teachers had it right, exemplifying a fundamental truth of the spiritual economy: the more we give, the richer we become.

Principles of Spiritual Guidance as Found in Psalm 119

Psalm 119, the longest of all the psalms, is an excellent summary of the principles of spiritual guidance. All the landmarks can be found in it, and all the issues discussed in the preceding chapters. One of its features is that it is an acrostic poem: beginning with *aleph*, the first letter in the Hebrew alphabet, the initial letters of the twenty-two stanzas follow the alphabetic sequence all the way to the end. A unique feature of this psalm is that the Hebrew word beginning each stanza may be seen to provide a thematic statement for the entire stanza. Examining each of these key words in order will bring together the fundamental concepts of spiritual guidance. Psalm 119 may be long, but as we study it, we come to understand it as a short guide to the spiritual way.

Stanza 1

> Happy [*ashrei*] are those whose way is blameless,
> who follow the teaching of Adonai [verse 1].

When approaching a psalm for the first time, we can listen for echoes of other psalms, other familiar texts. Here is what we might find:

> Happy is the one whom God corrects;
> Therefore do not despise the chastening of the Almighty.
> —Job 5:17

> Happy are all those who fear Adonai,
> who follow in God's ways.
> —Ps. 128:1

> Happy is the one whose help is the God of Jacob,
> Whose hope is in Adonai, our God.
> —Ps. 146:5

All these texts, like Psalm 119, define happiness in terms of a faithful relationship with God. It is the quest for happiness that also lies at the heart of the book of *Kohelet* (Ecclesiastes). "Vanity of vanities" says the king Kohelet, "all is vanity" (Eccles. 1:2). This notion that everything is merely a wisp of wind—nothing of substance—leads Kohelet to explore and then reject various possible sources of happiness: wisdom, wealth, and pleasure of the senses. The same quest is taken up by philosopher Baruch Spinoza in his autobiographical work *On the Improvement of the Understanding*. Like Kohelet, Spinoza also rejects riches, status, and sensate pleasure. He encourages us to search for the intellectual love of God, something that unites our head and heart. Spinoza may thus be considered one of the earliest Jewish spiritual guides. His work tries to join intellect with emotion so that we can come into a whole relationship with God.

We, like Spinoza, can recognize that whatever has made the world seem vain to us can serve the positive function of causing us to start on our way. It prompts in us a plea for guidance. Over time, we will discover that following the law is an intrinsic good. But it is a way of life that must be cultivated. The psalmist is not yet firm in it: "Would that my ways were firm in keeping your laws" (Ps. 119:5). Virtue, the life of *mitzvot,* is good in itself. It is a gift to us from God, because it provides us with direction for our lives. But we only make this discovery as we begin to live the religious life. So Psalm 119 begins with the idea of happiness as correctness, of doing no wrong, of not being ashamed (119:6). It offers us a place to begin as we move toward a relationship of love and intimacy.

Stanza 2

How [*bameh*, lit. with what] can people keep their ways pure? [verse 9]

Seekers and spiritual guides both recognize that it is hard to live by the values we have established as a moral compass for our lives. In a world that constantly bombards us with different standards (including a lack of standards) for ethical living, we need help remembering our own set of values. And we need help holding on to them in a society that measures progress by a different yardstick. The spiritual life is a quest for meaning and value in our daily experience. The world around us has become separated from a larger perspective, a story that lifts up and infuses all the small moments with significance, and so that world fails as a domain of happiness. We need to develop a relationship with reality. Stanza 2 of Psalm 119 urges us to find a road map for ethical living (described in Chapter One in the discussions of Exodus and the Song of Songs). It also encourages us to receive training. The focus here is not on the cognitive—that is, knowing—but rather on being and becoming.

If theology is the study of God's nature and actions, and ethics is concerned with human behavior, religion is the bridge that joins our notion of God to our behavior. As seekers and guides, we discover that this bridge is constructed through three types of experience. First, we may feel a divine imperative—a sense of God's love and presence, a demand for action. We then want our behavior to conform with our love of God. Second, in the face of evil, we may seek refuge in a genuine standard, one that reflects the divine relationship we have striven to achieve. When outrageously immoral conduct is displayed, we realize that the ways of the world are unacceptable. Finally, we may know the good but not follow it; our efforts are insufficient. We want to live a good life, one that we know to be right, but we seem helpless to achieve this level of living without God's help.

Addressing the needs of all three types of seeker, Stanza 2 is concerned with how we can we keep our way pure. It reinforces the idea that we may take delight in God's law. The text offers us a hint, but it will take a long time before glory in God's law emerges as a dominant theme in the psalm and in our lives.

Stanza 3

Deal kindly [*gemol*, grant] with Your servant
that I may live to keep your word [verse 17].

This stanza expresses the psalmist's plea for life and direction. The only way to keep God's word is to live. It is through living that we may find our way to God. Spirituality is "theology walking"; it is the way we live our life. Genuine spirituality is found in all that we do, every choice we make, each action we perform, the relationships into which we enter. In this stanza, the psalmist asks to be dealt with kindly but also expresses delight in the study of the law and makes of it an intimate companion (Ps. 119: 24). This notion of the sacred text as intimate companion, which transcends the idea that the law is a set of rules or a test to be passed, is a major step forward on our spiritual path.

Also hinted at in the term *gemol* is the idea of God's graciousness, or unconditional generosity. This concept, called "grace" in non-Jewish sources, is not alien to Judaism (it is generally referred to as *hein*), but we are rarely directed to notice the ever-present grace. Certainly the entire Exodus story—particularly the description of receiving manna in the wilderness—teaches us that we will receive exactly what we need, regardless of how much we appear to gather. Throughout the Israelites' forty-year journey, this is an ongoing lesson in grace. As spiritual guides, it is our responsibility to remind seekers that grace continues. This is best taught not by lecturing but by inviting those who come to us to do what we have done—to turn their lives to God.

Stanza 4

> My soul cleaves [*devakah*] to the dust [verse 25].

The crucial word in this verse is "cleaves," not "dust." Among the mystics, *devekut* (literally, adhesion) is associated with cleaving to God and raises certain other associations. In Genesis, the first covenant, between man and woman, models for us the covenant we are to have with God: "Hence a man leaves his father and mother and cleaves (*davak*) to his wife so that they become one flesh" (2:24). We learn about our relationship to God through our commitment to human relationships. As we examine those relationships, we recognize that the way we respond to human intimacy mirrors our response to God, which contains elements of both attraction and resistance. Frequently, seekers need to be reminded that their covenants with their spouses provide them with the best context for learning about their covenant with God. Just as the Israelites found it difficult to maintain their covenant with God in the day-to-day living of the wilderness, we find that there are difficult times in our marriages, times of desert-like aridity. We want intimacy with the other, but we fear it as well. Repeatedly in the *Tanakh,* we are told, "Be not afraid." We are also reminded, "You who cleave to Adonai are all alive today" (Deut. 4:4). Here the importance of cleaving is made abundantly clear. But how do we achieve such a level of devotion? That is the work of the spiritual journey. Though we will sometimes fail, relapse, and lose our footing on the path, thanks to *teshuvah* we are always able to find our true direction again and resume our efforts.

The stanza continues, "I have declared my way, and you have answered me." This statement gives us the sense that something more personal is developing. However, before we are able to believe that there is a real possibility of cleaving to God, we move back and forth in the relationship, sometimes toward God and sometimes away.

Stanza 5

Teach me [*horeini*], O God, the way of Your laws [verse 33].

Teaching is not simply the imparting of facts from one person to another. Teaching is the development of a transformative relationship. What is being sought here is a teaching that will unite head and heart. It is a way of life. We recognized in Chapter Seven two different forms of knowledge: performative (knowing how) and factual (knowing that). We are generally taught these forms of knowledge in schools. According to Genesis 3, both are part of the knowledge that led to the expulsion from Eden. One of Adam and Eve's first responses to having eaten from the fruit of the Tree of Knowledge was their awareness of and discomfort with their own nakedness. Previously they had been naked but at peace. It would be a long journey of building openness and trust in the face of vulnerability that would allow them once again to find comfort rather than shame in mutual nakedness.

There is a third type of knowledge, represented by but not limited to sexual intimacy, in which the knower and the known are mutually open to one another, with neither trying to control or possess the other. This type of knowledge—"Adam knew his wife and she bore a son"—is transformative and fruitful. It is the same category of intimate knowledge that is at stake in the spiritual way.

The psalmist repeatedly requests of God: "Train me in Your laws" (119:12, 26, 27). When we first look at the laws, they appear straightforward. We think we know what they mean and what God requires of us. Then suddenly we realize that we may not have fully understood what God wants of us. As we follow God's laws for living our life, they will gradually reveal to us the many levels of depth within them. As spiritual guides, therefore, we engage in a practice that is not measured in terms of expertise in text or psychology. Rather, the process emerges out of our relationship with God, which provides us with a model for the relationship we foster with the seeker. We find ourselves saying things we didn't know we knew, asking questions we had not planned to ask. We prepare for our meetings with the seeker not by reviewing history or law but by "getting out of the way" so that God's presence can be made manifest.

Stanza 6

May Your steadfast love come [*veyvoni*] to me, O God [verse 41].

Here the psalmist, only six stanzas into a psalm twenty-two stanzas long, already expresses a desire for closeness to God. But as spiritual guides, we know this apparent openness and receptivity is not yet well grounded. After moments of closeness and intimacy resistance is likely to arise.

Bert yearned for closeness to God and even asked for it, but he also feared it. My first task was to recognize this resistance to intimacy. His resistance took several of the many forms of inordinate busyness. He had no time for silence, no time to spend in engaging a text or letting it touch him—even though he spends a great deal of time at "reciting" prayers. He actually found a prayer community that moved him deeply, but "it's too much trouble to get there." It was my responsibility as his spiritual guide to point out that there was something paradoxical in what was taking place. He claimed to have found something that was deeply rewarding and satisfying, but then avoids it. By becoming conscious of his resistance, Bert can more easily overcome it. (Fear almost always plays a part in resistance to closeness.) This kind of fear can be overcome in part by Bert becoming more trusting. We might suggest that he repeat experiences that warrant trust. Bert is also greatly impatient. A high achiever in studies and work, he is not at all accustomed to waiting. But in Judaism, as in sound, the emphasis is on process and relationship, not on some final beatific vision. When we recall the shy, delightful unfolding of our human relationships, we begin to realize that instead of being a trial, patience can be a gift. I suggested that Bert open himself slowly to a deepening relationship. I also suggested that he establish routine times for coming into the presence of God in prayer, meditation, study, silence. In this way, Bert will become open and welcoming to God. I encouraged Bert to continue his other pursuits (nowhere in this psalm does the psalmist talk about abandoning his current life). Bert, like other seekers, must stand and wrestle with his daily commitments. He grows not by storming the heavens but by being patient, consistent, open, and welcoming. In this posture, he will find God.

Stanza 7

Remember [*zachor*] Your word to Your servant [verse 49].

According to Abraham Joshua Heschel, "the pious person lives always under the canopy of remembrance." And Nachman of Bratzlav, who taught a simple faith and emphasized the importance of prayer and music, said: "Forgetfulness is exile. Remembrance is redemption." Remembrance has always been central to our identity as a people and to the development of trust in God:

> God remembered Noah and all the beasts and all the cattle that were
> with him in the ark, and God caused a wind to blow across the earth,
> and the waters subsided [Gen. 8:1].

At one point, Bert described feeling as if he were in the midst of a flood. As he confronted the tasks of daily living, he felt overwhelmed and overburdened. It was hard for him not to believe that God had forgotten him. I suggested that he try to remember an experience he would label "God remembered." Because he did not experience this feeling in the present, I encouraged him to search his past. He recalled an experience and examined it as if he were looking at a rare animal. "Could that have been an occasion of God's remembering me?" When I assured him that it could, he quickly turned up four or five additional examples, saying, "I never knew how to name it before!" Having discovered God's caring presence during various occasions in his life, Bert became more interested in exploring this pattern of God's remembrance.

Stanza 8

Adonai is my portion [*ḥelki*] [verse 57].

Few people can say, "God is my portion" or "God is my central concern and is all I want." It is a difficult notion to accept, but the world looks very different to us if we truly mean it. To see God as our portion is to try to shape our life and consciousness in terms of our dedication to God. Once God has become real for us, we feel a sense of urgency to live in the context of that reality, of that covenant. Yet because so few people can affirm that God is indeed their portion, one of the tasks of spiritual guidance is to validate a relationship with God as the central reality in the seeker's life. But we can't just say "God is my portion" once and be done with it. We must reexamine our commitment to the covenant every day. And then we must reaffirm it. Every day we are offered alternatives to the covenant. They may not be bad in themselves, but they don't provide us with answers to the ultimate questions in life.

Stanza 9

> You have treated Your servant well [*tov*] [verse 65].

Discernment refers to our ability to recognize the signs that guide us on our way to a deeper relationship with God. Central to this ability is the capacity to accurately distinguish between good and evil, a key concept in spiritual guidance. In this stanza, the psalmist makes the further distinction between apparent evil and real evil; the psalmist had been humbled, but with a new capacity to discern, sees his humbling as having been for a greater good (verses 67, 71):

> Before I was humbled I went astray,
> but now I keep Your word. . . .
> It was good for me that I was humbled,
> so that I might learn Your laws.

The hardest day-to-day question is discernment. When must we struggle against the status quo? When must we accept it? Through what must we suffer? Where do we look for insight? In retrospect, the psalmist embraces his suffering as a great teacher. Sometimes we learn through joy, sometimes through humbling or affliction. When we can recognize affliction as a call, it ceases to control us. But the spiritual guide cannot tell the seeker that a particular affliction is a call, cannot label someone's pain and suffering as a positive experience. However, the guide can be present, reassuring, open to listening. Then the seeker might discover what lesson is meant to be learned from the experience.

Stanza 10

> Your hands [*yodekha*] made me and fashioned me [verse 73].

The imagery used in this verse suggests the intimacy of the relationship with God. Once we recognize that we are created by God—the source of all Creation—it changes our perspective on life. Suddenly, our daily routine becomes patterned, meaningful, and purposeful. Recalling that we are created by God's hands moves us out of the domain of randomness into the domain of eternal value. Having reached stanza 10 in the psalm, we are no longer at the starting point of our spiritual journey. Our seeker David, for example, could not have begun with the idea that God's hands had made and fashioned him. However, he did have great respect for the marvels of the world. He had studied enough science to develop a deep appreciation for many of the phenomena around him. Together, he and I would recall some of the wonders, and then he would be left to ponder more deeply so that he could move beyond cognition and experience a *feeling* of wonder.

Stanza 11

> I long for [*kaltah*] Your deliverance [verse 81].

Some of the people who have come to me for spiritual guidance seem to have started their journey with this verse. They did not come with a quest for happiness or purity. They came with an unnamed, unspecified yearning. Melanie was one such person. She had been very successful in business and had won the respect of those who worked with her. She was financially comfortable, and she was in a meaningful relationship. Yet she understood that something was lacking. Melanie did not enter spiritual guidance from a place of deprivation. She had hobbies and interests and many friends, and she was active in the community and generous with *tzedakah* (charitable giving). These words of Spinoza may have been written explicitly about her:

> After experience had taught me that all the usual surroundings of social life are vain and futile; seeing that none of the objects of my fears contained in themselves anything good or bad except as the mind is affected by them, I finally resolved to inquire whether there might be some real good [*On the Improvement of the Understanding*, p. 3].

Melanie began her quest for the real good. Within less than a year, she felt compelled to leave her work and return to school to become a rabbi.

Stanza 12

> Adonai exists forever [*l'olam*];
> Your word stands firm in heaven [verse 89].

Our initial desires are all framed in terms of time. Here the psalmist intro-
duces us to the notion of "forever," the enduring aspect of God that
changes our perspective. But with the concept of "forever" come both the
promise and the burden of time. After Noah lived through the destruction of the world's peoples (a calamity we too now face at the end of the
twentieth century), he was promised that

> So long as the earth endures,
> Seedtime and harvest,
> Cold and heat,
> Summer and winter,
> Day and night
> Shall not cease.
> —Gen. 8:22

This is not an unalloyed blessing. The ongoingness of time means the
ongoingness of time's trials. Noah's dominant experience had been one of
mass destruction, so he chose inebriation as a way out:

> Noah, the tiller of the soil, was the first to plant a vineyard. He drank
> of the wine and became drunk [Gen. 9:20–21].

The spiritual guide must encourage and support the seeker whether the
spiritual journey is perceived as desert, flood, or dark night.

Not every meeting between guide and seeker is concerned with life-
changing decisions. Frequently meetings focus only on supporting the person through the ongoingness of time.

Stanza 13

> O how I love [ahavti] Your teaching!
> It is my study all day long [verse 97].

In verse 75, the text refers to knowledge; here it refers to love. This change
represents significant spiritual growth. Initially the psalmist is concerned
with a fear of doing wrong, a desire to do right, and the search for a standard. Now, beyond fear and correctness, love comes to the fore. "[God's
teaching] is my meditation all day long" is not a mantra; it is a fundamental frame of reference. This kind of transformation really does occur.
Alan entered spiritual guidance with a desire for correctness, some degree
of fear about doing wrong, and very little apparent warmth or joy. There
were, however, areas of real love and joy in his life. He had not really recognized how his marriage, his love of music, and his appreciation of
nature might be connected to his spiritual quest. When he was asked dur-

ing guidance to find God in some of these experiences, the request was a catalyst for a breakthrough in his spiritual life. Suddenly he could *feel* the gifts of love that surrounded him.

Stanza 14

Your word is a lamp [*ner,* candle] unto my feet, a light for my path.

Lamp. Candle. God's word is the Pillar of Fire that led the way for the Israelites at night in the wilderness. The Children of Israel learned to trust in the fire and follow it. We no longer have the benefit of the fire and the cloud, so we need help in discerning something comparable to those guiding pillars. Like our ancestors, we cannot see ahead, but with the help of spiritual guidance, seekers can learn to sense what leads them and come to trust it over time.

Molly was very taken with the quotation from John Dunne's *The House of Wisdom* that I offered her: "Things are meant, there are signs, the heart speaks, there is a way" (p. 13). She could see that her belief in the God of Israel was a belief in a meaningful world. Also, she had come to learn that the signs that led the Israelites had not ceased to function. There *are* signs. One sign she was beginning to discern was the movement of her own heart, her deep sense of desire. And so, with guidance, she was beginning to discern a way.

Stanza 15

I hate those who are of a divided heart [*se'afim*] [verse 113].

Divided thoughts, branches, divisions—the opposite of *shelemut,* wholeness. Søren Kierkegaard defined purity of heart as being able to will one thing. We recognize the need to unify ourselves. The divisions we work to overcome include the artificial distinctions between heart and mind and between mind and body, separations that Jewish thinkers have always eschewed. Ultimately we must claim all of ourselves and bring the whole into our relationship with God. David's scientific appreciation had to transcend the cognitive in order to embrace the spiritual, emotional sense of awe. Another seeker's capacity for human love had to be expanded so that he could understand that this was one of the ways God loved him.

Stanza 16

I have done [*asati*] what is just and right [verse 121].

Belief and faith are not limited to states of being. Both must lead to action. Some people are afraid that spirituality might move them away from the prophetic call and the claims of social justice. The opposite is the case in Judaism. Belief always finds its foundation in the love of God, which is expressed as a concern for justice. There is change, however. What begins as a call to "do good" evolves into a natural response to the joy we feel in our own lives. There is a shift from "gritted teeth," the sense of having to do something, to the exuberant impulse to contribute.

Stanza 17

> Your decrees are wondrous [*pela'ot*] [verse 129].

This stanza contains several expressions of wonder: "[Your words] give light and grant understanding. . . . I pant, longing for Your *mitzvot*" (verses 130–131). We probably cannot always live at this level of wonder, but we have to periodically return to it so that we can water our arid soul. Our responsibility as spiritual guides is often simply to remind those who come to us about their past experiences of wonder. Sometimes we encourage them to observe something wondrous in the present—or we invite them to relate something they have experienced through their senses in the previous twenty-four hours. At first, they may draw a blank, but this is instructive. It allows them to see how rarely they are present to what is around them; they use their senses merely to navigate and not to take in the richness of God's world. After a while, they will report that they really do have a growing sense of wonder.

Stanza 18

> You are righteous [*tzaddik*], Adonai [verse 137].

God's righteousness as a standard should be apparent throughout the relationship between spiritual guide and seeker. What was initially accepted as a discipline, a way to grow in intimacy with God, is now embraced out of a sense of its intrinsic value and out of love for God. As the stanza continues, the psalmist declares that his smallness in the eyes of others does not diminish his consciousness of God's precepts (verse 141), nor do anguish and distress eclipse his joy in God's commandments (verse 143). He is embracing these precepts not out of fear but out of delight: "Though anguish and distress come upon me, Your commandments are my delight" (verse 143). The formula by which the first half of a verse expresses a condition of distress and the second a feeling of safety (or praise) is common in this psalm and in others. The juxtaposition can be interpreted to mean that in our lives we will suffer, but in the context of a life lived to God's standard—that is, a personal covenant with God—we can find the suffering meaningful.

Stanza 19

I call [*karati*, I have called] with all my heart [verse 145].

Out of all the abstract arguments for the spiritual way and our desire to enter into an intimate relationship with God finally comes a direct call, an expressed sense that we are ready to address God directly: "You, O God, are near" (verse 151).

Margot had been coming for spiritual guidance for two years. She had really grown through this experience. But one thing remained an obstacle for her: she did not know how to directly address God. She could talk about God, she could pray from the prayer book. She could ask about God and try to locate God in the context of a certain experience. But she could not form one sentence that addressed God directly. For some people, this is not a problem. We recall the ease and naturalness with which the character Tevye in *Fiddler on the Roof* addresses God. But what is easy and natural for Tevye seemed almost impossible for Margot—as it is for many of us. So I suggested that Margot write down some of the questions she was asking me and address this writing to God. She was able to write down her thoughts. Then I asked her to take home what she had written and read it out loud. It was amazing to her that she was able to do this. The final remaining hurdle had been traversed. As she read her own writing, it became an ongoing conversation with God.

Stanza 20

See [*re'eh*] my affliction and rescue me [verse 153].

See. Take notice of me. We do not want to pass through this world invisibly. We want God to recognize us, but we know that to be seen by God is to stand in nakedness before God. The Creator will not be deflected by our new haircut or artificial posture. God will see us as we are. It is difficult to come before God with all our flaws, but it is also very healing. That is what *teshuvah* (repentance) is all about. We acknowledge that we are accepted and loved by God even after all that we have done. To lead seekers before God, however unready they may feel, takes patience, encouragement, support, and confidence.

Stanza 21

Princes [*sarim*] have persecuted me without reason [verse 161].

These "princes" are the powers and forces of this world. In earlier times, such forces were given demonic names to arouse fear. In some cases, the names were euphemistic codes referring to those in power. Now we tend to give worldly forces names informed by our awareness of social psychology: status, the temptation of the inner circle, power—all of which can potentially lure us away from our center. No matter how long we have been on the spiritual way, we remain vulnerable to the powers of this world. The "princes" don't cease to attack because we have chosen the spiritual way—indeed, they may even become more subtle. It is therefore important that we continue in spiritual guidance as seekers so that we may be helped to examine our motivation and what is really at stake in every decision we make.

Stanza 22

May my plea reach [*tikrav*, approach] You, O Adonai [verse 169].

Let my cry come close to you—like a sacrifice (*korban*, rooted in the verb *to draw close*). The entire process of spiritual growth is one of drawing closer to God. The plea continues in the stanza's succeeding verses because the process continues. Just as a single breath is insufficient to maintain us in life, so a single moment of revelation cannot tell us everything of what God wants from us. The process must be ongoing. The covenant and the relationship continue through all the days of our lives.

We are always beginners. That is one of the magnificent aspects of growing in our relationship with the Infinite. It is an adventure that never pales, a task that is never completed, a way of life that remains engaging throughout our days. We are just as far from the end after a lifetime of growth as we were when we began. But the distance we cannot traverse can be—and is—traversed by God once we have become open and receptive.

We return again to our sacred texts, finding more and more detail in the maps of the spiritual way. We continue to pray and find that, over time, all of our inner dialogue becomes an unbroken conversation with God; we find that more and more of Creation speaks to us. Our powers of discernment grow. We will still be afraid, and will make the continuous choice against fear, but fear is subsumed in the larger trust of God. Our image of God expands and expands so that we are left as wordless as the mystic who said he had no name for God because God could not be contained in a name. When he was asked, "Then how do you call God?" he replied, "I say 'Ahhh.'"

———————— o ————————

Study remains a joy and a well from which we draw refreshment. There are temptations, but the fundamental temptation—to leave the spiritual way—no longer has power. We have reached life's "point of no return"; we are committed. So we endure the desert and the trials of dailiness and commit ourselves to those actions that will heal our world.

And the greatest aspect of all our striving is that it is liberating, joyous, and the product of love.

APPENDIX

THE "GOD" QUESTIONNAIRE

I

1. I feel / do not feel close to God because _____
2. The time of my life when I felt the closest to God was when I was _____ years old because _____
3. I think that in general, as a person I have pleased / dissatisfied God because _____
4. I think that God wants /does not want me to be good because _____
5. I believe / do not believe in a personal God because _____

II

6. The time in my life when I felt the most distant from God was when I was _____ because _____
7. My most important duties towards God are _____

III

8. For me, the love of God toward me is / is not important because _____
9. For me, my love for God is / is not important because _____
10. The feeling I get / used to get from my relationship with God is one of _____ because _____

From Ana-Maria Rizzuto, *The Birth of the Living God* (Chicago: University of Chicago Press, 1979), pp. 213–217. Copyright © 1979 by University of Chicago Press. Used by permission.

IV

11. I feel that the fear of God is not important because _____

12. What I like the most about God is _____ because _____

13. What I resent the most about God is _____ because _____

14. What I dislike the most about religion is _____ because _____

V

15. Emotionally, I would like to have the _____ that God has because _____

VI

16. Among all the religious characters I know, I would like to be like _____ because _____

VII

17. My favorite saint or Bible character is _____ because _____

VIII

18. I believe / do not believe in the Devil because _____

19. I think that he wants us to _____ because _____

20. Sometimes I have / have not felt that I hated God because _____ _____

IX

21. I feel that what God expects from me is _____ because _____

22. I feel that to obey the Commandments is / is not important because ___

23. I pray / do not pray because I feel that God will _____

X

24. I feel that God punishes / does not punish you if you _____ because _____

25. I think that God considers my sins as _____ because _____

26. I think that the way God has to punish people is _____ because _____

27. I believe that the way God rewards people is _____ because _____

XI

28. I think that God provides / does not provide for my needs because ____

29. The most important thing I expect from God is _____ because _____

XII

30. In my way of feeling, for me to fully please God I would have to _____ because _____

31. If I could change my past, I would like to change my _____ because _____

32. If I can change myself now, I would like to be _____ because _____

    to change my _____ because _____

    to improve my _____ because _____

    to increase my _____ because _____

XIII

33. If I am in distress, I resort / do not resort to God because _____

34. If I am happy, I thank / do not thank God because _____

35. Religion has / has not helped me to live because _____

36. If I receive an absolute proof that God does not exist I will ____ because _____

37. Prayer is / is not important to me because _____

38. I wish / don't wish to be with God after death because _____

XIV

39. I think that God is closest to those who _____ because _____

XV

40. I consider God my _____ because _____

41. I think that God sees me as _____ because _____

XVI

42. If I have to describe God according to my experiences with him, I would say that he is _____ because _____

XVII

43. The day I changed my way of thinking about God was _____ because _____

XVIII

44. Religion was always / never / at one time important to me (during the years from _____ to _____) because _____

45. For me, the world has / has not an explanation without God because _____

REFERENCES

Bakan, David. *The Duality of Human Existence.* Boston: Beacon Press, 1966.

Becker, Ernest. *The Denial of Death.* New York: Free Press, 1973.

Benson, Herbert, with Miriam Z. Klipper. *The Relaxation Response.* New York: Avon, 1976.

Birnbaum, Philip, ed. *Daily Prayer Book.* New York: Hebrew Publishing, 1949.

Birnbaum, Philip, ed. *High Holyday Prayer Book.* New York: Hebrew Publishing, 1951.

Buber, Martin. *Moses: The Revelation and the Covenant.* New York: Harper, 1958.

Buber, Martin. *Tales of the Hasidim: The Later Masters.* New York: Schocken, 1948.

Buber, Martin. *The Way of Man, According to the Teaching of Hasidism.* London: V. Stuart, 1963.

Cox, Murray, and Theilgaard, Alice. *Mutative Metaphors in Psychotherapy.* London: Tavistock, 1987.

Dan, Joseph, ed. *The Early Kabbalah* (trans. Ronald C. Kiener). New York: Paulist Press, 1986.

Dante. *Dante's Paradiso* (trans. John Sinclair). New York: Oxford University Press, 1977.

Dukas, Helen, and Hoffmann Banesh, eds. *Albert Einstein: The Human Side.* Princeton, N.J.: Princeton University Press, 1979.

Dunne, John. *The House of Wisdom: A Pilgrimage.* Notre Dame, Ind.: University of Notre Dame Press, 1993.

Eliot, T. S. *Four Quartets.* New York: Harcourt Brace Jovanovich, 1943.

Fischer, Kathleen R. *The Inner Rainbow: The Imagination of Life.* New York: Paulist Press, 1983.

Fischer, Kathleen R. *Women at the Well.* New York: Paulist Press, 1988.

Freud, Sigmund. *Beyond the Pleasure Principle.* London: Hogarth, 1961.

Freud, Sigmund. *The Future of an Illusion.* New York: Norton, 1989.

Freud, Sigmund. *Moses and Monotheism.* New York: Random House, 1987.

Hall, Donald. *Life Work*. Boston: Beacon Press, 1993.

Hammarskjöld, Dag. *Markings*. New York: Knopf, 1970.

Hillesum, Etty. *An Interrupted Life: The Diaries of Etty Hillesum, 1941–1943*. New York: Washington Square Press, 1985.

Hillesum, Etty. *Letters from Westerbork*. New York: Pantheon Books, 1986.

James, William. *The Varieties of Religious Experience*. Old Tappan, N.J.: Macmillan, 1986.

Jonas, Hans. *The Phenomenon of Life*. New York: Harper & Row, 1966.

Joyce, James. *Portrait of the Artist as a Young Man*. New York: Viking, 1956.

Kaplan, Aryeh. *Jewish Meditation*. New York: Schocken, 1985.

Kegan, Robert. *The Evolving Self*. Cambridge, Mass.: Harvard University Press, 1982.

Mason, Herbert. *The Death of Al Hallaj: A Dramatic Narrative*. Notre Dame, Ind.: University of Notre Dame Press, 1979.

Plato. *The Collected Dialogues* (eds. Edith Hamilton and Huntington Cairns). New York: Putnam, 1961.

Potok, Chaim. *The Chosen*. New York: Simon and Schuster, 1967.

Rilke, Rainer M. *Letters to a Young Poet*. New York: Norton, 1994.

Rizzuto, Ana-Maria. *The Birth of the Living God: A Psychoanalytic Study*. Chicago: University of Chicago Press, 1979.

Rosenfeld, Zvi Aryeh, ed. *Rabbi Nachman's Wisdom* (trans. Aryeh Kaplan). Brooklyn, N.Y.: Breslov Research Institute, 1973.

Sacks, Oliver. *The Island of the Colorblind*. New York: Knopf, 1997.

Scholem, Gershom G. *On the Kabbalah and Its Symbolism* (trans. Ralph Manheim). New York: Schocken, 1965.

Schwerin, Doris. *Diary of a Pigeon Watcher*. New York: Avon, 1976.

Shaw, Nate. *All God's Dangers: The Life of Nate Shaw* (ed. Theodore Rosengarten). New York: Knopf, 1974.

Spinoza, Baruch. *Ethics of Spinoza* and *On the Improvement of the Understanding* (ed. James Gutmann). New York: Hafner, 1949.

Tolstoy, Leo. *Anna Karenina*. New York: Heritage Press, 1952.

Wilner, Eleanor. *Sarah's Choice*. Chicago: University of Chicago Press, 1989.

Winner, Robert. *The Sanity of Earth and Grass: Complete Poems of Robert Winner*. Gardiner, Maine: Tilbury House, 1994.

GLOSSARY

Adonai	God. (Literally, my master.)
amidah	The central prayer of the Jewish liturgy, recited (commonly in an undertone) while standing. Also known as *Hatefillah* (the prayer) and the *Shemoneh Esreh* (eighteen [benedictions]). (Literally, standing.)
aseret hadibrot	The Ten Commandments. (Literally, ten words, or utterances.)
avodah	Worship. In the time of the ancient Temple in Jerusalem, the sacrificial service. (Literally, work.)
Avot d'Rabbi Natan	Short Talmudic commentary by Rabbi Natan on *Pirkei Avot* (see below), focusing on principles of daily ethical living.
bakashah	Petitional prayer.
Bamidbar	Hebrew name for the book of Numbers. (Literally, in the wilderness.)
beg meḥilah	To ask for forgiveness, particularly before Yom Kippur.
Berakhot	Blessings. Also name of a section of the Talmud dealing with this subject.
bikur ḥolim	Visiting the sick.
b'tzelem Elohim	In the image of God.
devar (pl. *divrei*) *Torah*	Minisermon explicating the sacred text. (Literally, words of Torah.)
devekut (devakah)	Cleaving; the state of ultimate union with God.
eved Adonai	Servant of God.
Gan Eden	Garden of Eden, Paradise.
Gehinnom	The approximation of hell.

Genesis *Rabbah*	Early collection of midrash (see below) on the book of Genesis.
hakshavah	Attentive listening.
Hamakom	Euphemism for God. (Literally, The Place.)
hanhagot	Medieval manuals of piety and ethical discipline.
Ḥasidism	Religious movement founded by the Baal Shem Tov in the eighteenth century. Devoted to strict observance of Jewish ritual and tradition, with focus on ecstasy and mass enthusiasm. Close-knit communal structure is headed by a charismatic rabbi (*rebbe*).
ḥazan	Cantor who leads the prayer service.
ḥein	Grace.
ḥeshbon hanefesh	Introspection, self-examination. (Literally, an accounting of the soul.)
ḥevruta	Study partner; classical method of studying with a partner.
hitlahavut	Religious ecstasy.
Ḥumash	Five Books of Moses.
Kaddish	Name of an Aramaic prayer recited, in different versions, throughout the worship service. Commonly associated with the version used as a memorial prayer.
kavanah	Single-minded focus on prayer; spontaneous (as opposed to fixed) prayer; mantra-like use of sacred texts in preparation for prayer. (Literally, intention.)
kedushah	Holiness.
keva	Fixed prayer.
kiddush	Prayer of sanctification, generally said over wine.
Klal Yisrael	The Jewish people as a whole.
korban	Sacrifice.
lashon hara	Slander, gossip. (Literally, evil tongue.)
lashon hatov	Positive things said of others. (Literally, good tongue.)
l'hitpalel	To pray; to place oneself in the position of judgment before God.
maḥzor	Festival prayer book.
manna	Mysterious food provided by God for the Israelites during their desert wanderings.

Meir Einei ha-Golah	Spiritual commentary on the Torah by Abraham Alter (1896–1943). (Literally, enlightened eyes of the exile.)
midrash	Nonlegal sections of the Talmud and rabbinic literature, containing biblical commentary, often in story or parable form.
minyan	Prayer quorum of ten; small worshiping community.
mi sheberakh	An intercessory prayer for healing or other blessings. (Literally, the One who blesses.)
Mitzrayim	Egypt. (Literally, the narrow places.)
mitzvah (pl. *mitzvot*)	One of 613 commandments, positive and negative, originating in the Torah or in ancient rabbinic decree; righteous act, good deed.
moreh (masc.) or *morah* (fem.) *derekh*	Spiritual guide. (Literally, teacher of the way.)
na'aseh venishmah	Declaration of obedience made by the Israelites when they were presented with the Torah at Sinai. (Literally, we will do and we will hearken.)
nigun (pl. *nigunim*)	Wordless song.
Olam k'negdo	Principle that "the world follows its own order."
pesukei d'zimra	Short songs, primarily drawn from the psalms, which introduce the liturgy and "warm up" the worshiper for prayer. (Literally, lines of song.)
Pirkei Avot	Chapters (or Sayings) of the Fathers: section of the Talmud containing pithy sayings and ethical teachings of rabbinic sages from the third century B.C.E. to the third century C.E.
piyyut (pl. *piyyutim*)	Liturgical poem.
rabbinic/Talmudic tradition	The divine law, excluding the Five Books of Moses, passed down orally from the time of Sinai to the period between 200 and 500 C.E., when it was committed to writing.
Rosh Hashanah	Jewish New Year, which occurs in September or October, depending on the Hebrew (soli-lunar) calendar.
Rosh Hodesh	The new moon and its liturgical celebration. Often celebrated by women in honor of their distinct gifts, responsibilities, and identity.
sefirot	According to mystical tradition, the ten emanations or attributes of God.

shalom	Peace.
shalshelet hakabalah	Chain of tradition.
Shekhinah	God's presence in our midst; God's feminine attributes.
shelemut	Wholeness, serenity.
Shema	Primary creedal statement in Jewish liturgy: "Hear O Israel, *Adonai* is our God, *Adonai* is One." (Literally, hear.)
Simhat Torah	Fall holiday celebrating the completion of one annual cycle of Torah reading and the beginning of another.
Tanakh	The entire Hebrew Bible.
teshuvah	Repentance, renewal, a return to God's ways.
tikun olam	Repair of the world.
tokheha	Righteous rebuke, as given by the prophets to the ancient Israelites, or by one person correcting another on a point of faith or religious practice.
tzaddik	Righteous person.
tzedakah	Charitable giving.
yetzer hara	The inclination to do evil; one's natural libidinal drives and urges.
Yom Kippur	Day of Atonement.
Zohar	Mystical commentary on sections of the Five Books of Moses, the Song of Songs, Ruth, and Lamentations. The *Zohar* dwells on the mystery of Creation and explains the stories and events of the Bible in a symbolic manner. Basic text of Jewish mysticism. (Literally, brilliant illumination.)

SAGES QUOTED

Rabbi Akiva
(ca. 40–135 C.E.)

Palestinian sage renowned for his
influence on the development of
Jewish law in the Mishnah (the core
of the Talmud). Became a scholar late
in life and attracted many students.
Headed a rabbinic academy. Was also
politically active in supporting a revolt
against Roman rule led by Bar Kohkba in
132–135 C.E.

Rabbi Alexandri
(third century C.E.)

Probably from Lyady, leading aggadist
of his time, hero of folk tales.

Al-Hallaj (Hallaj, al-Husayn
ibn Mansur) (858–922)

Sufi mystic.

Apter Rebbe

see Heschel, Abraham Joshua, of Apta

Baal Shem Tov (1700–1760)

(Literally, master of the good name.)
Israel Ben Eliezer, also called "the Besht,"
considered to be the founder of Hasidism.

Bachya ibn Pakudah (second
half of eleventh century)

Medieval philosopher and author of
Duties of the Heart.

Baruch of Medziboz
(1757–1810)

Grandson of the Baal Shem Tov,
Hasidic master and author of *Butzina
Kaddisha* (Holy Light).

Beruria (second century C.E.)

Spouse of Rabbi Meir (see below), one of
the few women mentioned in the Talmud
who participated in legal discussions.

Buber, Martin (1878–1965)

Israeli religious existentialist, born in
Austria. Was influenced by Hasidism
and is noted for his construct of a
dialogic (I-Thou) approach to relationship

	between God and human beings, as well as between people.
Chofetz Chayim (1838–1933)	Pen name of Israel Mayer Kagan, Polish author of *Shemirat Lashon* ("The Guarding of the Tongue"), a treatise on *lashon hara* that warns of the dangers of gossip and slander.
Gerer Rebbe (1845–1905)	Aryeh Leib Alter, leader of one of the most celebrated communities of Ḥasidim in Poland. Also known as the *Sefas Emes,* after a five-volume collection of his writings.
Heschel, Abraham Joshua (1907–1972)	Philosopher who focused on the relationship between God and people as the foundation for religion. Working from classical sources, developed a philosophy that shed light on contemporary problems and conflicts.
Heschel, Abraham Joshua, of Apta (d. 1825)	Distinguished author of *Torah emet.* Also known as the Apter-Rebbe.
Reb Hillel of Radoshitz (d. 1901)	An ascetic who spoke only Hebrew, son-in-law of the Rebbe Issachar of Radoshitz.
Rabbi Joshua ben Korcha (middle second century C.E.)	Lived to advanced age, argued with sectarians.
Rabbi Isaac (middle second century C.E.)	From Babylonia, engaged in mystical studies.
Rabbi Isaac the Blind (ca. 1160–1233)	Central figure among the early kabbalists.
Kaminker Rebbe (1815–1889)	Samuel Hirsch, son of Tzvi Hirsch of Kamensk, Poland, who was a follower of the Baal Shem Tov. Author of *Shem Mishmuel* (a Talmudic commentary). Immigrant to the United States.
Kaplan, Mordecai (1881–1983)	Philosopher and theologian, founder of Reconstructionist Judaism.
Kotzker Rebbe (1787–1859)	Menachem Mendl of Kotzk, a revolutionary among Ḥasidim,

	known for zealousness and harshness in the pursuit of truth.
Levi Yitzchak of Berditchev (1740–1809)	Leading figure of Hasidism in Poland and the Ukraine. Authored prayers and supplications in Yiddish. Was well-known for his arguments with God in the midst of his community.
Luria, Isaac (1534–1572)	Leading kabbalist in Safed.
Maimonides, Moses (1135–1204)	Moses ben Maimon, also called by the acronym Rambam. Physician, Torah commentator, and philosopher. One of the greatest thinkers in all of Jewish history. Was influenced by Aristotelian thought as articulated by Arabic philosophers. Author of *Guide for the Perplexed* and *Mishneh Torah,* an accessible compilation of Jewish law.
Rabbi Meir (second century C.E.)	Student of Rabbi Akiva. Wrote what became the basis of the Mishnah.
Nachman of Bratzlav (1772–1810)	Great-grandson of Israel Baal Shem Tov. One of the most influential Hasidic masters of his time. Taught a simple faith that emphasized the importance of prayer and music.
Rabbi Nissim (ca. 1310–1375)	Important Spanish Talmudist.
Rabbi Pinchas Shapiro of Koretz (1726–1791)	Emphasized the value of prayer and the primacy of the study of the *Zohar.* Author of *Beth Pinchas,* a collection of insightful commentaries on the Zohar text.
Shneur Zalman of Lyady (1745–1813)	Founder of Chabad Hasidism and patriarch of the rabbinic dynasty that continues to lead that community.
Spinoza, Baruch (1632–1677)	Dutch philosopher. Author of *Ethics,* one of the most influential works of Western thought. Excommunicated in 1656, reinstated in 1977.
Rabbi Zusya of Hanipul (d. 1802)	Early Hasidic leader.

FOR FURTHER READING
AND EXPLORATION

Adahan, Miriam. *Awareness: The Key to Acceptance, Forgiveness, and Growth.*
Spring Valley, N.Y.: Feldheim, 1994.

Blumenthal, David R. *God at the Center: Meditations on Jewish Spirituality.*
San Francisco: Harper San Francisco, 1987.

Buxbaum, Yitzhak. *Jewish Spiritual Practices.* Northvale, N.J.: Jason Aronson,
1990.

Buxbaum, Yitzhak. *Spirituality and Storytelling in Judaism.* Northvale, N.J.:
Jason Aronson, 1995.

Cohen, Norman J. *Self, Struggle and Change: Family Conflict Stories in
Genesis and Their Healing Insights for Our Lives.* Woodstock, Vt.:
Jewish Lights, 1995.

Gordis, Daniel. *God Was Not in the Fire: The Search for a Spiritual Judaism.*
New York: Scribner, 1995.

Green, Arthur, ed. *Jewish Spirituality.* New York: Crossroads, 1986–87.

Hoffman, Edward. *The Heavenly Ladder: A Jewish Guide to Inner Growth.*
San Francisco: Harper San Francisco, 1985.

Hoffman, Lawrence. *The Art of Public Prayer: Not for Clergy Only.* Washington, D.C.: Pastoral Press, 1988.

Kushner, Lawrence S. *Invisible Lines of Connection: Sacred Stories of the Ordinary.* Woodstock, Vt.: Jewish Lights, 1996.

Kushner, Lawrence S., and Olitzky, Kerry M. *Sparks Beneath the Surface:
A Spiritual Commentary on the Torah.* Northvale, N.J.: Jason Aronson,
1993 (rev. ed. 1996).

Ochs, Carol. *The Noah Paradox: Time as Burden, Time as Blessing.* Notre
Dame, Ind.: University of Notre Dame Press, 1991.

Ochs, Carol. *Song of the Self: Biblical Spirituality and Human Holiness.*
Valley Forge, Pa.: Trinity Press International, 1994.

Ochs, Carol. *Women and Spirituality,* 2nd ed. Lanham, Md.: Rowman & Littlefield, 1997.

Olitzky, Kerry M., and Sabath, Rachel T. *Preparing Your Heart for the High Holidays: A Guided Journal.* Philadelphia: Jewish Publication Society, 1996.

Olitzky, Kerry M., and Sabath, Rachel T. *Striving Toward Virtue: A Contemporary Guide for Jewish Ethical Behavior.* Hoboken, N.J.: KTAV, 1996.

Petsonk, Judy. *Taking Judaism Personally: Creating a Meaningful Spiritual Life.* New York: Free Press, 1996.

Pitzele, Peter. *Our Fathers' Wells: A Personal Encounter with the Myths of Genesis.* San Francisco: Harper San Francisco, 1995.

Umansky, Ellen M., and Ashton, Dianne, eds. *Four Centuries of Jewish Women's Spirituality: A Sourcebook.* Boston: Beacon Press, 1992.

Verman, Mark. *The History and Varieties of Jewish Meditation.* Northvale, N.J.: Jason Aronson, 1996.

Weintraub, Simkha Y., ed. *Healing of Soul, Healing of Body: Spiritual Leaders Unfold the Strength and Solace in Psalms.* Woodstock, Vt.: Jewish Lights, 1994.

Wolpe, David J. *In Speech and in Silence: The Jewish Quest for God.* New York: Henry Holt, 1992.

THE AUTHORS

CAROL OCHS has been engaged in spiritual guidance since the 1970s. In 1994, following a twenty-five-year career as professor of philosophy at Simmons College, Boston, she joined the faculty of Hebrew Union College–Jewish Institute of Religion (HUC-JIR), New York, where she now directs its Graduate Studies Program and serves as spiritual guide to rabbinic and Doctor of Ministry students. Her B.A. and M.A. degrees in philosophy are from City College and City University of New York, and she earned her Ph.D. degree in philosophy from Brandeis University. She is the author of *Behind the Sex of God* (1977), *Women and Spirituality* (1983; revised and expanded, 1997), *An Ascent to Joy: Transforming Deadness of Spirit* (1986), *The Noah Paradox* (1991), and *Song of the Self: Biblical Spirituality and Human Holiness* (1994). She has also written numerous essays and journal articles. Ochs and her work are recognized in *Who's Who in America*.

KERRY M. OLITZKY is national dean for Adult Jewish Learning and Living at Hebrew Union College–Jewish Institute of Religion (HUC-JIR), where he has developed a variety of pioneering programs, including a Doctor of Ministry and transdenominational training in spiritual counseling for Jews in recovery. Rabbi Olitzky received his B.A. degree in philosophy and his M.A. degree in social gerontology from the University of South Florida, having also attended the American College in Jerusalem. After graduating with honors, he went on to study at HUC-JIR, Cincinnati, where he was ordained and received master's and doctoral degrees in Hebrew literature. His earlier career included service at Congregation Beth Israel in West Hartford, Connecticut, and as national director of research and educational development for HUC-JIR. Olitzky is the author or editor of over thirty books and one hundred articles. His books include *Preparing the Heart for the High Holy Days* (1996) and *Striving Toward Virtue* (1996), both written with Rachel Sabath. He is well-known as the coauthor of "The Jewish Contribution to Twelve-Step Spirituality" and as the "how-to" rabbi—a result of his successful *How-to Handbooks for Jewish Living* series.

INDEX

death, 89–90; discernment of, 78; healing, through relationship with God, 100–101; of the holy, 91–94; of joy, 46, 85–87; of judgment, 94–95; of looking foolish, 83; and love, 99–101; of love, 84–85, 86; as motivation, 81; nature of, 81–83; and need to trust in God, 95–100; of not knowing the future, 83–84; as obstacles, 81–95; of our own unreadiness, 87–88; of transformation, 90–91; types of, 83–95; of union, 90–91; of the unknown, 89–90

Feminist theology: and God images, 108–111; and sacred texts, 129–130

Festival prayer book, 95, 207

Fiddler on the Roof, 197

Fifth Commandment, 152

First Commandment, 151

Fischer, Kathleen, 125, 129

Five Books of Miriam, The (Frankel), 130

Five Books of Moses, 15

Fletcher, Horace, 82

Foolish, fear of looking, 83

Forever, 193–194

Forgetfulness, 145

Forgiveness, and confession, 42. *See also* Repentance

Four Quartets (Eliot), 44, 55

Fourth Commandment, 152

Free will, 60; and sin, 146

Freedom: journey to, 27–28; trust in God and, 99–100. *See also* Exodus; Liberation

Freud, Sigmund, 14, 18–19, 33, 85–86, 89, 90, 113, 140, 170

Future: fear of not knowing, 83–84; inadequate knowledge of, 97

Future of an Illusion, The (Freud), 14

G

Gan Eden, 34, 85, 206. *See also* Paradise

Gehinnom, 85, 206

Gemol, 187–188

Gender images, 108–111

Genesis, 29, 70, 123–124, 127, 132, 152; 1:3, 147; 1:27, 103; 2:7, 127; 2:15, 33; 2:18, 37; 2:24, 188; 3, 189; 3:8, 127; 3:9, 15; 4:1, 127; 4:6–7, 135; 4:9, 15; 6:14, 15; 8:1, 191; 8:22, 194; 9:9, 15; 9:20–21, 194; 11:7, 65; 12:1, 15; 16:9, 15; 24:59, 110; 25:23, 15; 26:18, 174; 27:43, 58; 28:16, 18, 57; 28:20–21, 96; 32:3–5, 172; 32:11, 106; 32:24–29, 60 172; 35:8, 110; 45:5, 76; 49, 96; 50:20, 18, 76, 152

Gerer Rebbe, 23, 94–95, 177, 212

God: awareness of, 65–66; calling, 197, 198–199; clinging to, 21; distance from, 138, 145–150; fear of, 82; felt presence of, 37–38, 42, 88, 101, 109; hearing the call of, 58–61; love of, 37, 115–117, 142–143; as "my portion," 191–192; need for trust in, 95–100; proofs for existence of, 66; reality of, versus images of, 111; reaching, 198–199; righteousness of, 196–197; to be seen by, 197; sight of, 18, 56–58; sin as distance from, 138; as source of everything, 137–138; speech of, discernment of, 68–76; surrender to, 36–37, 96, 144; unity of, 140; voice of, 15–19, 42. *See also* Relationship with God

God images, 8–9, 103–118; adulthood expansion of, 25–26, 104–106, 183; apophatic theology and, 113–114; and atheists, 106; in case example, 24–25; cataphatic theology and, 114; childhood development of, 23–25, 104; evolution of, 103–108; feminine, 105, 108–111; God's love and, 115–117; inflexible, 113, 151; of kabbalists, 107–108; maternal, 108–111; parental, 111–112; patriarchal, 108–111, 112–113; in relationship with God, 23–26, 111–117; and relationships with others, 152; self-correcting, 104–106; and self-images, 106–107, 114; and self knowledge, 104; as tools for approaching reality, 111–117

God Questionnaire, 105, 200–202

Golden calf, 57–58

Good, relationship of the holy to, 144

Grace, 97–98, 188

Graven images, 113, 151

Greek world, 53, 123

Grow, refusal to, 143–144